1 MONTH OF
FREE
READING

at

www.ForgottenBooks.com

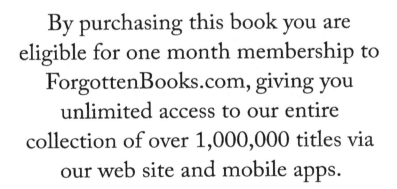

By purchasing this book you are eligible for one month membership to ForgottenBooks.com, giving you unlimited access to our entire collection of over 1,000,000 titles via our web site and mobile apps.

To claim your free month visit:

www.forgottenbooks.com/free997354

ISBN 978-0-260-98348-0
PIBN 10997354

I N D E X

BAY REGION BUSINESS
Vol. 20   1963

I N D E X

BAY REGION BUSINESS
Vol. 20   1963

on.
on.
/
I+
m:
. ¢
c

I N D E X

BAY REGION BUSINESS
Vol. 20   1963

I N D E X

BAY REGION BUSINESS
Vol. 20   1963

BUSINESS-EDUCATION DAY
Business Community Hosts 4,000 Teachers On Business-Education
    Day, October 11...No.   18... 9-27
4,000 Teachers Visiting Business and Industry Today............No.   19...10-11
More Than 50 Schoolteachers Were Hosted By The Chamber On
    Business-Education Day (with cut)...........................No.   20...10-25
CHAMBER CALENDAR
    Chamber Calendar...No.   2... 1-25
    Chamber Calendar...No.   4... 3- 1
    Chamber Calendar...No.   5... 3-15
    Chamber Calendar...No.   6... 3-29
    Chamber Calendar...No.   7... 4-12
    Chamber Calendar...No.   8... 4-26
    Chamber Calendar...No.   9... 5-10
    Chamber Calendar...No.   10... 5-24
    Chamber Calendar...No.   11... 6-14
    Chamber Calendar...No.   12... 6-28
    Chamber Calendar...No.   14... 7-26
    Chamber Calendar...No.   15... 8- 9
    Chamber Calendar...No.   16... 8-23
    Chamber Calendar...No.   18... 9-27
    Chamber Calendar...No.   19...10-11
    Chamber Calendar...No.   20...10-25
    Chamber Calendar...No.   21...11-15
    Chamber Calendar...No.   22...11-29
    Chamber Calendar...No.   23...12-13
    Chamber Calendar...No.   24...12-27
CHAMBER HISTORY
    Chamber Is Now 113 Years Young (with cut)..................No.   9... 5-10
CHAMBER STAFF
    The 1962 Chamber Staff (with cuts).........................No.   1... 1-11
    1964 Retirement Set For Chamber Executive Vice President...No.   2... 1-25
    Stanley Allen New Research Manager (with cut)..............No.   2... 1-25
    Charles Ayres New Publicity Department Assistant Manager
        (with cut)...No.   11... 6-14
    Borek Is Named Research Manager of The Chamber (with cut)..No.   19...10-11
    K. C. Chamber Executive Named Successor To G. L. Fox (with cut)No. 21...11-15
CHINESE NEW YEAR
    Gala Parade For Year of The Hare...........................No.   2... 1-25
    These Bay Area Chinese-American Beauties Face Competition
        Aplenty In Balloting For The Title of "Miss Chinatown,
        USA." (with cut).......................................No.   2... 1-25
CIVIC DEVELOPMENT
    Casey Named Head of Regional Problem (with cut)............No.   8... 4-26
CONSTRUCTION
    Allstate Building New Office (with cut)....................No.   4... 3- 1
    Standard Oil Company Building (with cut)...................No.   8... 4-26
    Bank of America Building (with cut)........................No.   8... 4-26
    Chamber Moves to Coordinate South-O-Market Development.....No.   8... 4-26

PAGE III

I N D E X

BAY REGION BUSINESS
Vol. 20   1963

I N D E X

BAY REGION BUSINESS
Vol. 20   1963

I N D E X

BAY REGION BUSINESS
Vol. 20   1963

I N D E X

BAY REGION BUSINESS
Vol. 20   1963

MISCELLANEOUS (Continued)

I N D E X

BAY REGION BUSINESS
Vol. 20   1963

WORLD TRADE

###

BAY REGION BUSINESS

SAN FRANCISCO CHAMBER OF COMMERCE

VOLUME 20 • NUMBER 1 • JANUARY 11, 1963

New Chamber Officers and Directors Begin 1963 Term

President
HARRY A. LEE

Vice President, Pacific Area Manager, J. Walter Thompson Company. Born in Santa Monica, Calif. Graduated Stanford University, 1931. Joined J. Walter Thompson Co. 26 years ago in San Francisco. Served in World War II as Lt. Commander, Naval Air Transport Service. For ten years following war (1945-55) lived in Far East; established and managed own advertising agencies in Manila and Tokyo. Rejoined J. Walter Thompson in present capacity in 1955.

Vice President
D. C. SUTHERLAND

D. C. Sutherland, Senior Vice President, loan administration, Bank of America NT & SA. Sutherland joined the Bank of America in Los Angeles in 1947 as Assistant Vice President in special administration following a distinguished career in banking in Nevada which started in 1925. Transferring to Pasadena, he later became vice president and manager of the Pasadena main office. Since 1955 he has been at the bank's San Francisco headquarters, where he was appointed senior vice president in 1959.

Treasurer
B. M. EUBANKS

General Partner, Stewart, Eubanks, Meyerson & Co., Investment Bankers, Owner, B. M. Eubanks Company. Born Jan. 8, 1909, Big Spring, Texas. Graduate, University of California, 1932. Member, New York Stock Exchange. Board of Trustees, California Historical Society. Director, San Francisco Bond Club. Member, San Francisco Stock Exchange Club, the Pacific Union Club, Bohemian Club, Commonwealth Club, San Francisco Commercial Club and the Navy League of the United States.

Vice President
GEORGE F. HANSEN

Assistant to the President, Matson Navigation Company. Born in San Francisco. Entire business career with Matson, having joined the company in 1926. Served in various sales management positions, becoming Vice President-Passenger Traffic in 1949. Vice-President-Secretary from 1958. Appointed to present position in 1962. Member, San Francisco Public Utilities Commission; Director and Treasurer, San Francisco United Community Fund. Director, Marine Exchange and Down Town Association. Director and Secretary, Jr. Achievement. Trustee, World Affairs Council.

Executive Vice President
G. L. FOX

Executive Vice President, San Francisco Chamber of Commerce. Born in Stockton. Attended University of California with major studies in industrial engineering and management. Spent 3 years as working newspaper-man and managing editor. Was industrial and traffic director of Parr - Richmond Terminal Co. for 6 years before joining San Francisco Chamber in 1943. Former manager, industrial department, Stockton Chamber.

Assistant Treasurer
GEORGE S. REPPAS

Partner, Reppas & Bradshaw, CPA's. 36th President of the San Francisco Junior Chamber of Commerce. Graduated high school in Oakland and earned his B.A. at Stanford, 1951, his M.B.A., Stanford, 1953. Organizer, rugby team, San Francisco Olympic Club. Trustee of Crystal Springs School, Hillsborough. Director, Beta Rho Assn., Delta Tau Delta. Director, Alec Membership Shopping Center. Director, Rugby Football Union of Northern California.

Vice President
WILLIAM J. BIRD

Western Vice President, John Hancock Mutual Life Insurance Company (senior officer in 12 western states). Native of Missouri. Graduate, University of Nebraska. Member, Board of Directors: Golden Gate Chapter, The American Red Cross; S. F. Council, Boy Scouts of America. Director, Junior Achievement; American Cancer Society; Chairman, Membership Committee, San Francisco Chamber; Chairman, Sustaining Fund Drive, Boy Scouts of America, San Francisco Council. Former Executive Vice President, Greater Boston Chamber of Commerce. Former Manager of External Affairs, Chamber of Commerce of the United States.

General Manager
S. H. KEIL

Born in Tacoma, Washington. Joined Safeway Stores, Inc. in Seattle upon graduation from the University of Washington. Graduate studies at the University of Chicago. Employed as supplier company plants manager for Safeway in San Francisco, Omaha and national purchasing office, Chicago. Active in the Naval Reserve since 1940, including five years' active duty during World War II—currently in grade of Captain, USNR.

Secretary
MARIE A. HOGAN

Secretary, San Francisco Chamber of Commerce, since 1929. A native of Grass Valley, California. Member, American Chamber of Commerce Executives and Central and Northern California Chamber of Commerce Executives. Serves as Secretary to the Board, custodian of Chamber records, and executes assignments directed by Executive Vice President.

ROSS BARRETT

President, Foster and Kleiser Division of Metromedia, Inc. Born in Washington, D. C., April 21, 1911. Attended Georgetown University, Washington, D. C. In World War I was Assistant Director of Press, Radio and Advertising for the first War Bond Campaign. Naval Officer from 1943 to 1946 attached to office of Secretary Forrestal. Vice President and Advertising Director of Foreman & Clark from 1946 to 1954. Vice President of Byron Jackson Division of Borg-Warner Corporation from 1954 to 1958. A director of the San Francisco Chapter of the American Cancer Society. A trustee of the Boys' Clubs Foundation of Southern California. Member of the San Francisco Golf Club.

ELLIS C. BROOKS

Ellis C. Brooks, President of Ellis Brooks Chevrolet, Inc., was born in Canton, North Carolina in 1907. Brooks adopted San Francisco as his new home in 1929 after receiving his discharge from the U. S. Navy. Brooks has been in the automobile business in the Bay Area since that date and is a past president of the Motor Car Dealers' Assn. He is an active member of the King Solomon Masonic Lodge, Lions Club, the Olympic Club, the St. Francis Yacht Club, and the U. S. Power Squadron. Brooks resides with his family at 1200 Sloat Boulevard, San Francisco.

G. E. COON

Regional Vice President, American Airlines. Born Fort Worth, Texas. Attended Rice University and Southern Methodist University. Joined American Airlines in 1930. Served in the Air Transport Command as Lieutenant Colonel. Vice President and Director of the San Francisco Convention and Visitors Bureau. Member Commonwealth Club and Olympic Club.

STEWART S. CORT

Vice President, Bethlehem Steel Co., Pacific Coast division. Cort has been associated with Bethlehem Steel since shortly after graduating from the Harvard School of Business Administration in 1936. Before entering Harvard, he received his B.A. at Yale. The Pennsylvania-born executive is considered to be one of the foremost rising young executives on the Pacific Coast. His management career has encompassed virtually every phase of management in the Bethlehem Company.

J. R. DANT

President, States Steamship Company. Born in Portland, Oregon. Graduate University of Oregon. Affiliated Pacific Coast shipping and lumber interests for over 25 years. Prior to World War II, he was engaged with Dant & Russell, Inc., founded by his father, the late Charles E. Dant. After World War II Navy duty, entered steamship activities of family. Appointed General Manager of States Steamship Company. Married, father of four. Member of Board of Trustees, San Francisco Maritime Museum, Board of Trustees, Mills College.

MELVILLE H. DeVOTO

General Manager, The Emporium, and Vice President, The Emporium Capwell Company. Born, 1906, Santa Rosa, California. Educated at Santa Rosa and the University of California. Colonel, U. S. Army, World War II. Director: The Emporium Capwell Company; Associated Merchandising Corporation; Downtown Association of San Francisco; City of San Francisco Downtown Parking Garage; San Francisco Region, American Red Cross.

PRESTON G. DREW

Manager, Shell Oil Company, San Francisco division. A Colorado native and an engineering graduate of Oregon State, he joined Shell in 1928 as a salesman in Junction City, Ore. Throughout the next decade he held sales positions at various West Coast points prior to becoming wholesale manager for the Portland marketing division in 1939. During the next 10 years he held assignments there as retail department manager and sales manager. He was appointed sales manager of the Boston marketing division in 1949 and in 1955 he went to the head office marketing organization in New York as an assistant sales manager. Drew was named special assistant to the manager, head office marketing departments in 1957. He moved to the West Coast in 1958 on special assignment on the staff of the vice president in charge of West Coast marketing.

HARRY P. GOUGH

Regional Vice President, General Electric Company. Born in Greencastle, Indiana. Graduate of DePauw University, 1929. Affiliated with General Electric Company and General Electric Credit Corporation, 1929-43. Lieutenant, Supply Corps, U.S. Navy in World War II, 1947-53, General Electric Credit Corp. 1953-61, Regional Manager, GE Appliance & TV Division and Manager for Northern California distributorship. Member: San Francisco Rotary Club, San Francisco Electric Club, Stock Exchange Club. Member and Director: California Manufacturers Association, Northern California Electrical Bureau, Pacific Coast Electrical Association.

Hitting the High Spots

With JOE HAUGHEY

THE AMERICAN CANCER SOCIETY has named 1963 as "The Year of the Volunteer," according to J. W. Mailliard III, president of ACS's San Francisco branch. Men and women of all skills are needed to supplement the corps of more than 5,000 volunteers now at work, he said. Call YU 2-0777 or TU 5-5822. . . .

TEMPORARY APPOINTMENT of John A. O'Kane as state Superintendent of Banks has been made permanent by Governor Brown. O'Kane was vice president and general counsel of the Federal Reserve Bank before taking his present post. . . .

H. M. ECKERT, after more than 50 years of service, retired last month as chief clerk in the freight traffic office of the Santa Fe Railway. His retirement was honored at a luncheon in the Commercial Club on Dec. 26. . . .

AMERICAN TRUCKING ASSOCIATIONS president, Clinton L. Sanders, said 1962 business will add up to one of three best years since the end of World War II. Sanders predicted total revenues for ICC regulated freight carriers are expected to reach $7.9 billion. . . .

CALIFORNIA EMPLOYMENT DIRECTORY for 1963 will be off the press by February 1. Book, including 4500 new listings of California employers with 100 or more employees, is published by Jobs in California Newsletter, 582 Market St. Directory price is $10 plus four per cent tax, but will be available at $7.50 for orders placed before Feb. 1. . . .

ELTON LAWLESS, chairman of the state's industrial Accident Commission, was appointed to San Francisco municipal judgeship by Governor Edmund G. Brown. . . .

RETAIL DRY GOODS ASSOCIATION stores will remain open on Washington's Birthday, Feb. 22. . . .

GREATER GROWS GEARY GREENERY — The Greater Geary Merchants Association has begun a program to plant more than 200 trees from Masonic Avenue to 28th Avenue. Inaugurating the drive are (l. to r.) Brian Fewer of the Department of Public Works; Leland Barrett, realtor; Peter Tamaras, Supervisor; Steve Chipralis, Geary Merchants; and Nowel Martin, landscape artist.

NEW LISTING of Business Schools in San Francisco is now available from Research Department of the Chamber, 333 Pine St. . . .

U. S. NAVY spent more than $2 billion in Northern California, Nevada and Utah in 1962, according to Rear Admiral E. E. Yeomans, Commandant of the 12th Naval District. He said 41,500 civilian employes picked up a total of $280,813,000 during the year. . . .

SAN FRANCISCO STATE'S Advanced Acting Workshop presents "The Diary of Anne Frank" tonight (Friday) at 8:30 p.m. in State's main auditorium. Presentation is part of burgeoning program activities of the school's Creative Arts Division. . . .

LOCKE-HURST GALLERIES, 124 Columbus, is displaying works of the expressionist painter, E. John Lanners, through Feb. 1. Galleries are open 11 a.m. to 7 p.m., at other times by appointment. . . .

UNIVERSITY OF PENNSYLVANIA announces availability of funds for fellowships in Public Finance, Taxation, Accounting, Statistics, Public Administration and related subjects. Applications should be addressed to Director of Admissions of the Graduate Division of the Wharton School of Finance and Commerce. Deadline is March 1. . . .

JOHN H. HALL has become vice president of Shell Oil Company's Western Marketing Region, succeeding Selwyn Eddy, who undertakes a special assignment until his retirement on March 31. . . .

MRS. CALVIN L. LUBRAN, Saratoga, mother of a cancer-stricken child, won the San Francisco Symphony for a day in a contest sponsored by KABL and the San Francisco Examiner. Her Jan. 24 concert will be performed for the benefit of the City of Hope. . . .

SYMPHONY directors have instituted new policy for purchase of tickets for next two weeks' performances. Box office will open at 7 p.m. before performances for advance ticket sales, and at 1 p.m. on matinee performance days. . . .

ST. FRANCIS HOTEL remodeling ended with opening of the new Cafe Medallion on Jan. 2. Completion of new gourmet restaurant marked the end of the half-million-dollar remodeling job, according to managing director Dan E. London, former Chamber president. . . .

LABOR UNION MEMBERSHIP in California was 1,752,400 in July, 1962, a slight drop from all-time high of 1,755,700 in 1960, according to Margaret R. O'Grady, director of the Department of Industrial Relations. . . .

SHOWS CURRENTLY SCHEDULED by Palace of the Legion of Honor include Fourth Winter Invitational Exhibition (through Jan. 27), photographs by Nichole Schoening and drawings by Claire Mahl, both opening January 12. . . .

BAY AREA RAPID TRANSIT DISTRICT gave a Recognition Award to the Chamber for its work in support of successful bond issue on November ballot. . . .

J. WESLEY HOWELL, former executive of El Dorado Oil Co., has taken over Reno Ski Bowl and renamed it Slide Mountain Ski Bowl. . . .

EVENING CLASSES of San Francisco Law School in San Francisco and Oakland will begin Monday, January 21. . . .

INTERNATIONAL HARVESTER received congratulations of Governor Edmund G. Brown for expansion of its operations into the San Leandro area. Brown said, "This forward step will make a significant contribution to the economy (of the Bay Area). . . .

WORK on an ultra-modern illuminated news tower at Fourth and Market Streets in downtown San Francisco will be begun January 15, according to KGO-TV. The 40-foot structure, resembling the Space Needle at the Seattle World's Fair, will flash news headlines and bulletins to passersby. It will be constructed by the Electrical Products Corporation of San Francisco. The news tower was designed by KGO-TV's design consultant, G. Dean W. Smith.

GOVERNOR BROWN will be the featured speaker at the 13th annual meeting of the Governor's Industrial Safety Council at the Biltmore Hotel in Los Angeles, Feb. 7 and 8. . . .

PROF. J. KEITH MANN of Stanford headed a three-man Presidential emergency board recommending furlough benefits equal to 70 per cent of their regular pay for Southern Pacific employes displaced by automation. . . .

RANSOM M. COOK, president, Wells Fargo Bank, said the bank's assets, deposits, loans, etc., reached new highs in 1962. The bank reported total assets of $3,231,228,716, a gain of more than $237 million over 1961. . . .

LOUIS B. LUNDBORG, former general manager of the Chamber, and executive vice president of the Bank of America, moves to newly created general administrative post in Los Angeles. He will work closely with board chairman Jesse W. Tapp, former Chamber president and director.

BANK OF AMERICA boasted a record of balanced growth in its year-end report. Total resources moved up to $13,417,140,809. Loans outstanding reached $7,587,992,697. Securities investments totaled $3,104,506,581. . . .

T. G. HUGHES has been elected president of California Chemical Company (subsidiary of Standard Oil of California). He succeeds Fred Powell, who becomes chairman of the board of the company. . . .

ERNEST ROVERE has been appointed San Francisco tournament director of the Second Annual North American Rubber Bridge Tournament. . . .

GORDON NEWSFILMS is producing a series of film clips for UC's Davis Campus, featuring new developments in food technology. Series is supervised by Henry Schacht, director of information at UC Agricultural Extension. . . .

NORMAN R. SUTHERLAND, PG&E president, estimated a $238 million expenditure for construction in northern and central California in 1963. The estimate tops all previous annual capital expenditures, he said. . . .

erving the Membership, Business and the Community

The 1962 Chamber Staff

Agriculture, Public Affairs

Randle P. Shields
Manager

Civic Development

Harold V. Starr
Manager

Industrial Department

Lewis M. Holland
Manager

Harold T. Wood
Assistant Manager

Membership Department

Farmer B. Smith
Special Repr.

Ralph Miller
Special Repr.

Walter Maxwell
Special Repr.

Herbert H. Harmon
Manager

Transportation Department

Charles C. Miller
Manager

James M. Cooper
Assistant Manager

Publicity

Joseph I. Haughey
Manager

Charles Morgan
Assistant Manager

Research

Fritz Albershardt
Manager

World Trade

James P. Wilson
Manager

Howard Stephenson
Assistant Manager

(Continued from page three)

'OSS R. YERBY

ce President-Marketing, California Packing orporation. Born in New York City. Attended eorgetown University d New York University. Itered the food business 1932. Joined his pres-It company in 1937 as a bbing salesman in the ew York office. Became ssistant Division Sales lanager in New York in 346. Appointed Division sles Manager, Eastern erritory, 1949, also ected to Board of Di-Ictors the same year.

1955 he was appointed Assistant General ales Director with headquarters in San Fran-isco. Appointed General Sales Director in 958 and Vice President-Marketing in 1959.

Ex-Officio Directors

LESTER GOODMAN

Born in Phoenix, Arizona. Attended San Francisco schools and Hastings College of Law, also graduate of Columbia School of Military Government and Administration. Joined Getz Bros. & Co. in 1922. Lived many years in the Far East, as Vice President and Area Supervisor for Getz Bros. Returned to San Francisco in 1939. Lt. Commander, U. S. Navy, in Military Government in World War II. Became President of Getz Bros. in 1958 and

Chairman of the Board in 1962. Elected Director of San Francisco Area World Trade Association in 1961 and became president of the association in January, 1962. Vice President and Director, British American Chamber of Commerce; Director, Japan Society; Chairman, San Francisco-Osaka Affiliated Cities Committee; Member, U. S. Selective Service Board.

JACK PODESTA

Partner Podesta Baldocchi Florists. Born 1922, San Francisco. Educated Galileo High School; graduate, University of California. World War II paratroop captain (101st Airborne Division). Member, Sales & Marketing Executives International, Sales and Marketing Executives of San Francisco, San Francisco Retail Florists Assn., San Francisco Kiwanis Club. President, Retail Merchants Assn. of San Francisco. Member, Press & Union League Club, UC Alumni Assn., UC Business Administration Alumni Assn., Masonic Fraternity, Native Sons of the Golden West, Parlor I.

WILLIAM M. JAEKLE

Assistant Vice President-System Operations, Southern Pacific Company. Born in Portland, Ore., August 25, 1912. Attended Berkeley elementary and high schools. Graduated from Stanford University and joined Southern Pacific in 1934. Various engineering department assignments until his appointment as Assistant Engineer, Maintenance of Way and Structures in 1951. Became Assistant Engineer in 1953, Chief Engineer in 1955 and General Manager, Pacific Lines, in 1960. Assumed his present position in 1962.

IRVING M. LEVIN

Executive Director, San Francisco International Film Festival for the San Francisco Art Commission. Born in San Francisco, October, 1916. Managed many theatres before becoming Divisional Director of San Francisco Theatres, Inc. circuit in 1945. Originated and is head of the S. F. Film Festival (the only recognized international motion picture competition in the United States). On Board of Directors of S. F. Theatres Inc. since 1945; Chief Barker of Variety Club of Northern California, 1957-58; President, Northern California Theatre Owners, 1958-60.

RAY B. MATTSON

President, Wilbur-Ellis Company since Dec. 14, 1959. Graduated, University of California. Resident of Atherton. Joined Wilbur-Ellis in 1923 in San Francisco. Since has worked for company in Vancouver, B. C., New York City, Chicago, Los Angeles and Seattle. Returned to San Francisco in 1957 as Executive Vice President of Wilbur-Ellis. Since then has traveled extensively inspecting domestic and foreign operations of Wilbur-Ellis and its export division, Connell Bros. Company, Ltd.

LEONARD S. MOSIAS

Head of his own architectural firm in San Francisco since 1945. Member, American Institute of Architects. Born in San Francisco in 1909, educated in local schools, Northeastern University school of law, Harvard University school of architecture. Member San Francisco Council, Boy Scouts of America (scoutmaster and cubmaster), founder and president, Troop Service Association, sponsors of Scout units for ill and handicapped boys, holder of Silver Beaver Award. Consultant to Urban Renewal Agency, City and County of San Francisco, and Architects Advisory Panel, Union of American Hebrew Congregations. Member San Francisco Consistory Scottish Rite and Islam Temple American Society of Military Engineers.

WILLIAM A. McAFEE

Director and Vice President, Supply and Transportation, Standard Oil Company of California, Western Operations, Inc. Born in Fresno, California, in 1910. Graduated from Stanford in 1931 and has been associated with Standard Oil continuously since, except for service with the United States Navy in the Pacific during World War II. Director and Vice President of the Boy Scouts of America, San Francisco Council. Member of the Executive Committee of the United Bay Area Crusade. Director of the United Community Fund. An active member of the Scottish Rite, the Commonwealth Club of California, and the Stock Exchange Club. Resides with his family at 15 Longview Court, Hillsborough.

EDWARD C. SEQUEIRA

Edward C. Sequeira, General Manager, Hotel Sir Francis Drake. Born in San Francisco, November 27, 1907; St Ignatius High School (San Francisco) and St. Mary's College. Assistant Manager and Resident Manager, Hotel St. Francis from 1943 to 1957. Presently, Chairman of the Board and Director of the San Francisco Convention & Visitors Bureau, Director of the California State Hotel Association, Director of the California Northern Hotel Association, Director of the San Francisco Rotary Club, Director of the City of San Francisco Uptown Parking Corporation. Member of the Presidio Club.

EDWARD LEE SOULÉ, JR.

President, Soulé Steel Company. Born in Berkeley, 1917. Attended University High School in Oakland. Was graduated from the University of California with a degree in Business Administration. Joined Soulé Steel Company in 1939. Became President of the firm in February, 1954. He is a member of the Kiwanis Club, the Diablo Country Club, California Tennis Club and Beta Theta Pi Fraternity.

GEORGE W. VAUGHAN

Vice President, Utah Construction & Mining Co. Born in Oklahoma City, March 21, 1918. Graduated from Stanford University. During World War II served from Ensign to Lt. Commander with U. S. Navy, primarily with carrier force in the Pacific Ocean area. Later assigned to the staff of the Secretary of State and assisted in the organization of the United Nations Conference in San Francisco in 1945. Associated with the Howard Automobile Co. until 1950. Subsequently owned and operated General Motors franchises until 1958. Served as Assistant Secretary of Defense (for Legislative Affairs) until 1960. Director of American Red Cross (San Francisco Chapter). Member of San Francisco Golf Club, The Family and Los Angeles Country Club. Home address: 2614 Jackson Street, San Francisco 15.

ROBERT W. WALKER

Vice President-Executive Representative, The Atchison, Topeka and Santa Fe Railway Company, San Francisco. Born in Salt Lake City, Utah, November 8, 1913. Educated in the public schools of Long Beach, Calif. Graduate of the University of California, 1935, and of the University of California School of Jurisprudence, 1938. Entered service of the Santa Fe as an attorney in 1945; was General Attorney in charge of the California Law Department of the Santa Fe at Los Angeles from 1948 to 1962. Appointed to his present position in 1962. Member of the Bohemian Club of San Francisco and the California Club, Los Angeles.

DONALD WATSON

President, Weyerhaeuser Steamship Company. Born in Oakland. Attended University of California. Serves on Advisory Board of Pacific American Steamship Association, Board of Directors of Pacific Maritime Association. Past President of Marine Exchange, Inc. Past President of Propeller Club of Port of San Francisco. Past President, San Francisco Commercial Club. Director, California Growth Capital Co., Inc. Member, Board of Governors, S. F. Bay Area Council; Advisory Board, Liberty Mutual Insurance Co. Past President, San Francisco Maritime Museum Association. Rear Commodore of the Great Golden Fleet and of the Marin Yacht Club.

ROY M. WESTLY

President, Lucky Lager Brewing Co. Born in Hawaii and grew up in the Philippine Islands. Attended Stanford University and the University of Southern California. Affiliated with the beverage industry in various capacities for more than 20 years, including five years with the parent Coca-Cola Co., five years with Pabst Brewing Co., and 10 years with Lucky Lager Brewing Co. Served as a bomber pilot in World War II, rank of Major, United States Air Force. Married, father of three children. Director of United States Brewers Association and Lucky Lager Brewing Company.

KING WILKIN

Chairman of the Board, Zellerbach Paper Company. Born in Robinson, Illinois. Attended University of California (at Berkeley), graduating in 1927. Entered business as a newspaperman. Joined Zellerbach Paper Company in 1937 as Director of Training; successively became Assistant to the President, General Sales Manager, Executive Vice President and General Manager and then President (in 1957). He was appointed Vice President for Marketing of Crown Zellerbach Corporation in 1959 (retaining this post as President of Zellerbach Paper Company). He is a member of the Board of Directors of the Commercial Club and a Director of the Better Business Bureau and of The Downtown Assn. Clubs: The Family, Circle de l'Union, Commonwealth Club.

(Continued on page four)

New Chamber Members

Edward J. Cory   Rolf Ruud   Alexander Black   Thos. F. Mulvihill   Mary Louise Boim

MEMBERS NEW TO THE CHAMBER ROSTER include (above, l. to r.):
Edward J. Cory, president, *Cory Imports, Inc.*, 311 California St.; Rolf Ruud,
District Sales Manager, *Bennett Tours, Inc.*, 323 Geary St.; Alexander
Black, Managing Associate, *Boyden Associates, Inc.*, 1616 International Bldg.;
Thomas F. Mulvihill, *Certified Public Accountant*, 1255 Post St.; Mary Louise
Boim, *Public Accountant*, 755 Flood Bldg.

Business Cycle Merrily Rolling
Along to New Crests of Activity

San Francisco and Bay Area business activity continues to improve, the Chamber research department reports. The general business activity index for November was 4.1 per cent higher than for November, 1961, and dropped less than one
per cent from the 1962 high reached in October. An eight per cent gain in bank
debits over the same month of 1961 was the chief reason for the rise. Department
tore sales rose 2.3 per cent and electric energy
ales were up 0.7 per cent. Freight carload-
ngs declined by 9.9 per cent. For the nine-
ounty Bay Area, freight carloadings were off
.5 per cent.

Bank debits in Oakland rose 21.4 per cent
ver November, 1961, although department
tore sales remained at about the same level.
an Jose recorded a similar spectacular jump
n bank debits of 23.8 per cent, while depart-
nent store sales showed a 4.4 per cent gain
ver November, 1961.

For the first time in the history of the Bay
rea, building permits issued in the nine-
ounty Bay Area totalled more than a billion
ollars.

Permits issued during November in San
rancisco added up to more than $20 million.
he bulk of this ($12,890,000) was for con-
truction of three 22 and 23-story apartment
uildings in the Golden Gateway redevelop.
nent area. The November figure for the Bay
rea was $95 million, of which $64 million
as for residential construction. The residen-
al figure brought the 1962 total for such
onstruction to a record high also—$637 mil-
on for the building of a record 54,812 homes
nd apartments.

California
FIRST
In Population

Shop-owners Form
Union-st. Ass'n

A new Union Street Association has been
formed by shop-owners and merchants of the
Cow Hollow area to cooperate with the Chamber to beautify the Union Street area.

Goal of the association is to retain the historical flavor and individuality of district
shops.

A four-man executive board has been set up
to guide the organization in place of the usual
president. Members of the executive board are
Mrs. Marian Britton, Ennis Bromfield, Mau-
rice Samter and Eugene DeVencenzi. Secretary
is Mrs. Helvi Walmsley.

School 'Drop-outs' Concern of Chamber Education Committee

The Chamber education committee plans to
help implement local projects under the new
Manpower Development and Training Act, according to committee chairman Kenneth R.
Rearwin.

Chamber action will include assistance to
CSES in finding areas of training need, publicity for the program and encouragement to
employers to cooperate and committee members to find part-time jobs for some potential
drop-outs who, in committee language, could
be expected to "cut the buck."

The Congress has appropriated $70 million
for solution of the program, and California
has been allotted $6 million from this fund.
Under the retraining act, CSES will determine
areas of need.

STATEMENT REQUIRED BY THE ACT OF AUGUST 24,
1912, as amended by the Acts of March 3, 1933, July 2, 1946
and June 11, 1960 (74 Stat. 208) showing the ownership, management, and circulation of Bay Region Business, published
semi-monthly at San Francisco, California, for October, 1962.
1. The names and addresses of the publisher, editor, managing
editor, and business managers are:

Publisher, San Francisco Chamber of Commerce, 333 Pine St.,
San Francisco 4, Calif.

Editor, Joseph I. Haughey, 333 Pine St., San Francisco 4,
Calif.

Associate Editor, Charles Morgan, 333 Pine St., San Francisco
4, Calif.

Business Manager, Joseph I. Haughey, 333 Pine St., San Francisco 4, Calif.

2. The owner is: (If owned by a corporation, its name and address must be stated and also immediately thereunder the names
and addresses of stockholders owning or holding 1 per cent or
more of total amount of stock. If not owned by a corporation, the
names and addresses of the individual owners must be given. If
owned by a partnership or other unincorporated firm, its name
and address, as well as that of each individual member, must be
given.)

San Francisco Chamber of Commerce, 333 Pine St., San Francisco 4, Calif.

3. The known bondholders, mortgagees, and other security holders owning or holding 1 per cent or more of total amount of
bonds, mortgages, or other securities are: (If there are none, so
state.)

None.

4. Paragraphs 2 and 3 include, in cases where the stockholder
or security holder appears upon the books of the company as
trustee or in any other fiduciary relation, the name of the person
or corporation for whom such trustee is acting; also the statements in the two paragraphs show the affiant's full knowledge
and belief as to the circumstances and conditions under which
stockholders and security holders who do not appear upon the
books of the company as trustees, hold stock and securities in a
capacity other than that of a bona fide owner.

5. The average number of copies of each issue of this publication sold or distributed, through the mails or otherwise, to paid
subscribers during the 12 months preceding the date shown above
was: (This information is required by the Act of June 11, 1960
to be included in all statements regardless of frequency of
issue.) 7,500.

JOSEPH I. HAUGHEY, Editor.

Sworn to and subscribed before me this 9th day of October,
1962. Alice E. Lowrie, Notary Public in and for the City and
County of San Francisco, State of California.

(My commission expires May 23, 1964.)

BAY REGION BUSINESS

SAN FRANCISCO CHAMBER OF COMMERCE

VOLUME 20 • NUMBER 2 • JANUARY 25, 1963

EARLY "SPRING"—*Regardless of the thermometer or the calendar, "spring" came to San Francisco last weekend with the planting of 50,000 packets of wildflower seeds on the Market-street side of Twin Peaks. Boy Scouts and Girl Scouts, about 700 of them, turned out to sow the hillside—pointing up the Chamber of Commerce "Plant-a-Tree" Week (April 1-6). Sponsors of the seed-planting included the Chamber, San Francisco Beautiful, and the Department of Public Works. Richfield Oil Co. donated the seeds.*

Chamber Approves Hunters' Point Freeway Route

San Francisco Chamber of Commerce is on record in support of "Alternative Route C" of the proposed Hunters Point Freeway.

Several plans were advanced for the freeway to link the Southern-Embarcadero Freeway extension with a point on State Sign Route 253 which branches off Highway 101 near the San Francisco-San Mateo county line.

Other routes proposed, the Chamber board said, would impinge on existing residential and industrial areas, while Route C would skirt these areas. It would be constructed on fill areas currently under water.

California
FIRST
In Population

Radio Programs

SAN FRANCISCO IN THE SIXTIES: *An Analysis of President Kennedy's Budget Message*—S. C. Worthington, Division Commercial Manager, PT&T; George Johns, Sec-Treas., S. F. Labor Council. 8:05 p.m., Saturday, KNBR.

SAN FRANCISCO PROGRESS REPORT: *A New Cathedral for the Archdiocese*--The Most Rev. Joseph T. McGucken, Archbishop, Archdiocese of San Francisco. 10:30 a.m., Sunday (Jan. 27), KFRC.

CONFERENCE CALL: *A Peace Corps for San Francisco?*—Irving J. Kriegsfeld, Director, Mission Neighborhood Centers; John Dervin, President, USF Student Body. 8 p.m., Sunday (Jan. 27), KFRC.

1964 Retirement Set for Chamber Executive V.P.

G. L. Fox, executive vice president of the Chamber, will retire on July 1, 1964, in accordance with the Chamber's pension program, according to Harry A. Lee, president of the Chamber.

Lee said the announcement was being made to answer questions which have arisen as a result of forward-planning discussions by the Chamber board of directors. He was highly complimentary about the work which has been and is being done by Fox, who will attain age 65 in 1964.

Lee said the executive committee of the Chamber will direct an orderly transition in the Chamber's management and make its recommendations to the Chamber's board in due course.

Fox is one of the most widely known Chamber executives in the nation. He is a director of the American Chamber of Commerce Executives, a director of the California Association of Chamber of Commerce Managers, and president of the Central and Northern California Chamber of Commerce Executives.

Upon retirement he will have served the Chamber for more than 21 years.

Stanley Allen New Research Manager

Stanley C. Allen, former location site analyst for the Crocker-Anglo National Bank, has been named manager of the Chamber's Research Department, according to executive vice president G. L. Fox.

Allen replaces Fritz Albershardt, who resigned the Chamber post to accept a position with Medical Management Control, 1906 Irving Street, San Francisco.

Prior to his association with Crocker-Anglo, Allen was market analyst for the Belgian consulate in San Francisco.

Education Committee Outlines Eight Point Program

An eight-point program outlining areas of activity in behalf of the betterment of education in the interests of the business community has been announced by the Chamber education committee.

Goals of the Chamber — disclosed by Harry A. Lee, Chamber president—were approved by the organization's board of directors following the recommendation of its education committee of which Kenneth R. Rearwin, vice president and manager of Merrill Lynch, Pierce, Fenner & Smith, is chairman.

The program of the Chamber education committee will include activity in these areas:

- school budgets (both operations and capital outlay);
- the student "drop-out" problem;
- curriculum, involving general content, basic fundamentals, American political and historical heritage, the free enterprise system, and vocational skills;
- summer school objectives and duration;
- possibility of a centrally-located, citywide academic four-year high school;
- methods of selecting and appointing Board of Education members;
- special events to encourage and recognize scholastic achievements;
- ways to increase the excellence of public school education and offer fuller cooperation with parochial and private schools.

This Calendar has been prepared on basis of laws as of December 1962.

TAX CALENDAR—1963

NOTE: Dates reported are for taxpayers on a calendar year basis. Those whose fiscal year ends on other than Dec. 31 should use dates corresponding to the calendar year.

FEDERAL TAXES

(all payable to District Director of Internal Revenue unless otherwise indicated)

INTERESTED PARTIES	FORM	Description	JAN.	FEB.	MARCH	APRIL	MAY	JUNE	JULY	AUG.	SEPT.	OCT.	NOV.	DEC.
Individuals	1040 1040A	PERSONAL INCOME TAX: 1962 final return—file and pay balance due by 15th day of the 4th month following end of the taxable year.				15th Return and tax								
Individuals	1040ES	1963 ESTIMATED TAX: declaration and ¼ of estimated tax due on the 15th of 4th month of taxable year. Additional payments due on 15th of 2nd, 5th, and 9th months following.	Balance 1962 estimate			15th Return and ¼ 1963 tax		17th ¼ 1963 tax			16th ¼ 1963 tax			
Corporations	1120	INCOME TAX: domestic and resident foreign corporations file 1962 returns and pay 50% of balance due by 15th of 3rd month after end of taxable year. Final 50% due 15th of 6th month after end of taxable year.			15th Return and ½ tax			17th Balance of tax						
Corporations	1120ES	1963 ESTIMATED TAX: above corporations which expect tax liability to exceed $100,000, file estimate and pay 25% on May 15th day of the 9th month of the taxable year, and 25% by 15th day of the 12th month of the taxable year.									16th Return and 25% tax			16th 25% tax
Employers	941 (return only) 450 (with deposit) W2 W3	PAYROLL TAXES: when combined social security and income taxes withheld exceed $100 in any month, amount must be deposited in authorized depository by 15th of following month. Payment for third month may be made with quarterly return instead of deposited. Individual withholding and reconciliation statements (W2, W3) accompany January 31 return and payment.	31st 4th quarter 1962 Return and payment	15th Deposit if Jan. tax over $100	15th Deposit if Feb. tax over $100	30th 1st quarter return and payment	15th Deposit if April tax over $100	17th Deposit if May tax over $100	31st 2nd quarter return and payment	15th Deposit if July tax over $100	16th Deposit if Aug. tax over $100	31st 3rd quarter return and payment	15th Deposit if Oct. tax over $100	16th Deposit if Nov. tax over $100
Employers, Corporations	1099 1099L 1096	INFORMATION RETURNS: on wages and payments of interest, rents, royalties, annuities, etc. of $600 or more in total, or dividends exceeding $10, or compensation paid to employees but not reported on form W2A. Send to Dir., Midwest Service Center, Ogden, Utah.		28th Returns										
Partnerships, Joint Ventures	1065	PARTNERSHIP INCOME: due 15th day of 4th month following end of taxable year. No tax due. Income reported in partner's individual returns.				15th Return								
Estates	1041	ESTATE INCOME: Return due 15th day of 4th month following end of taxable year. Information returns (Form 1041-A) of certain non-taxable trusts due April 15.	15th Balance 1961 tax			15th Return and ¼ 1962			15th ¼ 1962 tax			15th ¼ 1962 tax		
Trusts	1041	TRUST INCOME: Return and tax due 15th day of 4th month following end of year. Information returns (Form 1041-A) of certain non-taxable trusts due April 15.				15th Return and tax								
Non-resident Foreign Corporations	1120NB	INCOME TAX: Return due 18th day of 6th month following end of year. Tax due with return.						17th Return and ½ tax						
Tax Exempt Corporations, Trusts and Cooperatives	990 990A	EXEMPT CORPORATIONS: Corporations claiming exemption from income tax. Return due 15th day of 5th month after close of calendar or fiscal year. (Forms 990, 990-A). (Exempt Employees Trust, Form 990-P). (Except unrelated business income on Form 990-T). Exempt Cooperatives, Return (Form 990-C) due 15th day of 9th month following end of taxable year. If filed, Form 990 not required.					15th Returns							
Retailers, Manufacturers, Amusements, Cabarets	720	EXCISE TAXES: if more than $100 collected in either of first two months of a quarter, pay to authorized depository by 15th of following month. Taxes for 3rd month of quarter may be paid with quarterly return, due at end of month following end of quarter. If tax for each month is deposited in time, date for filing quarterly return is extended 10 days.	31st 4th quarter 1962 Return and payment	15th Deposit if Jan. tax over $100	15th Deposit if Feb. tax over $100	30th 1st quarter return and payment	15th Deposit if April tax over $100	17th Deposit if May tax over $100	31st 2nd quarter return and payment	15th Deposit if July tax over $100	16th Deposit if Aug. tax over $100	31st 3rd quarter return and payment	15th Deposit if Oct. tax over $100	16th Deposit if Nov. tax over $100
Liquor Dealers, Wholesale and Retail	11	EXCISE STAMPS: apply for stamps with certified check, cash or money order by July 2.							2nd Application					

INTERESTED PARTIES	FORM		RESPONSIBLE AGENCY	JAN.	FEB.	MAR.	APRIL	MAY	JUNE	JULY	AUG.	SEPT.	OCT.	NOV.	DEC.
Retailers and purchasers of personal property subject to tax	S401 et al.	SALES AND USE TAX: File return and pay tax on or before last day of month following end of taxable quarter. If required to pay on monthly basis, do so by last day of month following.	State Board of Equalization	31st 4th quarter 1962 return and payment			30th 1st quarter 1963 return and payment			31st 2nd quarter return and payment			31st 3rd quarter return and payment		
Employers	DE3	UNEMPLOYMENT AND DISABILITY INSURANCE: File return and pay by end of month following the taxable quarter. Disability insurance—1% deducted from employee's gross earnings up to $4600 each for 1963, unless covered by voluntary plan. Unemployment tax in 1963 rises to a maximum of 3.5% for employer on first $3,300 in wages of each employee.	State Dept. of Employment	31st 4th quarter 1962 return and payment			30th 1st quarter 1963 return and payment			31st 2nd quarter return and payment			31st 3rd quarter return and payment		
Individuals	540 540A	INCOME TAX: First payment of $50 or ½ of tax, whichever is greater, by 15th of 4th month after taxable year; second payment=50% of remaining balance, due 15th of 8th month; third payment=remainder, due 15th of 12th month following close of taxable year.	State Franchise Tax Board				15th Return and all tax, or ½ tax if over $50				15th ½ of tax if total over $50				16th ½ of tax if total over $50
Banks and Corporations	100	INCOME TAX: Minimum tax, even though corporation is inactive or operates at a loss, is $100. Banks pay full tax with return.	State Franchise Tax Board			15th Return and ½ tax						16th ½ tax			
Motor Vehicle Owners		REGISTRATION AND LICENSE FEE: Plate fees $8 per year plus 2% of market value of vehicle. Fee for calendar year becomes delinquent and subject to penalties after first Monday in February.	State Dept. of Motor Vehicles and fees		4th Registration and fees										
Employers	599 596	ANNUAL INFORMATION RETURN: Payments to individuals of (1) interest, rent, royalties, annuities, etc., of $1500 or more in total, (2) compensation of $1,500 or more to single person or $3,000 to married person, or (3) dividends of $100 or more.	State Franchise Tax Board		28th Return										
Employers	591 592	File return and pay tax on amounts withheld from non-residents of California.	State Franchise Tax Board				15th Return								
Public utilities, owners of state assessed property		File statement of property owned or used, money and solvent credits owned at noon, March 4, 1963.	State Board of Equalization				1st Statement								
Liquor licensees, other than on-sale retailers		License renewal—apply between May 1 and June 30. File report for year ending June 30 and pay additional license fee by July 31.	Dept. of Alcoholic Beverage Control					1st through 29th Application for renewal		31st Report and additional fees					
Liquor retailers		Make "on-sale" retailers license renewal application between November 1 and December 31.	Dept. of Alcoholic Beverage Control											Nov. 1 thru Dec. 31 Application for renewal	

CITY AND COUNTY TAXES

INTERESTED PARTIES	FORM		RESPONSIBLE AGENCY	JAN.	FEB.	MAR.	APRIL	MAY	JUNE	JULY	AUG.	SEPT.	OCT.	NOV.	DEC.
Property owners		REAL PROPERTY TAX: Payable in two installments: last half 1962 tax due February 1 through April 10; first half 1963 tax due November 1 through December 10. Penalty for delinquency, 6% plus costs.	Tax Collector		Feb. 1st through Apr. 10th 2nd half 1962 tax payable Delinquent 4/10 at 5:00 p.m.									Nov. 1 thru Dec. 10 1st half 1963 tax payable Delinquent 12/10, 5:00 p.m.	
Property owners		PERSONAL PROPERTY TAX: File statement by May 27 of property owned as of noon, March 4. Tax becomes delinquent with 8% penalty after August 31.	Assessor ; Tax Collector			4th List property owned at noon		27th File Statement			31st Pay tax				
Property owners on leased land		File for separate tax bill by 5 P. M. first Monday in March.	Assessor			4th Return									

OFFICES OF TAX AGENCIES

Assessor, City and County of San Francisco, City Hall — KL 2-1910
Tax Collector, City and County of San Francisco, City Hall — HE 1-2121
State Board of Equalization, Stevenson and Fifth Streets — UN 1-3700
State Franchise Tax Board, State Building Annex, 345 Larkin — UN 1-7234

State Department of Motor Vehicles, 250 Baker — UN 3-0500
State Department of Insurance, 1182 Market Street — KL 2-0212
State Controller, 515 Van Ness Avenue — UN 1-3700
District Director of Internal Revenue, 100 McAllister Street — UN 3-4900

If any date falls on a Sunday or legal holiday, the return is due the following day.

With *JOE HAUGHEY*

)ON MILLS, veteran broadcasting and publish-ıg figure in the Bay Area, has been named di-ector of public relations for KQED, the educa-ional station announced this week. He replaces Iarianne Goldman, who resigned in December fter serving as publicity director for the station ince its inception in 1954. . . .

.ELAND BUTLER has been appointed attorney ı the Santa Fe rail lines' legal department, ac-ording to Starr Thomas, the lines' general ounsel in Chicago. . . .

:. RONALD LONG, president of San Francisco 'ederal Savings, announced expansion plans for 963. They include plans already approved for a ew office adjacent to the Japanese Cultural Center in San Francisco, another at El Camino Real and California Avenue in Palo Alto. Expan-ion of other facilities is also on the program, .ong said. . . .

:RUCIBLE STEEL COMPANY, specialty steel ıroducer, is expanding its Bay Area operation vith a lease on one floor concrete clear-span ıuilding at 1255 22nd St., according to Damon t-ike and Company. . . .

;PUR (San Francisco Planning and Urban Re-ıewal Assn.) will stage its third annual confer-:nce at the Fairmont Hotel, Jan. 29. Subject of his year's discussion will be "Neighborhoods ınd Our City." . . .

:TALIAN GOVERNMENT will again enter the San Francisco National Sports and Boat Show ²ebruary 1-10 at the Cow Palace, according to Dr. Alessandro Savorgnan, consul general, and :ommercial attache Dr. Emanuele Costa. . . .

SAN FRANCISCO COUNCIL of District Mer-:hants Associations will stage its 11th annual .nstallation and Dinner Dance at Del Webb's TowneHouse, Saturday, Jan. 26. Officers to be nstalled are Paul V. Gill, president; Mike Salarno, 1st vice president; Leonard S. Bacci, !nd vice president; Harry J. Aleo, 3rd vice ıresident; Frank Tarantino, treasurer; James Iurley, sergeant at arms, and Harold V. Starr, :xecutive secretary.

JNITED AIR LINES passenger traffic in De-:ember set industry record for the month . . . :35,000,000 revenue passenger miles, a gain of even per cent over December, 1961. Total of ¹42,000 passengers was up two per cent, mail ton niles rose 10 per cent and freight ton miles, 12 ıer cent. . . .

RETIREMENT OF JOHN PETTIT, Yellow Cab vice-president emeritus for community re-ations, was announced at a luncheon in his ıonor on Jan. 17. . . . Born on Christmas Day, 891, Pettit has acted as the Chamber's unoffi-:ial "Ambassador Extraordinary" in travels hrough Europe, Africa, Canada, Mexico and he United States. . . .

New Chamber Members

Winfield S. Rumsey   Chris Borden   Robert B. Rorick   Paul F. Barnum   George V. Sweeney

MEMBERS NEW TO THE CHAMBER ROSTER include (above. l. to r.): Winfield S. Rumsey, executive director. *San Francisco Lighthouse for the Blind*, 1097 Howard St.; Chris Borden, owner, *Chris Borden School of Modern Radio Technique*, 259 Geary St.; Robert B. Rorick, president, *Games Imported of San Francisco*, 117 Post St.; Paul F. Barnum, owner, *San Francisco Potato Processing Co.*, 1991 Oakdale Ave.; George V. Sweeney, president, *San Francisco International Tourama*, 516 Geary St.

Gala Parade for Year of the Hare

More than a quarter-million celebrants are expected to line San Francisco's streets for the annual Chinese New Year's Day parade Feb. 9.

Route of the parade has been lengthened this year to accommodate the throngs expect-ed to join San Francisco's Chinese colony as it ends its week-long celebration of Chinese lunar year 4661—the Year of the Hare.

The parade will form at First and Market Streets at 7 p.m. Marchers will proceed up Market to Grant, through the style-conscious section of Grant Ave., and then through Chinatown.

For the first time, the New Year's parade will be telecast nationwide by ABC-TV.

Highlight of the famous parade will be, again, the Golden Dragon, the 125-foot long serpentine beast which weaves along the en-tire parade route.

THESE BAY AREA *Chinese-American beau-ties face competition aplenty in balloting for the title of "Miss Chinatown, USA," with entries still arriving from the Mainland and Hawaii. Contending for the honor of sitting in the Queen's throne in the New Year's Day parade are (l. to r.) Cecilia Wu, San Francisco; An-toinette Jay, Alameda; and Jennie Yep, San Francisco.*

SUZY STRAUSS has been appointed press and public relations director for Fairmont Hotel and Tower, according to president and managing director Richard L. Swig. . . .

NATIONAL AIRLINES president L. B. Maytag, Jr. said the firm showed an increase of 27 per cent in revenue-passenger miles during first half of 1962-63 business year. . . .

STANFORD UNIVERSITY professor Edward S. Shaw says California should charter practi-cally no new savings and loan associations for several years and should approve only "selec-tive mergers" of existing firms. Comment was made in a report to Savings and Loan Commis-sioner Preston N. Silbaugh. . . .

Calendar

January 25 — SOUTH AFRICAN TRADE DELEGATION LUNCHEON, no-host—World Trade Club, noon.

January 28—TRAFFIC SAFETY & CONTROL SECTION MEETING—Rm. 200, Chamber Building, 333 Pine St., 10:30 a.m.

January 29 — SAN FRANCISCO MUNICIPAL CONFER-ENCE—Rm. 200, Chamber Building, 333 Pine St., 3:00 p.m.

January 30—WORLD TRADE ASSOCIATION LUNCHEON MEETING—World Trade Club, noon.

February 3-6—GIFT AND HOUSEWARES SHOW—Brooks Hall, Western Merchandise Mart.

February 6—CONTACT CLUB MEETING—3rd floor, Sig-nature Room, John Hancock Building, 255 California St., 10:15 a.m.

HARRY A. LEE, President
C. L. FOX, Executive Vice President
M. A. HOGAN, Secretary
JOSEPH I. HAUGHEY, Editor
CHARLES MORGAN, Associate Editor

Published monthly and owned by the San Francisco Chamber of Commerce, a non-profit organization, at 333 Pine St., San Francisco, Zone 4, County of San Francisco, California. Telephone EXbrook 2-4511. (Sent free to sub-scription, $5.00 a year.) Entered as Second Class matter April 26, 1944, at the Post Office at San Francisco, Cali-fornia, under the Act of March 3, 1879.

Circulation: 7,500

BAY REGION

SAN FRANCISCO CHAMBER OF COMMERCE

VOLUME 20 • NUMBER 3 • FEBRUARY 15, 1963

BUSINESS

1962 Annual Edition

Agricultural Department — Chairman and Vice Chairman — Carl L. Garrison and W. Hunt Conrad, Agricultural Committee; Carl L. Garrison and Ed Le Vesconte, Livestock Sales Committee; Henry Schacht, Livestock Man Award Committee. Manager: Randle P. Shields.

Striving to develop greater understanding between San Francisco and the agricultural industry — with special attention to the generally unrealized interdependence of both — this department last year:

• Acted to protect northern California's interests in water quality under the State Water Plan, and to safeguard against soil salinity.

• Helped to clarify and declare agriculture's viewpoints on farm-labor problems.

• Studied application of agricultural fire control methods to suburban residential areas.

• Recommended policy on ballot proposition affecting assessments of agricultural lands. (Prepared detailed report on this issue for information statewide.)

• Promoted 1962 Grand National Junior Livestock Exposition and the 1962 Grand National; raised funds to assure premium prices for exhibit animals; sponsored "Salute to Rural Youth" luncheon; presented merit awards to outstanding farm youngsters; elected and honored California's Livestock Man of the Year; promoted San Francisco Chamber Night at Grand National.

• Conducted special events and luncheons to commemorate "burning of the mortgage" on San Francisco Farmers' Market; promoted "June is Dairy Month."

• Helped promote state-wide observance of National Farm-City Week.

• Prepared and widely distributed a special report on "What Agriculture Means to San Francisco," including three special mailings to farm leaders.

• Acted to expedite construction of $93 million dollar new Don Pedro Dam on the Tuolumne River as a project vital to San Francisco and Valley irrigation districts.

• Sought convention of National Cotton Council for San Francisco.

• Alerted members to possible effects of European Common Market on world market for California farm commodities.

• Activated new Nominating Section and enlarged the Agricultural Committee through screening and election of additional farm leaders as new members.

• Arranged and staffed 17 meetings involving the attendance of 563 persons.

• Answered hundreds of inquiries.

• Represented Chamber on various state-wide farm councils.

Civic Development — Chairmen and Vice Chairmen: Edward C. Sequeira, Civic Development Committee; F. Marion Donahoe and Dan A. Giles, Capital Improvement & Land Use; John J. Conlon and Myron Bird, Fire Safety; V. S. Herrington and Gustave E. J. Jamart, Mass Transit; Roy N. Buell and Robert Parlett, Regional Problems; Leonard S. Mosias and Oscar H. Fisher, Jr., Street, Highway and Bridge; H. A. Dunker and Roy E. Matison, Traffic, Safety and Control. Manager: Harold V. Starr.

Striving to develop the City and County of San Francisco's current and future municipal and related government programs through its own studies and recommendations, this department:

• Studied Community Renewal Program and approved the request to file application with HHFA for a $663,000 federal assistance grant to enable city departments to undertake a two-year study leading to city-wide program for community renewal.

• Recommended land acquisition for park and recreational purposes, but disapproved the $150,000,000 State Park & Recreation Bond Act.

• Requested delay in sale of Old Hall of Justice until study of best use of property can be made by City Planning Commission.

• Disapproved comprehensive sign control ordinance in existing form.

• Fire safety section and building code section members worked to eliminate duplications existing in Fire, Building and Housing codes.

• Mounted educational campaign to insure passage of the $792,000,000 San Francisco Bay Area Rapid Transit District Bond Issue.

• Studied San Francisco Bay barrier proposals and inspected Bay model at Sausalito.

• Studied Department of Public Works alternate plan to freeway program.

• Studied proposed freeway route through Panhandle to connect with Central Freeway through Golden Gate Park to Presidio Blvd.

• Made recommendations to California Highway Commission at Sacramento for construction projects, right-of-way allocations, surveys, design and rights-of-way acquisition for inclusion in 1963-64 budget.

• Studied proposed legislation to control signs on Southern-Embarcadero Freeway Extension regulating advertising structures. (Board approved requested action to support City Planning Commission resolution to amend Building Code Section to include Southern-Embarcadero Freeway Extension).

• Studied Alternate Routes, A, B, and C, Hunters Point Freeway, Legislative Route 253. (Section favored Route C.)

• Held fifth Annual Voluntary Community Vehicle Safety Check for three days in May. 99,728 cars checked.

• Distributed 85,000 Welcome to San Francisco driving tips leaflets.

Industrial Department — *Chairmen and Vice Chairmen: Wesley T. Hayes, Building Code Section; John A. Gast and A. W. Werry, Chemical Industries Section; C. D. Lafferty and Joseph K. Allen, Industrial Development; George A. Vosper, Manufacturers; Edward V. Wisser, Mining; William B. Swan and H. P. Stewart, Shipbuilding and Ship Repair; William W. Moore and D. I. Anzini, Technical Projects. Manager: Lewis M. Holland; Assistant Manager, Harold T. Wood.*

• Coordinated and arranged details for the Western Space Age Industries and Engineering Exposition, (April 24-29) at Cow Palace.

• Cooperated in studies leading to the recommendation for location on the Hunters Point Freeway.

• Attended 142 meetings, held nearly 6,500 telephone conversations, conducted 750 interviews and wrote 896 letters relating to industrial development.

• Conferred and corresponded with more than 150 industrial prospects regarding new plant locations in the San Francisco Bay Region.

• Compiled, tabulated and distributed information about new plants and expansions in San Francisco, the Bay Region and northern California.

• Distributed Architects and Engineers Directory, Aero-Space Electronics Directory and Plant-Tour list.

• Published Aero-Space Electronics Directory.

• Continued activity to solve problems in disposing building debris and other waste material economically.

• Successfully cooperated with Western Shipbuilding Association to defeat legislation which would have eliminated the six per cent differential on West Coast shipbuilding.

• Reviewed legislative proposals affecting local manufacturing and recommended suitable changes.

• Fought vigorously for the retention of the San Francisco Mining Exchange.

• Continued campaign to re-locate printing and others firms displaced by Golden Gateway Project.

• Held meetings with technical and building industry groups to coordinate annual amendments to the San Francisco building code.

• Reactivated the South of Market Redevelopment Subcommittee.

• Instituted studies on newly-proposed fire code with relation to San Francisco building code.

• Formed subcommittee to study manufacturing costs which could be detrimental to industrial development in San Francisco and the Bay Area.

Cover Illustration

by Jim Ballance

Available at Chamber Publicity Office

• *Suitable for framing*

• *50 cents each*

Domestic Trade Department — *(hereafter to be known as Business and Trade Department)— Chairman, Ralph J. Wrenn; Section Chairmen: F. T. Garesche, Inter-City; John O'Brien Cullen, Hawaiian Affairs; Daniel K. Beswick, Business Headquarters Promotion; Donald Hietter, Small Business; Dan E. London (Commodore), Great Golden Fleet.*

With its objectives to promote the sale of San Francisco products and services and San Francisco as the business headquarters of the Pacific Coast, and to create and sustain harmonious relationships between the business communities, organizations and individuals in the western states and San Francisco, this department last year:

• Launched a national promotional campaign among 2,800 corporations to attract new executive offices to San Francisco.

• Coordinated San Joaquin Valley Days on June 28 and 29. (Approximately 200 civic business leaders were provided conducted tours and entertained in San Francisco during the two-day event).

• Conducted trade development tours to 25 communities in Northern California.

• Counseled prospective new business owners and entrepeneurs on San Francisco business and market conditions and location factors.

• Responded to 2,525 written and 5,400 telephone inquiries relating to San Francisco products and services.

• Answered approximately 2,560 personal inquiries regarding business conditions and business opportunities in San Francisco Bay Area.

• Published 1962 Annual edition of the *Directory of Large Manufacturers—13 Bay Region Counties.*

• Participated in and promoted several major trade events.

• Published listings of 135 business opportunities in San Francisco for manufacturers and manufacturers' representatives.

About Our Cover Artist

The cover of this issue of *Bay Region Business* was created by Jim Ballance, a native San Franciscan and history buff who is a staff artist on the *San Francisco Examiner.* A former advertising manager and also creative head of an ad agency, Ballance has worked for the old *S. F. Call-Bulletin* and the

Chicago Sun-Times in addition to free-lance illustrating following a 5½-year stint in the Army Air Corps during World War II. Ballance calls his cover "a historical panorama of San Francisco from 1849 until 1906."

The inside illustrations are by Ballance and Hank Jackson and Don Irwin, who are fellow staffers on the *Examiner.*

Jackson, another native of San Francisco, is his colleagues' favorite cartoonist on the staffs of local newspapers—an artist's artist. Except for a three-year tour as a maritime purser during WWII, he has been an *Examiner* man most of his adult life and is famed as the creator of *Monk Sez,* a popular daily racing panel.

Jim Ballance   Irwin is a 29-year-old Canadian national who joined the *Examiner* in 1958 following service with the U. S. Army in Europe. He was educated at Beal Tech in Ontario and worked on the *L. A. Examiner* before "graduating" to the S. F. *Examiner.*

'ublic Affairs Department —*Chairmen*

ld Vice Chairmen: Major Gen. Stuart D. Menist, USAR, rmed Forces Section; George Rhodes and Edwin M. 'ilson, Aviation Section; Arnold E. Archibald, Business-lucation Committee; Kenneth R. Rearwin and John G. evison, Education Committee; S. G. Worthington, Legi-ative and National Affairs Section; Clarence C. Walker ld Victor B. Levit, Practical Politics Program Commit-c; Randell Larson and H. J. Brunnier, Redevelopment ordinating Committee; H. C. Tyler and J. Wesley Huss, 'ax Section. Manager: Randle P. Shields.

In considering and recommending action on pu)lic sues concerning aviation, armed forces, redevelopment, xation and other governmental matters, and in seeking increase general understanding of the American eco-)mic, educational and political systems, this department - with its 240 committeemen — accomplished the fol-wing:

RMED FORCES SECTION

- Led community efforts to retain vital military)ases, including the Presidio (Letterman General Hospital), Treasure Island and Fort Mason.

- Commemorated Armed Forces Week with a civic luncheon and other ceremonies.
- Assisted federal agencies in nuclear fall-out shelter survey.
- Helped promote civic program recognizing ROTC in local high schools.
- Visited military installations on liaison missions.
- Participated in U. S. Sixth Army ceremonies honoring e Cham)er for outstanding efforts toward civilian-military amwork.

VIATION SECTION

- Campaigned successfully for passage of $9.8 million irport Garage Bond proposal. (Prop. A on the June, 1962 unicipal Ballot.)
- Sought improved rates and facilities for general avia-)n.
- Urged compliance with laws providing that federal ;encies at San Francisco International Airport should pay nt for space used.
- Studied potential impact of proposed supersonic jet ansports and X-15 developments on aviation and the over-l economy.
- Helped on air line promotional ceremonies.
- Strongly supported principle of financing through non-'ofit corporation of major air line facilities at the Airport.
- Aided helicopter service for Bay Area.

USINESS-EDUCATION COMMITTEE

- Sponsored San Francisco's 12th annual Education-Busi-'ss Day (660 representatives of the)usiness community sited local schools), and the 13th annual Business-Educa-)n Day (over 4,000 teachers visited some 200 local)usiness rms).

DUCATION COMMITTEE

- Sponsored "Salute to Scholarship" luncheon honoring p students in San Francisco's pu)lic, private and parochial hools.
- Acted on pro)lems involving proposed Central Junior igh School, economic education, school curriculum, etc.
- Assisted school and PTA officials in o)taining speakers 1)usiness-education su)jects.
- Presented scholarship award to high school showing '')st scholarship attainment.
- Visited with officers and faculty of San Francisco State o!!cg .
- Re presented Cham)er at meetings of the Board of Edu-tion and its sub-committees.

Membership Relations Department

— *Chairman and Vice Chairman, Membership Committee: William J. Bird and Burt W. Pickard. Section Chairmen: Burt W. Pickard, Re-evaluation; Alan K. Browne, Retention. Contact Club officers: Gene Fox, Chairman, Dick Huss, Co-Chairman, Gene Whitworth, Program Incentives and Awards Chairman; Executive Committee and Team Captains: Ray Bartlett, Carl Brune, Chuck Coombs, Jack Cunningham, Trev Cushman, Stan Dubois, Al Enderlin, George Ford, Gene Fox, Allen Hanner, and Dick Huss.*

Membership Department Manager: Herbert H. Harmon. Special Representatives: Earle L. Hawkins, Farmer B. Smith, Ralph F. Miller, and Walter J. Maxwell.

With its o)jective of increasing the Cham)er's strength and effectiveness by expanding and maintaining mem)ership)ase fostering community support of Cham)er activities, stimulating member participation in Committee programs and informing in depth the)usiness community and Cham)er mem)ership by relating the "Chamber Story," this department:

- Secured 407 new mem)ers. An increase of exactly 100 over 1961.
- Organized the 1962 Contact Clu))y recruiting 75 volunteer executives from Cham)er mem)er firms and sold 75 mem)erships.
- Organized the 1962 Re-evaluation Committee which contacted)y)y)usiness categories Cham)er mem)er firms to increase Fair Share Dues Support.
- Organized the 1962 Retention Committee which contacted firms in resignation status to lower attrition rate.
- Held 13 orientation and assimilation meetings for Chamber mem)ers (5,250 invitations were sent and 1,950 telephone calls made).
- Trained its professional sales staff.
- Developed a program which added 67 firms to those which had already honored the 16⅔ per cent increase in the)asic dues rate.
- Increased efficiency of monthly dues)illing system which resulted in the further reduction of monthly delinquent accounts and the increase of cash receipts.
- Pu)lished a four color)rochure entitled "Fascinating San Francisco — Your Guide to . . . Hotels — Motels — Restaurants — Sightseeing" which was selected)y printers nationwide for a national award. This)rochure, as a sales tool, produced over 100 new Cham)er mem)ers.

LEGISLATIVE AND NATIONAL AFFAIRS

- Co-sponsored day-long AIRCADE FOR CITIZENSHIP ACTION (attended)y more than 500)usiness leaders).
- Recommended, assisted in wording of and successfully supported Prop. C on the June, 1962, Municipal Ballot, improving operations of City and County purchasing department to the advantage of the city and)usiness concerns.
- Devoted two meetings to study of postal-rate increase legislation in Congress; expressed businessmen's viewpoints on Department of Ur)an Affairs issue, etc.
- Spent hundreds of man hours in studying and recommending Cham)er policy on 17 State and local propositions on the June and Novem)er 1962)allots.
- Extensively studied King-Anderson Bill in Congress; (recommended opposition to medical care for the aged under Social Security and favored extension of program under Kerr-Mills Act).

(Continued on page five)

Publicity Department — *Chairman, Publicity Committee, Ross Barrett; Manager: Joseph I. Haughey; Assistant Manager: Charles Morgan.*

Pu)licizing and advertising the City and County of San Francisco and its economic and cultural development locally, nationally and internationally for the)enefit of local)usiness and informing its mem)ers and the pu)lic regarding the aims, actions and accomplishments of the Cham)er, this department:

• Prepared and distri)uted 536 news releases, captions, memos and fact sheets relating to Cham)er or civic events to hundreds of pu)lications, radio and television stations throughout the United States.

• Prepared and distri)uted 295 news photos and 929 mats to Northern California daily and weekly newspapers.

• Sent 2,429 captioned scenic photographs of San Francisco to 1,250 pu)lications and organizations throughout the world.

• Sent 1,995 magazine service)ureau articles a)out San Francisco to pu)lications all over the glo)e.

• Developed 35 new captioned scenic photographs of San Francisco.

• Lent 112 negatives, slides and transparencies to pu)lications and individuals throughout the world.

• Lent 77 cuts of San Francisco to various individuals and pu)lications.

• Handled 200 requests from press, radio and television and from organizations and individuals for information a)out the City and the Cham)er.

• Sent out 707 posters, 202 water-color lithographs, 193 four-color photo murals and 19,630 post cards of San Francisco to organizations and individuals in the far corners of the glo)e.

• Prepared and edited semi-monthly pu)lication, BAY REGION BUSINESS.

• Provided 14,000 reprints of features from BAY REGION BUSINESS for special mailings and distri)ution to pu)licize aspects of San Francisco.

• Handled press, radio and television relations for approximately 40 special events, including Cham)er luncheons, Education-Business and Business-Education Day, London Week, Vehicle Safety Check, Plant A Tree Week, Grand National, Jr. Grand National, Livestock Man of the Year, Seattle Fair Exhi)it, KQED Auction, Invest in America Luncheon, Armed Forces Day Luncheon, World Trade Week Luncheon, Navy Day Luncheon, "E" For Export Luncheon, West-Gate California, Corp. Luncheon, Muni Railway's 50th Anniversary, LOOK Magazine Luncheon, Salute to Western Packaging Luncheon, Valley Days Western Space Age Exposition, Seattle World's Fair and International Film Festival.

• Prepared two folders, one for the Strybing Ar)oretum and one for The California Academy of Sciences.

• Handled press, radio and television relations for Cham)er affiliates — The Retail Merchants Association, San Francisco Area World Trade Association and San Francisco Beautiful.

• Set up 52 radio programs for the Cham)er's "San Francisco Progress Report" on KFRC.

• Set up 52 radio programs for the Cham)er's "San Francisco in the Sixties" on KNBR.

• Set up 42 radio programs for the Cham)er's "Conference Call" on KFRC.

• Wrote copy, suggested editing and selected photos for SAN FRANCISCO QUARTERLY, pu)lication of Executive Headquarters Promotion project.

Retail Merchants — *President: Jack Podesta; Managing Director: Harold V. Starr.*

Constantly striving to promote and protect the interests of the city's retail industry, this segment of the Cham)er:

• Opposed issuance of second-hand store licenses to non-profit stores in neigh)orhood shopping districts.

• Studied Sunday Closing legislation. (This proposal, studied throughout the year, is of vital importance to all retailers.)

• Studied)ond issues on June Municipal Ballot.

• Worked to have parking garage)uilt in Japanese Cultural Center in Western Addition.

• Kept retailers advised on all legislation affecting)usiness and community welfare on local, state and federal levels.

• Heard Parking Authority General Manager present reasons why he)elieves a downtown parking survey is necessary (the)oard withheld action).

• Followed progress of the Neigh)orhood Parking Program.

• Worked on the 36)allot propositions on the November 6, 1962 election.

• Carried out fund-raising campaign with Retail Merchants Assn. mem)ers on Prop. A, the $792,000,000 Bay Area Rapid Transit Bond Issue. Letters and telephone calls raised an approximate $2,500.

(Continued from page four)

• Participated in and helped arrange numerous radio programs on legislative issues.

• Planned active program on issues)efore 88th Congress.

• Represented Cham)er interests in Sacramento during the 1962 legislative session.

PRACTICAL POLITICS COMMITTEE

• Sponsored civic luncheon on "FREEDOM VS. COMMUNISM" and conducted two courses on this su)ject.

• Assisted mem)er companies in esta)lishing Action Courses in Practical Politics for their employees. Helped on programming and furnishing material.

• Prepared and distri)uted more than 30,000 *Know Your Elected Representatives* pamphlets showing elected officials and political-district maps for six counties.

• Prepared and distri)uted voting recommendation cards showing Cham)er stand on 45 measures on the June and Novem)er 1962)allots.

REDEVELOPMENT COORDINATING COMM.

• Paved way for sound development of old Hall of Justice site and environs;)acked delay of Hall sale pending determination of the area's potential.

• Worked continually to keep new Islais Creek Produce Market Project on the track.

• Supported needed renewal studies.

• Continued to foster Golden Gateway Project; saw first ground)reaking there, crowning years of Cham)er leadership.

TAX SECTION

• Acted on 16 Propositions on the June and Novem)er Ballots after many meetings on pros and cons of each issue.

• Conducted joint meetings with Agriculture Committee on question of agricultural land assessment.

• Met with University of California and San Francisco State College officials in study of college tax fund requirements; supported State school)uilding)ond issue (Proposition 1-A) on Novem)er ballot.

• With other committees, studied and successfully supported Pu)lic Welfare Building Bond Proposal — Proposition B on the Novem)er)allot.

• Researched and wrote 41 detailed Board Reports recommending Cham)er policy on as many issues.

ransportation Department — *Chair-*
ın and Vice Chairman: A. D. Carleton and R. A. Morin.
ınager: Charles C. Miller, Assistant Manager: James
Cooper.

Determined to assure San Francisco of adequate rail, ıter, highway and air transportation facilities and serv-ıs at fair and reasona)le rates and fares, and to attract d hold industry and increase)usiness volume, port ıffic and tourist travel, this department:

• Succeeded, with others after many years of concerted ort to secure passage of legislation repealing excise tax on ssenger travel)y railroad, bus and water and reducing ʳ travel tax to 5 per cent (to expire in June).

• Vigorously opposed California Public Utili-ties Commission investi-gation, (Case 7372), in-to operations, public utilities and air trans-portation companies re-quiring sealed)ids for purchase of equipment.

• Participated in 13 individual cases)efore Civil Aeronautics Board, Maritime Com-mission, California Pub-lic Utilities Commission

ıd state legislative committees (requiring 25 days in "court" ıpearances on)ehalf of San Francisco interests).

• Rendered 6,321 direct services to Cham)er mem)ers ıd others; answered 427 travel information requests from l parts of the country, and attended 323 meetings involving ınsportation matters.

• Succeeded, with others,)y Civil Aeronautics Board No. 19124, awarding expedited hearing in Docket No. 12029, ın Francisco and Oakland Helicopter Airlines, Inc., San ·ancisco Bay Area Service.

• Succeeded, with others, in gaining favora)le decision)y ıvil Aeronautics Board which awarded, among other things, ghts and routes for new and extended local air service four San Francisco)ased air lines.

• Participated in special events program honoring new ute services)y two local airlines)etween San Francisco ıd Nevada and Southern California points.

• Honored Philippine Air Lines re-entry in trans-pacific ʳ service with special luncheon program.

• Assisted in arrangements for programs for an eastern ʳ carrier and a western air carrier to hold)oard of direc-ʳ meetings in San Francisco for the first time.

• Furnished comprehensive distri)ution cost studies on ᵇ different commodities involving over 2,000 freight rates industrial prospects interested in San Francisco Bay Area cation.

• Secured cooperation of motor carrier officials and rate ıreau to maintain reasona)le differentials from northern evada to California points to protect San Francisco trade ·eas.

• Favora)le report and findings made)y Interstate Com-erce Commission examiner in the two-year old cases ICC ockets 33590/91 which upheld Cham)er's stand that it is scriminatory to exempt certain Southern California areas ʳom general six per cent increase applica)le to the San ʳancisco Bay Area. (Final ICC decision still pending.)

• Presented Cham)er's statement of position, involving)8 rate proposals, at nine pu)lic hearings)efore freight ıte tariff)ureaus held in Los Angeles, Portland, Reno, San ateo and San Francisco.

• Filed six pages of Exceptions with the California Pub-ᵉ Utilities Commission to examiner's report, Case 7024, ʳoposed Distance Ta)le No. 5, concerning proper place-ent of San Francisco)asing point near to center of industry ıd commerce.

• Maintained 450 volume tariff li)rary, 500 volume trans-ortation case histories and San Francisco transportation

Research Department — *Manager: Fritz*
Albershardt. Information Assistant, Ida Mae Berg; Re-search Assistant, Ellen Welles.

Purposes: to generate and collect significant)usiness and economic data, provide a basic central source of information for market research and analysis of San Francisco and the Bay Area and to respond to more than

90,000 inquiries an-nually relating to tour-ists, newcomers and re-lated su)jects.

Major 1962 accom-plishments:

• 12 monthly reviews of San Francisco and Bay Area)usiness activ-ity, presenting current data on approximately 86 items.

• Complete revision of Cham)er's annual Economic Survey.

• Pu)lished quarter-ly editions of "Calendar of Events of Pu)lic In-terest" in San Francisco.

• Assisted editors of several pu)lications in presenting statistical)ackground for articles a)out San Francisco, in-cluding *Encyclopaedia Brittanica, Encyclopedia Americana, Newsweek, Home Builders Journal, Sales Management, Edi-tor & Publisher, California Real Estate* magazine, *Printers Ink* and *Trailer Topics,* R. L. Polk & Company's *City Direc-tory of San Francisco,* and all local and regional papers.

• Answered a total of 88,600 inquiries a)out events, points of interest, census data, economic indicators, organizations, companies, new construction projects, and countless unusual requests.

• Maintained active reference li)rary with over 350 city directories and 200 telephone directories from cities all over the United States and Canada.

• Issued two comprehensive semi-annual reviews of con-struction activity in San Francisco, and a 1961 Bay Area re-view of construction.

• Compiled a listing of all Cham)er publications.

• Prepared calendar of Federal, State and local taxes.

• Produced two maps of San Francisco—a street map with guide to points of interest, and a census tract map.

---

service directories for use)y San Francisco traffic executives and others.

• Successful, with San Francisco grain interests and others, in securing pu)lication of long-sought adjustments in local grain rates to place Port of San Francisco in favor-a)le competitive position with other California ports.

• Successful, with others, in securing railroad approval for pu)lication of local and transcontinental export freight rates on California canned goods and grain, Colorado ore, Arizona safflower seed and Idaho grain to aid Port of San Francisco water commerce.

• Department manager honored)y appointment to Na-tional Executive Committee of Association of Interstate Com-merce Commission Practitioners, Washington, D. C.

• Successfully opposed, with others, proposed elevator storage rate increases that would create undue financial hard-ship to San Francisco rice interests.

• Aided in arrangements and presentation of special plaque honoring arrival of American President Lines' newest luxury liner SS *President Roosevelt.*

• Cooperated with maritime industry urging that Federal Maritime Commission hearing Docket S-137, American-Hawaiian Trailership application be held in San Francisco.

• Prepared and distri)uted 1,770 copies of Transcon-tinental Freight Bureau Advance Docket Listings to inter-ested San Francisco Bay Area shippers.

• Manager was elected secretary of American Marketing Association's Northern California chapter for 1962-63 year.

World Trade — *President of the San Francisco Area World Trade Association (a Chamber affiliate): Lester L. Goodman; Chairman of the World Trade Week Committee: Daniel Polak. Manager: James P. Wilson. Assistant Manager: Howard R. Stephenson.*

Promoting expansion of two-way commerce for the Port of San Francisco and the San Francisco Bay Region through educational and service programs and preparing and distributing current commercial information on San Francisco throughout the world, this department has:

• Served as secretariat for the San Francisco Area World Trade Association (about 500 members).

• Sponsored 35 world business meetings of the Association with total attendance over 2,500.

• Invited ambassadors or ministers of 14 nations throughout the world, and high officials of U. S. and U. N. and other international agencies to speak at SFAWTA luncheons.

• Met with official business development groups for Taiwan, Korea, Japan, West Africa, Finland, Chile, plus business leaders from 46 overseas nations.

• Cooperated in the staging of "Holland Week," "London Week" and "Swiss Week."

• Sponsored and organized World Trade Week.

• Prepared and printed a brochure on world trade and ts impact on San Francisco economy (distributed to 50,000 high school and junior college students in Northern California).

• Published twice during the year a listing of official representatives of other nations in the San Francisco Bay Area.

• Organized a plant tour for consular corps residents in San Francisco.

• Distributed trade and commercial material on San Francisco to 800 overseas international trade promotion offices and organizations.

• Participated in TV and radio programs on world trade, plus newspaper interviews and releases.

• Made personal appearances and talks before many school, professional and civic groups.

• Printed more than 2,000 export-import business opportunity tips in the International Bulletin.

• Serviced more than 13,000 callers who used the world trade department as a source of information on world business contacts in the San Francisco area.

• Received and answered some 5,400 written requests for commercial information.

• Received more than 13,000 telephone calls seeking information regarding world trade activities and opportunities.

• Certified more than 20,000 certificates of origin for export documentation.

• Received the Presidential "E for Export Award" for its contribution to the National Export Expansion Program.

• Sponsored a seminar on foreign Credit Insurance.

• Appointed to serve on Regional Export Expansion council.

• Obtained wide-spread and effective support for Administration Foreign Trade Expansion bill.

Marsh Appointed Industrial Manager

Harold C. (Bud) Marsh, director of industrial and economic development of the Greater Bakersfield Chamber of Commerce, has been appointed manager of the industrial department of the San Francisco Chamber of Commerce.

Marsh's appointment is effective today, according to G. L. Fox, executive vice president of the San Francisco Chamber.

"Marsh, who has a fine background in his field, will be responsible for re-energizing the Chamber industrial development program, including all Fox commented.

aspects of research and promotion of job-creating activities in San Francisco and the Bay Region,"

Marsh succeeds Lewis M. Holland, who left to become Commissioner of the California State Economic Development Agency, January 1.

Prior to his appointment as director of industrial and economic development of the Bakersfield Chamber in 1960, Marsh was secretary-manager of the Delano District Chamber of Commerce for nearly two years. Under his aegis at Bakersfield, 17 new industries were located there, creating 428 new jobs and bringing in an annual payroll of more than $2,700,000. He also played a key role in developing Bakersfield's first industrial park near the Meadows Field Airport.

Marsh is a director of the California Association of Chamber of Commerce Managers, a member of the American Chamber of Commerce Executives and the American Industrial Development Council. He attended the University of California and served with the U. S. Navy for nearly three years during World War II, including 22 months of duty in the South Pacific.

Marsh, 39, is a native of Bakersfield. He is married to the former Alta Stockton, also a native of Bakersfield. They have two children, Elizabeth, 15, and Sidney, 10.

ARTIST'S VIEW of Idea Center

Trans World Airlines To
'Road Show' Here For S

BAY REGION BUSINESS

PUBLISHED BY THE
SAN FRANCISCO CHAMBER OF COMMERCE

HARRY A. LEE, President
G. L. FOX, Executive Vice President
N. A. HOGAN, Secretary
JOSEPH I. HAUGHEY, Editor
CHARLES A. ORGAN, Associate Editor

Published semi-monthly and owned by the San Francisco
Chamber of Commerce, a non-profit organization, at 333
Pine St., San Francisco, Zone 4, County of San Francisco,
California. Telephone EXbrook 2-4511. (Non-member sub-
scription, $5.00 a year.) Entered as Second Class matter
April 20, 1946, at the Post Office at San Francisco, Cali-
fornia, under the Act of March 3, 1879.

Circulation: 7,500

Manufacturers in the San Francisc
application are invited to attend the T
Area-Business" on Wednesday, March
Jointly sponsored by TWA and th
and east bay chambers of commerc
will be in the Champagne Room proce
a luncheon in the Peacock Court.

Purpose of the road show is to se
more competitive bidding for TWA's
purchases which totals more than $140 m
ing items from jet engine parts to
bookends. TWA's annual distributio
area is $15 million.

BAY REGION BUSINESS

SAN FRANCISCO CHAMBER OF COMMERCE

VOLUME 20 • NUMBER 4 • MARCH 1, 1963

Site of New Produce Mart

Completion of Islais Creek Mart a 'Victory' for Chamber

ARTIST'S VIEW *of Islais Creek produce market ...*

Completion of the Islais Creek produce market will mark a signal victory for the agricultural committee of the San Francisco Chamber of Commerce, according to Chamber president Harry A. Lee.

Ground for the new terminal was broken by Mayor George Christopher February 4, following dissension which had stymied plans for establishment of the new site for years.

Lee pointed out that the Chamber had)een active in establishment of the new site since formation of its agricultural committee in 1941.

He said that 34 produce firms are committed to the Islais Creek site. All will move from the present area, center of the Golden Gateway Redevelopment Project, which will see the rise of new apartment and office buildings.

Further, he said, under the presidency of Angelo J. Scampini, the Islais Creek Produce Market Corporation "will well serve agriculture and allied industries which, together, form the number one industry of both San Francisco and the state of California."

Cost of the new produce market will be about $4,460,000.

Trans World Airlines To Hold 'Road Show' Here For Suppliers

Manufacturers in the San Francisco Bay Area producing goods for airline application are invited to attend the Trans World Airlines' road show "TWA Means Business" on Wednesday, March 20, Mark Hopkins Hotel.

Jointly sponsored)y TWA and the Cham)er in association with peninsula and east bay cham)ers of commerce, the afternoon display of purchasing power will be in the Champagne Room preceded by a luncheon in the Peacock Court.

Purpose of the road show is to encourage more competitive bidding for TWA's supply inventory which totals more than 130,000 separate items from jet engine parts to gourmet foodstuffs. TWA's annual purchasing power exceeds $70 million.

Prepackaged exhibits of the airline's supply needs covering everything from nuts and bolts to tractors are being transported from major cities on TWA's domestic system in a giant 35-foot-long trailer-van.

(Turn to page 2)

Carleton Chairman of Transportation Group

A. D. Carleton, manager of the traffic department, Standard Oil Co. of California, has been re-named chairman of the transportation committee of the Chamber.

R. A. Morin, director of traffic for Fibreboard Paper Products, was re-named assistant chairman of the committee.

A. D. Carleton

Carleton and Morin will direct activity of the 53-man committee with special emphasis on three major points:

• Elimination of freight surcharges within 14 counties of the bay region levied by carriers who claim labor costs in the area justify extra freight charges.

• Maintaining a favorable freight rate structure commensurate with the geographic location of San Francisco in relation to other major industrial areas in interstate and foreign commerce.

• Encouraging use of new and improved types of equipment and facilities by all forms of transportation serving San Francisco and the Bay Area.

Directors Reaffirm Position that Mining Exchange Should Stay

On recommendation of the Chamber's mining committee, the Chamber board of directors has reaffirmed its position to "support the retention of the San Francisco Mining Exchange as an institution which has rendered and should continue to provide essential services in the development of the mineral sources of the state of California and the West by making possible the financing of small mining enterprises."

Action of the Chamber was announced by Harry A. Lee, Chamber president.

"This action was taken with the knowledge that certain charges were made against the Exchange and certain of its members and determinations in this regard were the object of a hearing conducted in San Francisco by James G. Ewell as the hearing officer for the Exchange with Frank E. Kennamer serving as the Commission's counsel and Gardiner Johnson serving as counsel for the Exchange," Lee said.

"At no time has the Chamber endeavored to arrive at judgment on any of the charges which the Commission made," Lee continued, "but it has taken the position that San Francisco and the West need a mining exchange which has been and should continue to be subject to regulation and due scrutiny by the Securities and Exchange Commission as well as by state agencies.

"In response to a statement attributed to Mr. Kennamer, it should be obvious that the Chamber at no time has made representations 'that charges of fraud, dishonesty and manipulation of Securities prices be forgotten and brushed under the table without a hearing.' The facts are in direct opposition to this statement. The Chamber not only recognizes but encourages the functions of the Securities and Exchange Commission, but this has no direct relationship to the Chamber's support of the retention of the San Francisco Mining Exchange as an institution operating in full compliance with the law.

"It is possible that considerable liberty should be given to the Commission's counsel in such proceedings, but this is no justification for the misinterpretation of either the official statement of the Chamber's position or the testimony of the Chamber's representative."

PREVIEWING "Plant A Tree Week"—to be held this year from April 1 through April 7—are Mayor George Christopher (center), and Walter A. Lawrence (left) and Jerome A. Adams of the Adlaw Investment Company. The tree is one of 18 laurel trees gracing the front of the Whitcomb and enhancing upper Market Street.

TWA To Stage 'Road Show' for Suppliers

(Continued from page one)

"We think these programs will promote new business for local manufacturing firms and, at the same time, give us the advantage of more competitive bidding for our business," said J. A. Shaunty, TWA's purchasing vice president. "We spend more than $70,000,000 a year and want to buy material that meets our exacting specifications at prices reflecting true competitive values," he added.

One of the displays features sketches and broad specifications of equipment not yet available but which TWA envisions will be needed in the future and as such will offer manufacturers a challenge to develop and market new items.

Buyers will be on hand at the presentations to answer questions and distribute brochures outlining TWA's wide range of purchasing needs. The brochures will list buyers of specific items to facilitate follow-up contact with TWA by suppliers.

Marketing representatives also will be on hand to outline TWA services for the business traveler including its briefcase commuter and conference services, cargo service and its ability to serve businessmen interested in the common market or international trade. TWA is the only U.S. flag airline serving both principal American and European market centers.

TWA officials feel that their need to reduce purchasing costs through an expanded group of manufacturers, offering the required items, is consistent with the objectives of many state administrations faced with decreasing markets and the resulting unemployment.

This program is a continuation of the airline's vigorous approach to combat the fast-rising cost of its purchasing needs which was first dramatized in June of 1960 when some 150 representatives of manufacturers and suppliers met in Kansas City at TWA's invitation, to discuss ways of halting the skyrocketing price tags on many items.

New Chamber Members

A. D. Jamile   Hugh W. Hitchcock   Koichi Kurosaki   Francis J. Hayes   Irwin Welcher

MEMBERS NEW TO THE CHAMBER ROSTER include (above, l. to r.) Alexander D. Jamile, branch manager, Berry Travel Inc., 323 Geary St.; Hugh W. Hitchcock, West Coast manager, Advance Mortgage Corporation, 333 Montgomery St.; Koichi Kurosaki, president, Hitachi New York, Ltd. (S. F. office), 100 California St.; Francis J. Hayes, owner, Hayes Printing, 835 Howard St.; Irwin Welcher, owner, General Graphic Services, 880 Folsom.

By JOE HAUGHEY

WESTERN GIRL, INC. has inaugurated new bus service. In radio contact with head office, bus carries temporary office help who may be delivered to her destination within a matter of minutes. . . .

PACKAGING COMPANY OF CALIFORNIA, Berkeley, a division of Packaging Corporation of America, announced a new source of packaging supply for west coast farmers and produce shippers. Production has commenced in a 300,-000-square-foot plant (former H. J. Heinz process center) with the first of four $300,000 giant machines for molding of pulp. . . .

KSFO won top awards in Radio Men of the Year poll of Gavin Record Report. Jack Carney was named disc jockey of the year. Elma Greer Bomba, music librarian, was named musical director of the year for non-rock-and-roll stations. Al Newman was a runner-up for Program Director of the Year award. . . .

WILLIAM G. HAMILTON, manager of Department of Employment Industrial and Service Office of California State Employment Service, reported 19,881 job placements in San Francisco and South San Francisco in 1962. It's an all-time high, 33 per cent above record set in 1961. . . .

SAN FRANCISCO CONSERVATORY OF MUSIC has received full accreditation as specialized professional music school from Western Association of Schools and Colleges. . . .

JOHN J. PETERS, board chairman of Security Savings and Loan Assn., reported a rise in assets of 31 per cent in 1962 over 1961. The greatest rate of growth in Association's 36-year history left Security Savings with a year-end total of assets of $136,183,900. . . .

GEORGE KAY, assistant manager of Lane Bryant's New York store, has been appointed manager of the chain's San Francisco store, according to Larry Wollan, general manager in charge of operations for Lane Bryant. . . .

ROBERT A. JURAN is new editor of *San Francisco Progress*, succeeding the late Robert Krauskopf, brilliant young editor who passed away last Nov. 2. . . .

MAYOR LENARD GROTE of Pleasant Hill officially opened 13th Bay Area branch of Citizens Federal Savings and Loan Assn. on Jan. 15. F. Marion Donahoe, Citizens Federal president, Kevin Burke, manager of new branch, and Elmo Rose, Citizens Federal secretary, were on hand for mayor's unveiling of glass mosaic mural picturing features of Contra Costa County. . . .

HARRY P. GOUGH, General Electric regional vice president and Chamber director, and Percy A. Wood, United Air Lines vice president, were elected to board of directors of Junior Achievement, Inc. . . .

JOSEPH M. CULLEN, director of Internal Revenue for San Francisco district, reminded taxpayers they may take tax refunds in Series E Savings Bonds. . . .

KTVU (CHANNEL 2) won the American Municipal Association's International Award for film depicting linking of sister cities of Oakland and Fukuoka, and the fifth anniversary of the like affiliation of Osaka and San Francisco. Film, "Bridge to the Orient," won A.M.A.'s Committee of International Cooperation citation, given in conjunction with Civic Committee of the People-to-People program. . . .

MARKET STREET VAN & STORAGE has purchased new all-electronic van for cross-country use. Forty-foot vehicle is powered by 220 horsepower Cummins diesel. . . .

KRON'S TOM MULLAHEY will direct one of the discussion groups at statewide conference on juvenile delinquency in Sacramento, March 13 and 14. . . .

ADVANCE MORTGAGE CORPORATION has opened new western headquarters for FHA and conventional financing at 333 Montgomery St. Hubert W. Hitchcock manages new headquarters. . . .

"SAN FRANCISCO, MY ENCHANTED CITY"—*a record which the Chamber publicity department long has promoted, will be used as a basis for "an impressionistic documentary" production by KRON-TV. Well-known San Francisco columnists mentioned in the record were photographed aboard the Matson liner Lurline in a press conference announcing the enterprise. Above are (l. to r.) Jack Rosenbaum of the S.F. News Call Bulletin, TV actress Marie Wilson, and News C B columnist Paul Speegle.*

HARRY McCUNE SOUND SERVICE has adopted the name "Channel X" to cover closed circuit TV rentals, while retaining McCune name for rental of sound and projection equipment. . . .

FOUR CALIFORNIA POWER POOL COMPANIES have advanced proposal to reduce federal expenditures $100 to $245 million and increase tax revenues by at least $110 million over a 20-year period. Companies are PG and E, Southern California Edison, California Electric and San Diego Gas and Electric, serving more than 75% of California's power users. . . .

CONGRESSMAN JOHN F. SHELLEY has introduced a Mass Transportation Act, providing for federal grants and loans for development of comprehensive and coordinated transportation systems. Bay Area Rapid Transit stands in forefront for receipt of federal aid, Shelley said. . . .

PAN AMERICAN AIRWAYS announced acquisition of three Boeing all-cargo jets, the first of which will be put into service this spring . . . trans-Pacific from San Francisco, trans-Atlantic out of New York. . . .

AMERICAN PRIVATE SHIPYARDS began 1963 with smallest commercial order book in years. Only 54 ships were building or on order. Number reflects a constant downward slide from 1958 when year's beginning saw 93 ships building or on order. . . .

JUNE TERRY Finishing School and the J. T. Agency have opened their doors at 627 Sutter to offer courses in personal improvement, modeling, TV and drama, and a department for young men and young executives for courses in personal improvement for personal and business life. . . .

Well 'Staged' Opening

Allstate Building New Office

A TOUCH OF THE PAST POINTS UP THE FUTURE

E. A. Frederick rides shotgun on Wells Fargo Concord stage coach . . .

Allstate Insurance Company plans to construct a new $1.5 million regional office building in Menlo Park's Sharon Heights.

Construction of the building on a 12-acre site will house more than 250 employees, according to E. A. Frederick, vice president in charge of Allstate's Pacific Coast zone. The building will have a potential capacity of 435 employees.

Groundbreaking ceremonies featured an authentic Wells Fargo stage coach with more than 150 persons in attendance. The new 83,000 square-foot, two-floor building will serve Allstate's policy holders in the Bay Area and the state of Hawaii. Completion is scheduled by November of this year.

The Menlo Park regional office now has more than 180,000 policies in force and a total payroll of $3.2 million annually.

. S.F.'s home of opera and symphony . . .

hony Orchestra has a tradition which closely
of the city.
as come a long way since a woman violinist in
ength and muscle by alternating musical offer-
the city's El Dorado gambling saloon on the

ed in San Francisco, in 1850, was described as
classics on a trombone by Signor Lobero." A
user, led the city's first chamber music group,
l quadroloque of equally attuned souls." (The
to an attack of indigestion.)
prises more than 100 musicians. Its members
the ballet, the opera, and various other orches-
of a musical tradition as proud as the city itself.
usical organization was founded in 1911, the
by more than half a century. San Francisco's
s spawned in the opulent, turbulent period of

at Coloma, Rudolph Herold organized the city's
" in 1854, which continued to give concerts for
a pianist and conductor, led an orchestra of 60
erts in 1865. He was followed by such distin-
omeier, Gustav Hinrichs and Fritz Scheel. (The
a)ms, Tschaikovsky, and Von Bulow, founded
Orchestra.)
to allow women to perform, the San Francisco
fostered such prodigies as Yehudi Menuhin,
icci, Patricia Benkman and Grisha Goluboff.
rs Eliza Bisccianti, Catherine Hayes and Madam
sco its first reputation as an opera-loving com-
era House, beginning in 1879, had operatic per-
year without a break for 26 straight years (a
American theatre). The great Luisa Tetrazzini
ul manager of the Tivoli, William H. (Doc)

the Chamber Research Dept., 333 Pine St.

Hans Schmit-isserstedt will be guest conductor for the San Francisco Symphony Orchestra in a program which will include Haydn's *Symphony No. 92 in G Major* (The
Oxford); Boris Blacher's *Variations on A
Theme by Paganini*, and Brahms' *Symphony
No. 1 in C Minor.*

Tickets for Chamber Night, priced at $2 to
$3.50, are available at the Symphony Box
Office in the War Memorial Opera House or
at Sherman & Clay. Kearny and Sutter Streets.

Political Information Folder Reissued by Public Affairs Dept.

A brochure entitled *"Know Your Elected
Representatives and Get Them to Know You"*
has been updated and reissued by the Chamber public affairs department.

The folder lists representatives of state and
federal offices from the San Francisco-Oakland
Metropolitan Area's six counties, state and
federal office-holders, and elective officials of
the City and County of San Francisco.

(Metropolitan Area counties listed are Alameda, Contra Costa. San Francisco, San Mateo, Marin and Sonoma.)

The brochure, compiled under the direction
of Randle P. Shields, manager of the Chamber
public affairs department. is available in
quantity at two cents each at the Chamber.
333 Pine Street. San Francisco 4. (Single
copies are available to the public by sending
a self-addressed stamped envelope to the
Chamber.)

Calendar

March 4—LIVESTOCK SALES DEVELOPMENT COMMIT-
TEE, *Cow Palace, 3 p.m.*

March 5—TRAFFIC SAFETY AND CONTROL SECTION
MEETING: *Traffic Safety Check, Room 200, 10:30 a.m.*

March 5—WORLD TRADE ASSOCIATION LUNCHEON.
World Trade Club. 12 noon.

March 5—BOARD OF DIRECTORS' MEETING, Commercial
Club. Room 1. 12 noon.

March 7—LEGISLATIVE AND NATIONAL AFFAIRS SEC-
TION MEETING, Room 200, 10:30 a.m.

Francisco
n, at 333
Francisco,
mber sub-
ss matter
sco, Cali-

BAY REGION BUSINESS

SAN FRANCISCO CHAMBER OF COMMERCE

VOLUME 20 • NUMBER 5 • MARCH 15, 1963

Chamber of Commerce Symphony Night Is Held at Opera House

A night at the symphony was held for the Chamber by the San Francisco Symphony Orchestra last night at the Opera House.

—Courtesy Bank of America

Officials and directors of the Chamber were invited guests.

Hans Schmidt-Isserstedt, famed conductor of the North German Radio Symhony orchestra of Hamburg, was the onductor.

The program included Haydn's *Symhony No. 92 (The Oxford)*, Boris Blacher's *Variations on a Theme by Paganini*, and Brahms' *Symphony in C Minor*.

R. A. Peterson Is Appointed Chairman Of Invest-in-America

Rudolph A. Peterson, Vice Chairman of the Board of Directors, Bank of America, has been appointed chairman of the 1963

R. A. Peterson

Invest-in-America Northern California Council, according to Frederic A. Potts, chairman of the organization's national council.

Peterson, in accepting the position, said, "The continued strength and growth of our American enterprise system depend on every man, woman and child understanding how his own and the nation's economic future is an integral part of it."

The annual Invest-in-America program will be climaxed with Invest-in-America Week, April 28 to May 4.

Golden Gate World Trade-Travel Week Celebration Set May 19-25

Golden Gate World Trade and Travel Week will be held in San Francisco May 19-25, according to J. T. Buckley, general chairman.

The observance, which coincides with National World Trade Week—proclaimed by the President of the United States, and National Maritime Day, May 22—will be held locally under the auspices of the San Francisco Area World Trade Association of the Chamber.

World Trade Week, which has been held annually since 1927, concerns one of "the true boom industries of northern California," according to Buckley. Export-import trade through the Golden Gate totaled $375 million that year. A decade ago the figure for the San Francisco Customs District exports and imports was $733 milloin—today it is $1.3 billion.

Unlike some of northern California's other "boom" industries, international trade has been an integral and vital part of the California scene since Frederick W. Macondray—who later became president of the San Francisco Chamber of Commerce in 1856-57—collected hides with Richard H. Dana, (author of *Two Years Before the Mast*).

"Today this $1.3 billion-a-year volume of exports and imports is perhaps the major industry in northern California," Buckley continued. "Its impact reaches every segment of our economy, including agriculture, industry, commerce, shipping, banking, insurance, transportation, communications, research and education.

"Additionally, international travel has become an important industry within the framework of world trade. The tourist and businessman spend millions of dollars in our hotels, restaurants, theatres, and on ships, airplanes, trains and buses.

"Golden Gate World Trade and Travel Week is designed this year to broaden the public's knowledge and understanding of the

Large Manufacturers Directory for 1963 Published by Chamber

The 1963 edition of the *Large Manufacturers Directory* for the 13 counties of the San Francisco Bay Region has been published by the San Francisco Chamber of Commerce, according to Sidney H. Keil, general manager.

The directory, compiled through the cooperation of chambers of commerce in each of the counties, lists approximately 1,600 manufacturers who employ 25 or more workers in San Francisco and 50 or more workers in the counties of Alameda, Contra Costa, Marin, San Mateo, Solano, Napa, Santa Clara, Sonoma, Sacramento, San Joaquin, Santa Cruz and Yolo.

The directory is available at $1 to Chamber members, and $3 to non-members, according to Preston Drew, Chamber director, chairman of the Chamber business and trade section, and division manager of Shell Oil Company's San Francisco marketing division.

Copies are obtainable at the Chamber, 333 Pine Street, EXbrook 2-4511, extension 85.

Of the many publications issued by the Chamber, this directory—made very comprehensive by improved research techniques—has been expanded to 56 pages. The publication is of great value to those selling to manufacturing industries in the Bay Region.

immense importance of this multi-million dollar industry."

Opening ceremonies will be held Monday noon, May 20, at Union Square—featuring dancing and music from other nations and the choosing of a queen from among overseas students now on bay area campuses.

Welcome Wagon Founder Arrives March 20

Patricia Mackay

Thomas W. Briggs, founder and president of Welcome Wagon International, will arrive in San Francisco from Australia Wednesday (March 20).

Briggs went "Down Under" to establish Welcome Wagon headquarters there for the hospitality group which has its principal offices in Memphis.

He will be greeted in San Francisco by Mrs. Agnes Jenkins, area representative of the group, and by Mrs. Patricia Mackay, executive supervisor for the San Francisco bay counties.

Agnes Jenkins

Trans World Airlines To Hold $70 Million Suppliers' Road Show

The San Francisco Chamber and Trans World Airlines will join in sponsoring a community luncheon at which TWA vice president of purchasing J. A. Shaunty will speak on "TWA Means Business to You."

The luncheon, scheduled at the Mark Hopkins Hotel, Wednesday noon, March 20, will highlight a day in which items used by TWA planes will be displayed. Samples of the 30,000 items included in the airline's $70 million annual parts and equipment budget will be on display in the hotel's Champagne Room. These run from jet engine parts to gourmet foodstuffs.

TWA purchases through competitive contracts. Purchasing agents for the line will be present for discussions with potential bidders.

The luncheon is being staged with the cooperation of the Chambers of Commerce of Berkeley, Oakland, Palo Alto, Redwood City, San Jose, San Leandro, San Mateo, and the San Mateo County Development Association.

Also: the San Francisco Bay Area Council, the Marin County Development Foundation, and the United States Small Business Administration.

Tickets, $4 each, may be purchased, or reservations may be made, by telephoning the San Francisco Chamber of Commerce, EXbrook 2-4511, Extension 16.

FAMED SINGER TONY BENNETT—whose national bestselling record "I Left My Heart in San Francisco" has brought invaluable publicity to the city, was awarded the coveted "Ambassador Extraordinary" card of the Chamber at the March 6 banquet of the National Association of Record Merchandisers, Inc., in the Fairmont. William P. Gallagher, vice president of Marketing, Columbia Records (L), looks on as G. L. Fox, executive vice president of the Chamber, makes the presentation.

Transportation Dept. Issues Trucking List

A 23-page list of common carrier truck lines which service San Francisco has been issued by the Chamber transportation department, according to Charles C. Miller, manager.

More than 150 firms with San Francisco as their terminal and the territories which they serve are included.

The list can be obtained by contacting the Chamber transportation department.

Clifford Luster Named General Chairman of Vehicle Safety Check

Clifford M. Luster, division plant safety supervisor of the Pacific Telephone and Telegraph Company, has been appointed general chairman of the sixth annual Chamber voluntary community vehicle safety check, to be held May 15-16-17, inclusive, according to G. L. Fox, executive vice president of the Chamber.

The annual campaign, conducted by the Chamber traffic safety and control section, won the national award of excellence in 1962 for cities of more than 300,000 population.

Nearly 100,000 cars were checked last year by the Chamber in cooperation with the San Francisco chapter of the National Safety Council, the police and fire departments, private, public and parochial schools, the San Francisco Hi-Board Council, the San Francisco chapter of the American Society of Safety Engineers, industrial firms, civic organizations, the U. S. Army, Navy and Marine Corps, and hundreds of individuals.

G. C. Briggs Added to Board of Directors

G. C. Briggs, president, Standard Stations, Inc., and general manager, retail sales department, Standard Oil Company of California, has been elected to the 1963 board of directors of the Chamber.

Briggs replaced William A. McAfee, director and vice president, supply and transportation of Standard Oil Company of California, who was given another assignment outside the San Francisco bay area.

Briggs began his career with Standard in Los Angeles and Torrance in 1923. He subsequently served as a special agent at Van Nuys, San Francisco and La Mesa, as city sales superintendent at Medford, Ore. (1935), branch manager at Fresno (1938), and as assistant division manager, Standard Stations in Seattle (1941).

He was appointed Fresno district manager in 1948 and then regional manager. In 1955 he became assistant general sales manager, retail sales department, home office of Standard.

New Chamber Members

Winfield S. Rumsey   Chris Borden   Robert B. Rorick   Paul F. Barnum   George V. Sweeney

MEMBERS NEW TO THE CHAMBER ROSTER include (above, l. to r.): Winfield S. Rumsey, executive director, San Francisco Lighthouse for the Blind, 1097 Howard St.; Chris Borden, owner, Chris Borden School of Modern Radio Technique, 259 Geary St.; Robert B. Rorick, president, Games Imported of San Francisco, 117 Post St.; Paul F. Barnum, owner, San Francisco Potato Processing Co., 1991 Oakdale Ave.; George V. Sweeney, president, San Francisco International Tourama, 516 Geary St.

Below are Mort R. Feld, vice president, Harry McCune Sound Service, 960 Folsom St.; William H. Baldwin, president, Baldwin, Erickson & Tait, Inc., contractors, 2300 Mason St.; George V. Clark, vice president, Elder and Company, 333 Seventh St.; Noel Gravino, resident manager, Grolier Society, 15 Southgate, Daly City; Don C. Silverthorne, president, San Francisco National Bank, 260 California St.

Mort R. Feld   Wm. H. Baldwin   George V. Clark   Noel Gravino   D. C. Silverthorne

---

"HEAD FOR CHICAGO, MEN"—so says G. E. Coon, vice president, American Airlines, San Francisco (r.), to civic dignitaries A. D. Carleton and J. Max Moore who were on hand at the recent inauguration of new 990 Astrojet service between San Francisco and Chicago. Coon also is a director of the Chamber. Carleton is chairman of the Chamber transportation committee. Moore is a newly designated Supervisor of the City and County of San Francisco.

BUSINESS BEACON

By JOE HAUGHEY

CALIFORNIA Welding & Equipment Co. "cut the chain" to open its new $185,000 office and warehouse site at 2955 Third street with Sidney H. Keil, general manager of the Chamber, and Richard L. Bradley, president of California Welding, in attendance. Founded 16 years ago in a small warehouse on Bryant street, the company has grown to be one of the leading distributors of welding equipment and supplies in the Bay Area. . . .

SAN FRANCISCO MAIN LIBRARY has taken thousands of books from closed stacks and placed them on open shelves. Formal opening of Art and Music Department on March 7 made 50,000 books available on Art, Music, Theater and Recreational Arts. . . .

PROJECT MISSIONAIRE of Mission Neighborhood Centers has concluded its first year of successful operation. Project is concerned with helping corporations prepare personnel for retirement, and with aiding retired men and women in finding opportunities to use their talents. Emphasis has been on placing men and women over 50 in what the project calls "interesting and personally rewarding community service jobs." . . .

1962 AWARDS PROGRAM of the American Institute of Architects opens tomorrow (March 16) at M. H. de Young Memorial Museum in Golden Gate Park, as does showing of mosaics by Thomas Hunt. Museum's permanent collection of Greek Art will be specially displayed March 22-31 in observance of "Salute to Greece" week. . . .

DR. HANS KUNG, controversial leader of the liberal wing of Catholic theologians, will speak on "The Church and Freedom" at the University of San Francisco at 3 p.m., Sunday, March 31. Father Küng, professor of dogmatic theology at Germany's University of Tubingen, holds that to achieve reunion with other Christian faiths, the Church must begin with reforms within itself.

SAN FRANCISCO SYMPHONY Association has achieved $186,000 of its fund-drive goal of $270,000, according to Association president J. D. Zellerbach. Gifts and donations, tax deductible, may be sent to the association at the War Memorial Opera House. . . .

CALIFORNIA STATE CHAMBER says public and private construction in California will reach an all-time high of $8.488 billion in 1963. Figure will represent increase of 10 per cent or $779 million. . . .

UNITED AIR LINES placed a $19,800,000 order for three long-range, fan-jet cargo craft with Douglas Aircraft Co., according to UAL president W. A. Patterson. . . .

CONGRESSMAN JOHN F. SHELLEY has urged reactivation of San Francisco Mint or construction of a new and larger mint in the city. . . .

THE MILLION CELLAR, San Francisco's first young adult night club, opened on March 7. Club, with the backing of school and city officials, features musical entertainment. Drinks are non-alcoholic. Club is located at 960 Bush street. . . .

ROBERT J. MENNE has been named manager of San Francisco office of Bekins Van & Storage Co., according to regional manager W. F. Soines. . . .

WESTERN AIRLINES is seeking approval of Civil Aeronautics Board to cut jet fares by 50 per cent for military personnel on authorized leave. Plan, slated to start on March 29, would become effective in the line's 12-state system. . . .

JUNIOR ACHIEVEMENT reached $40,000 of its $75,000 fund drive total on Feb. 27. Final report is due soon from organization devoted to teaching young people the virtues of the free enterprise system. . . .

U. S. TRAVEL SERVICE and Trans World Airlines will cooperate in presenting the work of San Francisco landscape artist Ted Lewy in seven foreign countries. Lewy's "America the Beautiful" series is now on display at the White House, whose president, Reginald H. Biggs, says, "They are rugged, colorful, and create a desire to visit the scene painted." . . .

ADRIEN J. FALK, past Chamber president, has been re-elected president of the Bay Area Rapid Transit District for the fourth time. Marvin A. Joseph, Richmond attorney, was elected vice president, succeeding George M. Silliman. . . .

PAN AMERICAN AIRWAYS has filed for permission to cut group rates (for 15 or more) on jet flights between San Francisco and Sydney, Australia. If approved by both governments, fares would be cut from $1,008 to $744 in the economy section of Jet Clippers. . . .

FEDERAL URBAN RENEWAL Administration has advised the San Francisco Redevelopment Agency of a schedule of land prices which will apply to the local agency's program of moderate-priced private housing in Diamond Heights. Action is a green light for three sponsors whose plans were approved tentatively by the agency last November. . . .

WINE INSTITUTE says nearly 170 million gallons of wine—a new record—were distributed in the U. S. in the 12 months ending last July 1. California produced more than three-quarters of it. . . .

THE COW PALACE recorded new highs in attendance and variety of attractions in the period between Feb. 1 and March 3 when 518,000 people attended shows and events on 24 of the 31 days. . . .

NATIONAL VAN LINES has moved its regional offices from 2955 Third St. to 745 Airport Boulevard. . . .

SAFEWAY STORES reported sales for the second four weeks of this year were up 3.68 per cent over the comparable period of last year—a boost in consolidated sales of almost seven million dollars. . . .

A. KENT BROWN has joined San Francisco Federal Savings and Loan Association as an appraiser, according to Association president E. Ronald Long. . . .

SECOND EPISODE of KRON's Assignment Four, "The Mission," is due Monday (March 18) at 6:30 p.m. This one purports to offer a new approach to Mission redevelopment. Channel 4.

UNITED AIR LINES reported substantial earning gains in 1962, according to UAL president W. A. Patterson. Net earnings were $1.36 per common share, compared with 70 cents per share in 1961. . . .

INVEST-IN-AMERICA Northern California Council won George Washington Honor Medal of Freedom Foundation for its 1962 economic education program as "an outstanding accomplishment in helping to achieve a better understanding of the American way of life." . . .

SALVATION ARMY announced its annual "National Salvation Army Week"—May 19 through 26. . . .

NEW MARKET PUBLICATION—"The Public School Market in the Biggest State, 1963"—is now off the press. Listing public school enrollment in the 1600-plus school districts in the state's 58 counties, publication is available at $2.00, at P. O. Box 21344, San Francisco, 24. . . .

THIS LIGHTHOUSE *stands at Black Horse Pike in Atlantic City, marking the origination of U. S. Highway 40, which ends in San Francisco. The photo, together with the key to Atlantic City, was presented to Chamber executive vice president G. L. Fox by Ada Taylor, vice president of sales of the Claridge Hotel in the eastern seaboard city. Miss Taylor was formerly the chairman of the women's division of the Atlantic City Chamber.*

L. A. SEEBERGER has been appointed city freight agent for Santa Fe Railway in San Francisco, according to freight traffic manager F. J. Wright. . . .

FOSTER AND KLEISER advised clients that "Impeach Chief Justice Earl Warren" billboards are not the work of F and K. President Ross Barrett said F and K had been offered the contract, but "our judgment . . . was that these posters would degrade the medium and would thereby be harmful to the best interests of our advertisers." . . .

GORDON NEWSFILMS is filming the year-long ceremonies commemorating Saint Mary's College Centennial. . . .

SEARS ROEBUCK FOUNDATION has given University of San Francisco a $750 grant, money to go toward costs of educating a Sears merit scholar, Gordon J. Lau of San Francisco. . . .

JAPANESE MAESTRO Seiji Ozawa, 27, will conduct the San Francisco Symphony in concerts at the War Memorial Opera House, April 24-26. The young musician has conducted most of the world's major orchestras. . . .

SAN QUENTIN inmates are donating their art and handicraft work to the City of Hope's annual Town Fair to be held March 15 through 18 at the National Guard Armory, 14th and Mission streets. . . .

STATE LEGISLATURE has before it a new bill (AB 110) authorizing establishment of Apprenticeship Information and Training Centers to gather and disseminate information concerning current apprenticeships and other on-the-job opportunities, services and programs. . . .

TOKYO'S FIFTH BIENNIAL Trade Fair, with 100,000 exhibits from all parts of the world, will open on April 16. . . .

(Continued on page four)

State College Enrollment Tops the Nation

S.F. STATE'S *new Psychology-Air Science building . . .*

One of the most graphic illustrations of California's surge to the position of the No. 1 state is that of the development—in quantity and quality—of its state college system.

California's universities and colleges have the largest total enrollment of the higher educational system of any state in the nation. And perhaps San Francisco State College offers the clearest picture of the extent of that development.

State's 95-acre campus near Lake Merced was established in 1950. At that time the students numbered 5,100, the faculty, 299. Today, student lists at the school carry the names of 14,000, and the faculty nears 1,000.

San Francisco State was founded in 1899 on Powell Street between Bush and Pine, a block from the present location of its Downtown Extension Center. It was originally intended to offer a two-year course for elementary school teachers in a plan developed by Dr. Frederic L. Burk. Since then, its growth has been slow, sometimes painful—but always careful.

Under the leadership of Dr. Glenn Dumke, now chancellor of the state college system, its liberal arts program was extended. Today, it offers programs at the baccalaureate and master's levels and is cooperating with the University of California in the development of a program which will ultimately offer students the opportunity to participate in doctorate courses.

Professors, instructors and teachers have been carefully selected. Many offer living refutation of the cliché that those who teach cannot do. Members of the art department exhibit paintings and sculptures actively throughout the country, members of the literary staff are publishing writers, engineers and scientists and members of the telvision and radio schools are active participants in these fields.

The campus contains 18 permanent buildings. A nineteenth is now building. It is a $1.13 million Psychology-Air Science structure. It will contain the most complete laboratory psychological testing of any like facility in the state. A three-story library carries 180,000 volumes; it adds 18,000 annually and has 1,600 periodicals on hand.

At present, "State" is headed by Dr. Paul A. Dodd, economist and former Dean of the College of Letters and Sciences at UCLA. Dr. Dodd has carried forth the policy that "those who teach must also do," and the production of arts and sciences by faculty and students have borne ample proof of the reality of that goal.

As California grows, so grows San Francisco State, prime example of the growth of the state college system of the most burgeoning state in the nation.

Reprints available at the Chamber Research Dept., 333 Pine St.

BAY REGION BUSINESS

SAN FRANCISCO CHAMBER OF COMMERCE

VOLUME 20 • NUMBER 6 • MARCH 29 1963

Contact Club Holds Annual Awards Luncheon

1962 CONTACT CLUB WINNERS—*This team, which sold 15 member-ships at $84 each, received individual awards from Chamber president Harry A. Lee. Left to right are: Si Sellers, Foster & Kleiser; Trev Cushman, American Airlines; Beverly Lee, Citizens Federal Savings & Loan Association; George Ford, Soulé Steel Company; and Harry A. Lee, vice president, J. Walter Thompson Company.*

ALL WORK AND SOME PLAY—*It was an Admiral's Cabin at Trader Vic's last week for these captains of contact—the 1962 Contact Club award winners. The Contact Club, whose members form "the voluntary arm of the Chamber membership relations department," headed by Herbert H. Harmon, is comprised of 50 executives appointed by leading Chamber member firms to augment the Chamber membership program.*

AWARD WINNERS—*Back row (l. to r.): George Ford, Soulé Steel Company; Ray Bartlett, Standard Oil Co. of Calif.; Si Sellers, Foster & Kleiser; Cliff Walker, Crown Zellerbach Corp.; Justin Hills, Hills Bros. Coffee; Jim Field, BBD&O; Chuck Coombs, Standard Oil Co. of Calif. Front row: Al Enderlin, Crocker-Anglo; Gene Fox, United Air Lines; Harry A. Lee; and Beverly Lee, Citizens Federal Savings & Loan Association.*

Valley Days 1963 Slated June 13-14

Valley Days 1963 has been scheduled for Thursday and Friday, June 13 and 14, according to Paul Bissinger, 1950 Chamber president who is general chairman.

During these two days business, agricultural, and civic leaders from the greater Sacramento Valley will be guests of the San Francisco business community.

Activities chairmen for this event are: F. T. Garesche of Standard Oil Company of California, arrangements; Frank Grossman of Santa Fe Railroad, baseball chairman; Irving Danielson, Bank of California, finance chairman; Dan E. London, 1960 Chamber president, Commodore, Great Golden Fleet; Ivan Branson, Morning Glory Caterers, and Ian Russell, Wells Fargo Bank, hospitality; and Perry Spackman, Southern Pacific Company, transportation.

"An inter-city tour of 18 Sacramento Valley communities, conducted last month, presages an enthusiastic response for Valley Days this year," Garesche said.

Gene Fox Captures Top Sales Honors

The 1962 Contact Club Awards Luncheon was held last week in the Admiral's Cabin at Trader Vic's, according to Harry A. Lee, Chamber president and luncheon chairman.

The 1962 Contact Club produced 88½ sales at $84 for a $7,434 total, according to Contact Club chairman Gene Fox, city sales manager of United Air Lines who himself was the top individual producer with 11 sales at $84.

Tied for second place were Ray Bartlett, eight sales at $84, and Al Enderlin and Si Sellers.

Prizes were announced by Herbert H. Harmon, manager, membership relations department.

Chamber officers, directors and former directors who attended were:

Burt Pickard, vice chairman, 1962 membership committee, Chamber director, '60-'61-'62, director and vice president, Standard Oil Company of California Western Operations;

B. M. Eubanks, '63 Chamber treasurer, Stewart, Eubanks, Meyerson & Co.; Ross Barrett, president, Foster & Kleiser and Chamber director, '62-'63; S. R. (Speed) Newman, western regional sales manager, United Air Lines and past Chamber director;

George Hansen, Chamber vice president; Gene Fox, 1962 Contact Club chairman; Dick Huss, 1962 Contact Club co-chairman and partner-in-charge, Lybrand, Ross Bros. & Montgomery;

And members of the Contact Club executive committee: Fox and Huss; Ray Bartlett, special representative, aviation, San Francisco

(Continued on page four)

Progressogram No. 56

State College Enrollment Tops the Nation

S.F. STATE'S *new Psychology-Air Science building . . .*

One of the most graphic illustrations of California's surge to the position of the No. 1 state is that of the development—in quantity and quality—of its state college system.

California's universities and colleges have the largest total enrollment of the higher educational system of any state in the nation. And perhaps San Francisco State College offers the clearest picture of the extent of that development.

State's 95-acre campus near Lake Merced was established in 1950. At that time the students numbered 5,100, the faculty, 299. Today, student lists at the school carry the names of 14,000, and the faculty nears 1,000.

San Francisco State was founded in 1899 on Powell Street between Bush and Pine, a block from the present location of its Downtown Extension Center. It was originally intended to offer a two-year course for elementary school teachers in a plan developed by Dr. Frederic L. Burk. Since then, its growth has been slow, sometimes painful—but always careful.

Under the leadership of Dr. Glenn Dumke, now chancellor of the state college system, its liberal arts program was extended. Today, it offers programs at the baccalaureate and master's levels and is cooperating with the University of California in the development of a program which will ultimately offer students the opportunity to participate in doctorate courses.

Professors, instructors and teachers have been carefully selected. Many offer living refutation of the cliché that those who teach cannot do. Members of the art department exhibit paintings and sculptures actively throughout the country, members of the literary staff are publishing writers, engineers and scientists and members of the telvision and radio schools are active participants in these fields.

The campus contains 18 permanent buildings. A nineteenth is now building. It is a $1.13 million Psychology-Air Science structure. It will contain the most complete laboratory psychological testing of any like facility in the state. A three-story library carries 180,000 volumes; it adds 18,000 annually and has 1,600 periodicals on hand.

At present, "State" is headed by Dr. Paul A. Dodd, economist and former Dean of the College of Letters and Sciences at UCLA. Dr. Dodd has carried forth the policy that "those who teach must also do," and the production of arts and sciences by faculty and students have borne ample proof of the reality of that goal.

As California grows, so grows San Francisco State, prime example of the growth of the state college system of the most burgeoning state in the nation.

Reprints available at the Chamber Research Dept., 333 Pine St.

BAY REGION BUSINESS

SAN FRANCISCO CHAMBER OF COMMERCE

VOLUME 20 • NUMBER 6 • MARCH 29, 1963

Contact Club Holds Annual Awards Luncheon

1962 CONTACT CLUB WINNERS—This team, which sold 15 member-ships at $84 each, received individual awards from Chamber president Harry A. Lee. Left to right are: Si Sellers, Foster & Kleiser; Trev Cushman, American Airlines; Beverly Lee, Citizens Federal Savings & Loan Association; George Ford, Soulé Steel Company; and Harry A. Lee, vice president, J. Walter Thompson Company.

ALL WORK AND SOME PLAY—It was an Admiral's Cabin at Trader Vic's last week for these captains of contact—the 1962 Contact Club award winners. The Contact Club, whose members form "the voluntary arm of the Chamber membership relations department," headed by Herbert H. Harmon, is comprised of 50 executives appointed by leading Chamber member firms to augment the Chamber membership program.

AWARD WINNERS—Back row (l. to r.): George Ford, Soulé Steel Company; Ray Bartlett, Standard Oil Co. of Calif.; Si Sellers, Foster & Kleiser; Cliff Walker, Crown Zellerbach Corp.; Austin Hills, Hills Bros. Coffee; Jim Field, BBD&O; Chuck Coombs, Standard Oil Co. of Calif. Front row: Al Enderlin, Crocker-Anglo; Gene Fox, United Air Lines; Harry A. Lee; and Beverly Lee, Citizens Federal Savings & Loan Association.

Gene Fox Captures Top Sales Honors

The 1962 Contact Club Awards Luncheon was held last week in the Admiral's Cabin at Trader Vic's, according to Harry A. Lee, Chamber president and luncheon chairman.

The 1962 Contact Club produced 88½ sales at $84 for a $7,434 total, according to Contact Club chairman Gene Fox, city sales manager of United Air Lines who himself was the top individual producer with 11 sales at $84.

Tied for second place were Ray Bartlett, eight sales at $84, and Al Enderlin and Si Sellers.

Prizes were announced by Herbert H. Harmon, manager, membership relations department.

Chamber officers, directors and former directors who attended were:

Burt Pickard, vice chairman, 1962 membership committee, Chamber director, '60-'61-'62, director and vice president, Standard Oil Company of California Western Operations;

B. M. Eubanks, '63 Chamber treasurer, Stewart, Eubanks, Meyerson & Co.; Ross Barrett, president, Foster & Kleiser and Chamber director, '62-'63; S. R. (Speed) Newman, western regional sales manager, United Air Lines and past Chamber director;

George Hansen, Chamber vice president; Gene Fox, 1962 Contact Club chairman; Dick Huss, 1962 Contact Club co-chairman and partner-in-charge, Lybrand, Ross Bros. & Montgomery;

And members of the Contact Club executive committee: Fox and Huss; Ray Bartlett, special representative, aviation, San Francisco

(Continued on page four)

Valley Days 1963 Slated June 13-14

Valley Days 1963 has been scheduled for Thursday and Friday, June 13 and 14, according to Paul Bissinger, 1950 Chamber president who is general chairman.

During these two days business, agricultural, and civic leaders from the greater Sacramento Valley will be guests of the San Francisco business community.

Activities chairmen for this event are: F. T. Garesche of Standard Oil Company of California, arrangements; Frank Grossman of Santa Fe Railroad, baseball chairman; Irving Danielson, Bank of California, finance chairman; Dan E. London, 1960 Chamber president, Commodore, Great Golden Fleet; Ivan Branson, Morning Glory Caterers, and Ian Russell, Wells Fargo Bank, hospitality; and Perry Spackman, Southern Pacific Company, transportation.

"An inter-city tour of 18 Sacramento Valley communities, conducted last month, presages an enthusiastic response for Valley Days this year," Garesche said.

Plant-a-Tree Week Gets Underway Next Week

Section chairmen have been named for the Chamber Plant-a-Tree Week which begins Monday, according to Jim Kerr, "The Old Scotch Gardener" of radio and television and chairman of the event.

The section chairmen are:

• Peggy O'Brien, Area No. 1 (Russian and Telegraph Hills, Jackson Square and North Beach).

• Mitchel L. Mitchell, Area No. 2 (Central Business District).

• Mervyn Silberberg, Area No. 3 (Pacific Heights, Marina, Western Addition, Haight-Ashbury and Laurel Heights).

• Herbert E. Harris, Area No. 4 (Sunset, Parkside, Richmond, Midtown Terrace).

• Nicholas Perkocha, Area No. 5 (Potrero, Mission, Bernal Heights).

• Robert B. Olson, Area No. 6 (Ingleside, Bayview, Visitacion Valley and West Portal).

This is the fifth annual Plant-a-Tree Week, sponsored by the Chamber in cooperation with the Street Tree Planting Division of the Department of Public Works and San Francisco Beautiful.

Overall goal of the continuing campaign is the planting of 300,000 trees in the city. Thus far, more than 33,000 trees have been planted in different areas of the city.

Since inception of the program, Kerr said, many areas of the downtown business district have been planted. He pointed to Jackson Square, Maiden Lane, 200 Post and the 300 block of Pine Street as examples of successful planting in the central business district.

Chamber Suggests Objectives For Kennedy Tax Programs

Specific objectives in regard to federal tax reduction and reforms have been announced in behalf of the board of directors of the Chamber by Harry A. Lee, president. Lee outlined a set of five recommendations, approved by the Board after studies and recommendations by the Chamber tax section of which H. C. Tyler is chairman. The five-point recommendation, according to Lee:

• "tax reduction should be accomplished only in association with definite plans for reducing, or at least holding, the line on budget expenditures;

• "except where imperative to national defense, new government spending programs should not be launched during the period over which unusual budget deficits are expected from tax reduction;

• "tax reduction methods should be considered separately on their own merits;

• "tax reform should be considered as a separate objective to be accomplished through studied overall revisions of the Internal Revenue Code;

• "the objective of a tax reduction program should be to spur the economy."

On the last point, Lee stressed that, "to do this, it must provide strong incentive to various sectors of the economy, particularly to encourage increased private investment and business activity, which, in turn, will create additional payrolls and a broader tax base."

Produce Market Now Ahead Of Schedule

Produce merchants of San Francisco will move into their new home ahead of schedule, a spokesman for the developers of the $4.7 million project has disclosed.

"We have started to pour concrete for the foundations of four buildings," Herbert Ortman of the Dworman Development Co. said, "and we are working Saturdays and Sundays to speed the job."

Ortman estimated that the 25-acre market at Islais Creek would be "ready three weeks ahead of the July target date."

In addition to the 54 produce stalls in the four buildings, three restaurants, an office structure, bank, covered carports, loading docks and a service station will be constructed.

The move will end eight years of negotiation by the marketmen to find a location within San Francisco, with the Chamber playing a leading role from the start. Vacating of the old market will speed completion of another Chamber-initiated project—the Golden Gateway.

Supreme Court Office 'Should Stay in S.F.'

All Californians should urge their legislators and Governor Brown to allow the state's Supreme Court justices to "exercise their judicial independence in determining the headquarters of that court," according to action taken by the board of directors of the Chamber.

The Chamber board's resolution followed recommendations from the Governor's office that Supreme Court headquarters be transferred from San Francisco to Sacramento.

The Chamber resolution pointed out that transfer of Supreme Court offices to Sacramento "is not only unnecessary for efficient operation but is also undesirable in achieving the full benefits of the separation of governmental powers upon which our government is based."

The Supreme Court has "operated historically from central headquarters in San Francisco and has adopted the practice of holding sessions of that court in Los Angeles and Sacramento as well as San Francisco," the Chamber pointed out.

Street Tree-Planting Booklet is Re-issued

A street tree-planting booklet has been updated and re-issued by the Chamber publicity department.

The guide, designed for use by district associations and householders, is expected to be widely used during Plant-a-Tree Week, which begins Monday—an annual event sponsored by the Chamber, San Francisco Beautiful and the Department of Public Works.

Compiled by Brian Fewer of the Department of Public Works and published by the publicity department, it contains lists of trees adaptable to the varied climates within the city, tips and suggestions for sidewalk curb installation, and instructions on obtaining planting permits.

The tree-planting booklet is obtainable either from the Chamber publicity department or from the Department of Public Works, street tree-planting division, 2323 Army street.

Transportation Head Attends 10 Hearings

Charles C. Miller, manager of the Chamber's Transportation Department, attended 10 hearings before government regulatory bodies or meetings before carrier freight bureaus in the first two months of 1963.

The meetings required 21 days of hearing participation and more than 11,500 miles of travel, Miller said.

Miller presented the bureaus with arguments enforcing his department's objectives of assuring San Francisco an adequate transportation system in all fields. He argued for "just, reasonable and non-discriminatory rates, fares and charges to protect, hold and attract new industries, port traffic and tourist travel to this area."

Roy Matison Chairman of Traffic Safety

Roy E. Matison, personnel manager and safety director, Federated Metals Division, American Smelting and Refining Company, has been named chairman of the Chamber traffic safety and control section, according to Harry A. Lee, president.

The Chamber section, composed chiefly of industrial traffic safety engineers and insurance representatives, is concerned with all phases of traffic safety and works closely with law enforcement agencies.

It is responsible for directing the annual citywide voluntary vehicle safety check campaign, scheduled May 15-17.

In 1962 the Chamber program won a national award for cities of more than 300,000 population.

BUSINESS BEACON

By JOE HAUGHEY

BAY AREA RAPID TRANSIT program got a boost from West German transportation officials now conducting a five-week study of highway and mass transport facilities in U. S. and Canada. Horst Grabert, construction supervisor for Berlin's Senate for Building and Housing, said of BARTD, "Obviously it is very carefully planned." . . .

ROBERT M. HAYNIE, a former Chamber director, has been appointed by Governor Edmund Brown to the Governor's business advisory committee. Haynie, a Democrat, is a partner in Haas and Haynie, contractors. . . .

SANTA FE RAILWAY president Ernest S. Marsh reported the line's net income for 1962 was 28.9 per cent above that of 1961. Santa Fe reported a net of $70.7 million for '62, compared with $54.8 million in 1961. . . .

SAN FRANCISCO PAGEANT of KPIX (Channel 5) will trace the history of Lotta's Fountain in the fifth of its San Francisco Pageant series Monday, 8 p.m. Marvin Miller, familiar as the messenger of "The Millionaire," will host the show. . . .

ERICH LEINSDORF will conduct a special concert of the Boston Symphony at the War Memorial Opera House, 8:30 p.m., Monday, April 22. The concert, held under the auspices of San Francisco Symphony Association, marks Leinsdorf's first tour since he took the reins of Boston Symphony from Charles Munch in 1962. . . .

COMMITTEE FOR BAY AREA RAPID TRANSIT NOW asserts that suits against the system have brought delays which already have cost taxpayers about $24 million. Chairmen of new committee are Thomas J. Mellon (former Chamber president); A. Hubbard Moffit, Jr., Alameda, and Carl H. Rehfuss, El Cerrito. . . .

REP. JOHN F. SHELLEY has announced transfer of 517 acres of Angel Island from Department of the Interior to the State Parks System. Transfer leaves only three small navigational aid sites in federal ownership on the Island. . . .

E. W. (STACE) CAREY, president of Fibreboard Paper Products Company and Chamber director, has been named vice chairman of the 1963 drive of the five-county United Bay Area Crusade, according to chairman John R. Beckett. . . .

LANSING KWOK of Wing On Company, Inc., has been named deputy chairman of the subcommittee on Trade Relations with Asia of the Chamber's affiliated World Trade Association.

COW PALACE DIRECTORS unveiled plans for $3,011,561 expansion program on March 11. "Palace board president Fred P. Cox said "need for an expansion program is urgent." . . .

FRANK WERNER CO. marked beginning of its 3rd year on March 18 with opening of new financial district shoe store at 242 Montgomery Street. New store displaced the Exchange Club which has moved to rear of Werner store on Petrarch Place. . . .

FORMER CHAMBER PRESIDENT Dan E. London, managing director of the St. Francis Hotel, and Willard Abel, president of the St. Francis Hotel Corporation, have been named senior vice presidents of Western International Hotels. . . .

JAMES P. MITCHELL, vice president of Crown Zellerbach and former Secretary of Labor, will be honorary chairman of the Labor Department's 50th anniversary banquet, April 15 at the Fairmont Hotel. . . .

SAN FRANCISCO BOYS CHORUS is preparing for the spring concert season. Boys will participate in the Junior Bach Festival Sunday and will sing a free-will offering concert April 21 at the First Baptist Church, Market and Octavia streets. Admission to latter is free. . . .

SIR FRANCIS DRAKE'S historic "plate of brass" with which Drake claimed possession of California for England 400 years ago, will be returned on April 1 to Marin County. Bancroft library at UC lent the plaque to Citizens Federal Savings and Loan Association in San Rafael. It will be displayed there under heavy guard. . . .

MARITIME SUBSIDY BOARD granted States Steamship Company the right to make 26 calls yearly in each direction between California and Hawaii. Decision doubles the number for States, whose application had been challenged by Matson. . . .

MISS SAN FRANCISCO Pageant of 1963 will see the new Miss San Francisco crowned at the Jack Tar Hotel April 6. Eight finalists are contesting for the honor. . . .

SAN FRANCISCO ART INSTITUTE'S 82nd Annual Exhibition is on display at the San Francisco Museum of Art. Ford Foundation is considering possible purchase of works from the exhibit. . . .

J. A. SHAUNTY, vice president of purchasing, Trans World Airlines, discussed "TWA Means Business to You" at a civic luncheon last week in the Peacock Court of the Hotel Mark Hopkins under the sponsorship of the Chamber and TWA. Samples of 130,000 items included in the airlines' $70 million annual parts and equipment budget were displayed in the Champagne Room of the hotel. . . .

MIKE POWELL has been named assistant news director of KSFO, according to vice president and general manager William D. Shaw. He moves into early morning news slot formerly occupied by Chet Casselman, who will concentrate on station's public affairs schedules. . . .

UNITED AIR LINES inaugurated first and only nonstop jet service between San Francisco and Philadelphia on March 10, according to sales manager H. E. Morley. Flight will use DC-8s, leaving here at 8:45 a.m., returning from Philadelphia at 6:15 p.m., daily. . . .

AUTOMATION, a major concern of labor, will get classroom attention at Labor Management School of the University of San Francisco, Tuesday nights through May 7. The course, "Automation and Technical Change—Their Impact on 180 Million People," will deal with "changing production methods and their effect on every phase of American life—income, residence, social habits, education and mores," according to the Rev. Andrew C. Boss, S.J. Father Boss is school director and chairman of Governor Brown's statewide committee on automation and technical change. . . .

Kilmer Chairman of World Trade Group

David C. Kilmer, McKinsey and Company, has been named deputy chairman of the area affairs committee of the San Francisco Area World Trade Association, affiliate of the Chamber.

The area affairs committee includes five regional sub-committees which concentrate on development of trade relations with Asia, the Americas, Europe, Australia-New Zealand and Africa.

LURA RAE DALES, private secretary to Leonard K. Firestone, president of Firestone Tire and Rubber, Los Angeles, was in San Francisco last week to discuss plans for the national convention of Executives' Secretaries, Inc. Convention, to be held May 23-26 at the Mark Hopkins and Fairmont, is expected to attract 700 delegates. . . .

ED HILLYER, veteran newsman and public relations consultant, has been appointed public information and education director for the Bay Area Air Pollution Control District, according to chief administrative officer Jud Callaghan. . . .

PACIFIC FAR EAST LINES has shifted its Embarcadero base of operations from piers 40, 42 and 46A to piers 29, 31 and 33 between Chestnut and North Point streets. . . .

LINDE COMPANY Division of Union Carbide will build the west coast's first on-site oxygen-nitrogen plant at Antioch for E. I. DuPont de Nemours and Company. Construction begins this month with a final target date in August. . . .

MANAGEMENT DEVELOPMENT CENTER of the University of San Francisco will present 10 weekly seminars on "Building Effective Managerial Communication," Mondays, April 15-June 17. Center will also present six weekly seminars on "Making the Most of Meetings," April 11-May 16 (Thursdays). . . .

Directors To Back S. F. Film Festival

Directors of the Chamber have approved a resolution suporting the Seventh Annual San Francisco International Film Festival.

Chamber directors said that the festival, scheduled for October 30 - November 12 this year, "has succeeded in elevating San Francisco to a position of prominence in the world of motion pictures, and gives every evidence of continuing to add to the reputation and prestige of our city."

The Chamber statement added that the festival "has attracted many international visitors to our city, and has been mentioned prominently in magazines and newspapers of the world."

In recognition of "the valuable contributions the festival has made to the city," the directors said the Chamber will "encourage activities that will increase the international stature of the festival."

Calendar

April 2 — TRAFFIC SAFETY & CONTROL SECTION MEETING, *Room 200, 10:30 a.m.*

April 3—BUILDING CODE SECTION MEETING: Review of Proposed S. F. Building Code Changes; *Room 200, 6-11 p.m.*

April 9 — SALUTE TO RURAL YOUTH LUNCHEON, *French Room, Fairmont Hotel, 12 noon.*

April 10 BUSINESS EDUCATION COMMITTEE MEETING, *Room 200, 11 a.m.*

April 10 - WORLD TRADE ASSOCIATION LUNCHEON MEETING, *World Trade Club, 12 noon.*

April 11—EXECUTIVE COMMITTEE MEETING, *Room 200, 11 a.m.*

... for City, County Streets and
Highways Development Backed

Legislation to provide additional revenues to cities and counties through a highway users' gas tax for improvement and construction of streets and highway systems has been approved by the Chamber board of directors, according to Harry A. Lee, Chamber president. Action of the board resulted from recommendations of the Chamber civic development committee, of which Edward C. Sequeira, general manager of the Hotel Sir Francis Drake and a Chamber director, is chairman, and the Chamber street, highway and bridge section, of which Leonard S. Mosias, architect and also a Chamber director, is chairman.

Representatives of the State Chamber, the San Francisco Department of Public Works, California Trucking Association, State Division of Highways, Municipal Railway, California State Automobile Association, various oil companies and others, who met with the Chamber street, highway and bridge section to discuss the matter on March 13, also agreed "in principle," to support Senate Bill 344. (There is no known organized opposition to SB 344.)

"During the past few years there has been increasing concern that road and street development in the counties and cities is not keeping pace with demands of modern traffic," Mosias pointed out. "It seems that California's overall road program was destined to be somewhat out of balance in that a modern network of state highways was being provided but that the feeder and connector roads to the state system would not be adequate to provide a satisfactory overall transportation system.

"In some areas these deficiencies have had a serious impact on the safe and expeditious movement of traffic and constitute a critical need for improvement," Mosias continued.

"Some cities and counties have expended considerable effort in providing adequate roads. Others have done very little and some, nothing at all."

In approving the bill the Chamber recommended that:

• "funds for distribution to cities and counties should be limited to expenditure for acquisition of right-of-way and construction on major and collector systems;

• "availability of any new funds to a local agency should be contingent upon a reasonable degree of local matching effort;

• "allocation of more funds should be based on factors including registration, assessed evaluation and population;

• "any new legislation should include a provision to permit local agreements between counties and cities for distribution of new money within the county;

• "the program should provide funds which can be reasonably employed to good advantage and, which at the same time, will not impose unreasonable tax burden;

• "none of the present state highway allocation should be diverted to the improvement of city streets or country roads; all funds that can reasonably be anticipated for expenditure on the state highway system will be needed to meet future requirements of that system," the Chamber pointed out.

San Francisco would receive approximately $2,239,152 if the legislation is passed.

Inter-City Section Modesto Trek Slated

Members of the San Francisco Chamber will be guests of the Greater Modesto Chamber of Commerce on Friday, April 19, according to F. T. Garesche, regional public relations representative of Standard Oil Company of California and chairman of the Inter-City Section.

The Modesto visit is being sponsored by the Modesto Chamber inter-city relations committee in cooperation with the Modesto Trade Club.

Mark Nusbaum, owner of the Nusbaum Wholesale Hardware Co. here, trip chairman, said that the group will be taken on a tour of the city, including visits to one or more local manufacturing plants after meeting with chamber, city and other civic leaders at the Modesto City Hall.

Endures Like Iron

Guilfoy Cornice Works 76 Years Old in June

The Guilfoy Cornice Works, 1234 Howard Street, will celebrate its 76th anniversary as a sheet metal plant in June, John A. Guilfoy announced this week.

The plant was opened by James Guilfoy at 145 Second Street in June, 1887. The building was dynamited during the 1906 fire and quake, and during its reconstruction, business was conducted from the Guilfoy Capp street home.

The concern moved to its present location in 191.

The Guilfoy Cornice Works was involved in construction of the World Fairs of 1915 and 1939, the Palace of the Legion of Honor, the original Fairmont Hotel, the City Hall, St. Mary Cathedral and the Opera House.

...E LOYD and ROBERT VICKREY

S F. Ballet Open At Geary April 14

The San Francisco Ballet will climax its 43-city tour of the United States with its fourth annual spring season at the Geary Theatre, April 16-May 4.

The company will present a new ballet "Fantasma," choreographed by director Lew Christensen to music by Prokofiev. The work has won high critical praise throughout the nation.

The ballet will again offer special rates to groups of 15 or more — $3.50 orchestra seats for $2.50, according to managing director Leo Kalimos.

Contact Club

(Continued from page one)

region, Standard Oil Company of California; Cal Brune, staff assistant, S. F. division manager Pacific Gas & Electric Company;

Guck Coombs, associate editor, Marketing News, Standard Oil Company of California; Tre Cushman, sales representative, American Airlines; Al Enderlin, assistant vice president Crocker-Anglo National Bank; and George Ford, vice president in charge, purchasing, Soulé Steel Company.

BAY REGION BUSINESS
PUBLISHED BY THE
SAN FRANCISCO CHAMBER OF COMMERCE

HARRY A. LEE, President
G. L. FOX, Executive Vice President
M. A. HOGAN, Secretary
JOSEPH L. HAUGHEY, Editor
CHARLES MORGAN, Associate Editor

Published semi-monthly and owned by the San Francisco Chamber of Commerce, a non profit organization, at 333 Pine St., San Francisco, Zone 4, County of San Francisco, California. Telephone EXbrook 1-4511 (Non member subscription, $3.00 a year.) Entered as Second Class matter, April 28, 1911, at the P... Office ... San Francisco, California, under the Act of March ...

BAY REGION BUSINESS

SAN FRANCISCO CHAMBER OF COMMERCE

VOLUME 20 • NUMBER 7 • APRIL 12, 1963

WILLIE MAYS
... that $100,000 smile

—San Francisco Examiner Photograph

AND THERE WAS MADNESS ON MONTGOMERY STREET
... Pennant celebration, noisest day downtown since V-J Day.

Reno Odlin Speaker At Invest-in-America Week Civic Luncheon

Invest-in-America Week will be launched here at Monday noon, April 9, with a civic luncheon in the Garden Court of the Sheraton-Palace Hotel at which Reo Odlin, chairman and president of the Puget Sound National Bank, will speak on "Can We Afford Tomorrow?"

Chairman of the day is R. .. Peterson, vice chairman of the board of directors of the Bank of America NT & SA. Luncheon Committee chairmen are Walter A. Haas, Jr., and Wendell W. Witter.

Invest-in-America Week is sponsored by the Invest-in-America Northern California Council, the San Francisco Chamber of Commerce, the California State Chamer, Bay Area

(Continued on page two)

Giants Really Mean Business—For The Pennant and for the Economy

Northern California baseball fans expended about $17 million, by conservative estimation, to see the San Francisco Giants perform last year, according to the Chamber research department.

During the 1962 baseball season, 1,592,594 fans visited Candlestick Park to see 81 regular home season contests — an increase of 201,915 over the 77 game homestand in 1961. In addition, the National League playoff game in San Francisco drew 32,660 fans and the four games of the World Series here attracted another 176,738 fans. The 1962 home attendance total of 1,802,012 represented an overall increase of 411,333 over the previous season.

Revenue alone from 1962 ticket sales amounted to nearly $5 million. An estimated 50 per cent of the fans — or more than 900,000 — were out-of-towners who spent $2,476,000 for ducats. In all, fans expended some $17 million for ticket purchases, transportation, food, entertainment, overnight stays and other miscellaneous items. Total financial output from the World Series alone was an estimated $5 million.

Based on a Federal Reserve Bank formula, that each dollar spent changes hands on an average of 29 times, (withdrawals and time deposits), more than

(Continued on page two)

Port of S.F Celebrates its 100th Anniversary April 24

A REMINDER OF THE PORT'S PAST AND PRESENT
... the W. F. Babcock named after a man who was Chamber president twice in the '70's and thrice in the '80's — goes through the Golden Gate.

The 100th anniversary of the State's operation of the Port of San Francisco will be celebrated at a civic luncheon in the Main Concourse of the Ferry Building, Wednesday noon, April 24.

Governor Edmund G. Brown will speak on "California's Stake in the Port of San Francisco" at the affair, jointly sponsored by the Chamber, the Marine Exchange, the Propeller Club of the Port of San Francisco and the San Francisco Area World Trade Association.

Luncheon reservations—$4 each—may be obtained by phoning EXbrook 2-4511, Extension 17. Tables for groups of ten are available.

Bill For City, County Streets and Highways Development Backed

Legislation to provide additional revenues to cities and counties through a highway users' gas tax for improvement and construction of streets and highway systems has been approved by the Chamber board of directors, according to Harry A. Lee, Chamber president. Action of the board resulted from recommendations of the Chamber civic development committee, of which Edward C. Sequeira, general manager of the Hotel Sir Francis Drake and a Chamber director, is chairman, and the Chamber street, highway and bridge section, of which Leonard S. Mosias, architect and also a Chamber director, is chairman.

Representatives of the State Chamber, the San Francisco Department of Public Works, California Trucking Association, State Division of Highways, Municipal Railway, California State Automobile Association, various oil companies and others, who met with the Chamber street, highway and bridge section to discuss the matter on March 13, also agreed "in principle," to support Senate Bill 344. (There is no known organized opposition to SB 344.)

"During the past few years there has been increasing concern that road and street development in the counties and cities is not keeping pace with demands of modern traffic," Mosias pointed out. "It seems that California's overall road program was destined to be somewhat out of balance in that a modern network of state highways was being provided but that the feeder and connector roads to the state system would not be adequate to provide a satisfactory overall transportation system.

"In some areas these deficiencies have had a serious impact on the safe and expeditious movement of traffic and constitute a critical need for improvement," Mosias continued.

"Some cities and counties have expended considerable effort in providing adequate roads. Others have done very little and some, nothing at all."

In approving the bill the Chamber recommended that:

● "funds for distribution to cities and counties should be limited to expenditure for acquisition of right-of-way and construction on major and collector systems;

● "availability of any new funds to a local agency should be contingent upon a reasonable degree of local matching effort;

● "allocation of more funds should be based on factors including registration, assessed evaluation and population;

● "any new legislation should include a provision to permit local agreements between counties and cities for distribution of new money within the county;

● "the program should provide funds which can be reasonably employed to good advantage and, which at the same time, will not impose unreasonable tax burden;

● "none of the present state highway allocation should be diverted to the improvement of city streets or country roads; all funds that can reasonably be anticipated for expenditure on the state highway system will be needed to meet future requirements of that system," the Chamber pointed out.

San Francisco would receive approximately $2,239,152 if the legislation is passed.

Inter-City Section Modesto Trek Slated

Members of the San Francisco Chamber will be guests of the Greater Modesto Chamber of Commerce on Friday, April 19, according to F. T. Garesche, regional public relations representative of Standard Oil Company of California and chairman of the Inter-City Section.

The Modesto visit is being sponsored by the Modesto Chamber inter-city relations committee in cooperation with the Modesto Trade Club.

Mark Nusbaum, owner of the Nusbaum Wholesale Hardware Co. here, trip chairman, said that the group will be taken on a tour of the city, including visits to one or more local manufacturing plants after meeting with chamber, city and other civic leaders at the Modesto City Hall.

Endures Like Iron

Guilfoy Cornice Works 76 Years Old in June

The Guilfoy Cornice Works, 1234 Howard Street, will celebrate its 76th anniversary as a sheet metal plant in June, John A. Guilfoy announced this week.

The plant was opened by James Guilfoy at 135 Second Street in June, 1887. The building was dynamited during the 1906 fire and quake, and during its reconstruction, business was conducted from the Guilfoy Capp street home.

The concern moved to its present location in 1924.

The Guilfoy Cornice Works was involved in construction of the World Fairs of 1915 and 1939, the Palace of the Legion of Honor, the original Fairmont Hotel, the City Hall, St. Mary's Cathedral and the Opera House.

SUE LOYD and ROBERT VICKREY . . .

S. F. Ballet Opens At Geary April 14

The San Francisco Ballet will climax its 42-city tour of the United States with its fourth annual spring season at the Geary Theatre, April 16-May 4.

The company will present a new ballet, "Fantasma," choreographed by director Lew Christensen to music by Prokofiev. The work has won high critical praise throughout the nation.

The ballet will again offer special rates to groups of 15 or more — $3.50 orchestra seats for $2.50, according to managing director Leon Kalimos.

Contact Club

(Continued from page one)

region, Standard Oil Company of California; Carl Brune, staff assistant, S. F. division manager, Pacific Gas & Electric Company;

Chuck Coombs, associate editor, Marketing News, Standard Oil Company of California; Trev Cushman, sales representative, American Airlines; Al Enderlin, assistant vice president, Crocker-Anglo National Bank; and George Ford, vice president in charge, purchasing, Soulé Steel Company.

BAY REGION BUSINESS
PUBLISHED BY THE
SAN FRANCISCO CHAMBER OF COMMERCE

HARRY A. LEE, President
G. L. FOX, Executive Vice President
M. J. HOGAN, Secretary
JOSEPH J. HAUGHEY, Editor
CHARLES MORGAN, Associate Editor

Published semi-monthly and mailed by the San Francisco Chamber of Commerce, a non-profit organization, at 333 Pine St., San Francisco, Zone 4, County of San Francisco, California. Telephone EXbrook 2-4511. (Non-member subscription, $5.00 a year.) Entered as Second Class matter April 20, 1961, at the Post Office at San Francisco, California, under the Act of March 3, 1879.

(Advertisement 7,500)

BAY REGION BUSINESS

SAN FRANCISCO CHAMBER OF COMMERCE

VOLUME 20 • NUMBER 7 • APRIL 12, 1963

WILLIE MAYS
...that $100,000 smile

—San Francisco Examiner Photograph

AND THERE WAS MADNESS ON MONTGOMERY STREET
...Pennant celebration, noisest day downtown since V-J Day.

Reno Odlin Speaker At Invest-in-America Week Civic Luncheon

Invest-in-America Week will be launched here at Monday noon, April 29, with a civic luncheon in the Garden Court of the Shera-ton-Palace Hotel at which Reno Odlin, chairman and president of the Puget Sound National Bank, will speak on "Can We Afford Tomorrow?"

Chairman of the day is R. A. Peterson, vice chairman of the board of directors of the Bank of America NT & SA. Luncheon Committee chairmen are Walter A. Haas, Jr., and Wendell W. Witter.

Invest-in-America Week is sponsored by the Invest-in-America Northern California Council, the San Francisco Chamber of Commerce, the California State Chamber, Bay Area
(Continued on page two)

Giants Really Mean Business—For The Pennant and for the Economy

Northern California baseball fans expended about $17 million, by conservative estimation, to see the San Francisco Giants perform last year, according to the Chamber research department.

During the 1962 baseball season, 1,592,594 fans visited Candlestick Park to see 81 regular home season contests — an increase of 201,915 over the 77 game homestand in 1961. In addition, the National League playoff game in San Francisco drew 32,660 fans and the four games of the World Series here attracted another 176,738 fans. The 1962 home attendance total of 1,802,012 represented an overall increase of 411,333 over the previous season.

Revenue alone from 1962 ticket sales amounted to nearly $5 million. An estimated 50 per cent of the fans — or more than 900,000 — were out-of-towners who spent

$2,476,000 for ducats. In all, fans expended some $17 million for ticket purchases, transportation, food, entertainment, overnight stays and other miscellaneous items. Total financial output from the World Series alone was an estimated $5 million.

Based on a Federal Reserve Bank formula, that each dollar spent changes hands on an average of 29 times, (withdrawals and time deposits), more than
(Continued on page two)

Port of S.F. Celebrates its 100th Anniversary April 24

A REMINDER OF THE PORT'S PAST AND PRESENT
... the W. F. Babcock — named after a man who was Chamber president twice in the '70's and thrice in the '80's — goes through the Golden Gate.

The 100th anniversary of the State's operation of the Port of San Francisco will be celebrated at a civic luncheon in the Main Concourse of the Ferry Building, Wednesday noon, April 24.

Governor Edmund G. Brown will speak on "California's Stake in the Port of San Francisco" at the affair, jointly sponsored by the Chamber, the Marine Exchange, the Propeller Club of the Port of San Francisco and the San Francisco Area World Trade Association.

Luncheon reservations—$4 each—may be obtained by phoning EXbrook 2-4511, Extension 17. Tables for groups of ten are available.

Walter 'The Great' On KFRC Radio Program

Prospects of the San Francisco Giants in 1962 will be discussed by Walter (The Great) Mails, former major league and Pacific Coast League pitching star, on the San Francisco Progress Report program of the Chamber over KFRC Sunday at 9:45 p.m.

Moderator is G. L. Fox, executive vice president of the Chamber.

S. F. Giants—
(Continued from page one)

$493 million dollars turned over during the '62 season as a financial result of all 86 home games — including 81 regular season games, one playoff game and four series games.

"It is obvious that increased attendance is of great benefit to the local economy," said G. L. Fox, executive vice president of the San Francisco Chamber of Commerce.

"The Chamber, with the cooperation of all Northern California chambers of commerce, has done its best to deepen interest in the Giants since their arrival here in 1958.

"It also is significant that 50 per cent of the fans were from out of town last year, contrasted with 20 per cent the previous year.

"The Giants have obviously entrenched themselves in the minds of all northern California fans as a great ball club.

"The San Francisco Chamber, keenly aware of the intercounty and intercommunity cooperation which exists between the city and all northern California communities on all economic levels, is happy that the local and regional economies, as well as the coffers of the Giants, have been enriched.

"What is good for the Giants is good for the San Francisco Bay Area. What is good for the Area is good for the Giants."

Invest-in-America
(Continued from page one)

Council Investment Bankers Association (California Group), the San Francisco Real Estate Board and the San Francisco Life Underwriters Association.

Odlin, a native of Washington, has spent his entire banking career in that state after matriculating at Princeton, the University of Washington, and the University of Toulouse, France.

He is a director of several northwestern industries, president of the Washington State Historical Society and a National Associate of the Bank Club of America.

FOR OBSERVANCE of Public Schools Week, April 22-27, were discussed by L. to r., James F. Kearney, senior supervisor of Public Schools Week; Ronald P. Shields, manager, Summer Public Affairs Department; Dr. Edward I. Goodman, assistant superintendent, Unified School District; and attorney Raymond H. Levy, chairman of the Citizens Committee for Schools Week. Highlight of the week will be the Chamber's annual Education-Business luncheon, April 25, when businessmen visit schools to "bone up" on newest teaching methods.

Chamber Directors Vote Support for Anti-Sunday-Selling Measure

...the Senate Bill 345, which, if passed, would make it a misdemeanor for any... to sell "non-essential articles" in "specified areas of the state" on Sundays, ...ven voted support by the Chamber board of directors, according to Harry A. ...hamber president.

...ard action followed the recommendation of the San Francisco Retail Merchants Association, of whom Jack Phoenix is a Sacramento...

Senate bill, authored by Senators Harman (Santa Rosa) and Hugh M. Fross..., would affect the Sunday of clothing accessories, furniture, appliances, television, radios, cameras, jewelry, dishes, and other goods not considered as to public health and safety.

Affected by the proposed law would be ...gas and automobile supplies, food, ...dairy, newspapers, souvenirs and similar goods used primarily for recreational ...ds and in recreational areas.

...hree to states primarily allied in supporting...e the Retail Merchants ...lliance.

...erally in thousands of ...t of reduced and... ...on hours... ...e the sole practice as...

...sociation and community participation:

• "To protect thousands of small shopkeepers and large merchants from being driven into Sunday business slavery;

• "To protect the state and its communities from the moral, social and economic damage caused by Sunday selling."

The Rattigan-Burns Bill also is supported by the California Retailers Association, the Retail Dry Goods Association and the San Francisco Council of District Merchants Associations.

Coordinating the campaign for passage of the measure is the Californians Against Commercializing Sunday Committee, of which Ernest L. Malley, president of Macy's, is area chairman, Area Three, of which the Bay Area is a part.

Ted Lewy to Exhibit His Paintings on the Continent

...ableoise artist Ted Lewy ...for "America the..." ...of paintings in Eu- ...is the man of the United ...ted in Spain. ...on of these and...

...artistic, yet they are rugged, colorful and create a desire to visit the scene painted. We are arranging to have the paintings exhibited in the several Britain and the Continent...living that Secretary of Commerce Luther Hodges joined with the USTS in the project with the full cooperation of Trans World Airlines...

...oil and watercolor paintings depicting such attractions as the Golden Gate Bridge, Fisherman's Wharf, Grand Canyon and New England... to have the exhibit. In connec...

tion with Trans World Airlines' overseas offices, the USTS will present the exhibit in England, France, Germany, Switzerland, Italy, Greece and Spain.

Lewy also recently was lauded by Mayor George Christopher for having "depicted a wide and colorful variety of San Francisco scenes" and for having brought "further renown to San Francisco" by his original oil paintings and water colors.

BUSINESS BEACON

By JOE HAUGHEY

WALTER J. BROWN, former publicity manager for the Chamber, has been named head of the newly-created public relations department of the State Chamber here. New department supplants former publicity and marine services headed by Will Williams, who has resigned to take a new post in Los Angeles.

SEVEN BAY AREA COLLEGES have entered the campus competition in the Furniture Fashions Exposition in Brooks Hall, May 22 to 29. Schools are Stanford, San Jose State, College of Marin, Oakland City College, College of San Mateo, California College of Arts and Crafts and Rudolph Schaeffer School of Design.

BAY AREA AIR POLLUTION CONTROL directors have endorsed federal aid for air pollution control.

MAYORALTY CANDIDATES, Supervisor Harold Dobbs and Congressman John F. Shelley, have joined Committee for Rapid Transit Now, respective officials announced.

TRANS WORLD AIRLINES increases its nonstop San Francisco-to-Europe schedules to four a week by June 3. Elapsed flying time on nonstop trips to Paris is 10 hours, 55 minutes.

E. MICHAEL COSTELLO has been appointed to designer staff of Albert-Crown Associates, Inc., according to chief designer Bert Franklin.

THREE ADDITIONAL FLOORS in the Western Merchandise Mart will be redecorated before Summer Market, July 22-26. New floors make total of seven to be redecorated. Remaining three will be designed and completed at a later date.

CALIFORNIA SAFETY CONGRESS and Exhibits has been set for the Jack Tar Hotel, May 1 and 2. Congress is sponsored by the San Francisco Chapter, National Safety Council.

J. D. ZELLERBACH, chairman of the board of Crown Zellerbach, has been named chairman of 1963 National Library Week, to be observed here April 21-27.

KRON-TV's "ON CAMPUS" show will feature panel discussion of new book, The Teaching of Anthropology, Sunday, April 14, at 2:30 p.m.

MONDAY, APRIL 29, is date set for the door-to-door drive of American Cancer Society, according to Cancer Crusade chairman O. Cort Majors, who said advance contributions are up-grading their gifts this year.

WELLS FARGO BANK president Ransom M. Cook announced after-tax earnings for first three months of this year were up 17 per cent over the comparable period of 1962. On per-share basis, earnings returned 89 cents as compared with 75 cents in 1962.

WORLD AFFAIRS COUNCIL, schedule of April lectures and addresses: April 18, Gerald Clark, associate editor, Montreal Star, "The Latin-American Tragedy—and Ours"; April 19, Satellites in Communications, a seminar; April 20, a panel discussion of France, Germany and European Unity; and April 23, Gunnar Myrdal, Swedish economist, subject to be announced.

QANTAS AIRWAYS will commemorate issue of Cocos Islands postage stamp on June 11 with specially-designed flight covers for American philatelists. Applications at 370 Post Street will close May 13.

GEORGE E. MAHONEY of W. R. Grace & Co. has been named chairman of the San Francisco Area World Trade Association subcommittee on trade relations with the Americas. The subcommittee works closely with members of other American councils who are assigned to San Francisco, and with U.S. government and chamber of commerce officials.

PREMIERE EPISODE of "Sam Benedict" series, seen locally on KRON-TV, has been nominated for American Bar Association's 1962 Gavel Awards. Winners will be named at a 1963 Chicago convention, Aug. 12-16.

PROBLEMS AND TECHNIQUES of communicating for management will be analyzed in two seminars of the University of San Francisco Management Development Center. One series, "Making the Most of Meetings," began tomorrow (Thursday); a five-week series, "Building Effective Managerial Communication," begins Monday, April 15.

KPIX (CHANNEL 5) has made its library of Encyclopaedia Britannica educational films available to educational station KQED, General Manager Louis S. Simon announced the move; the films were accepted by KQED general manager James Day.

SPECIAL DISCOUNT RATES for groups of 15 or more have been announced for some dates in the season of the San Francisco Ballet. Rates apply to Wednesday and Thursday evening performances April 17, 18, 24 and 25, and May 1 and 2, and Sunday matinees April 21 and 28.

NEGOTIATIONS for construction of a $27 million atomic reactor plant in Fayetteville, Arkansas, are under way, according to J. Robert Welch, president of Southwest Atomic Energy Associates, group of 17 investor-owned utility companies in the south and southwest.

PAUL MASSON Wines has announced Music at the Vineyard Series for 1963. Music of the Baroque is scheduled Saturday and Sunday, June 22 and 23; Sonatas and Trios of Boccherini, July 27 and 28; and a Chamber Choir and Brass Instruments Ensemble, August 24 and 25.

HAROLD B. GOODWIN, vice president of Pacific Steamship Company for the past eight years, has been appointed northern California director of sales for States Steamship Company, according to States vice president R. G. Julien, Jr.

PAUL E. HOOVER, board chairman of Crocker-Anglo National Bank, announced all-time highs in loans and capital accounts for first three months of the year. Net operating income, after taxes, showed increase of 14 per cent.

PAN AMERICAN AIRWAYS has scheduled two "Yacht Race Special" flights for trans-Pacific yacht races to July. Passengers will be able to talk with boat of their choice at radio time, as named, the Lucky Bear, to via line.

S. FURMAN, president of Paradise Park Marina, Inc., Tiburon, announced construction plans for new yacht center and country club at Paradise Cove. New facilities will berth 127 boats.

SUMITOMO BANK opened its San Jose branch at 615 North First St. on March 15. Mayor Robert Welch presided at ribbon-cutting and opening ceremonies.

Large Manufacturers' Directory Available

The 1963 edition of the Large Manufacturers Directory for the Bay Region's 21 counties is still available, though it is selling rapidly, Chamber general manager Sidney H. Keil said this week.

Copies of the directory are available at $5 each to Chamber members, $8 to non-members at the Chamber, 333 Pine Street, EXbrook 2-4511, extension 65.

LANS FOR OBSERVANCE *of Public Schools Week, April 22-26, were discussed by (l. to r., ove) James W. Kearney, school coordinator for Public Schools Week; Randle P. Shields, man- er of the Chamber Public Affairs Department; Dr. Edward D. Goldman, assistant superintend- t, Unified School District; and attorney Raymond H. Levy, chairman of the Citizens Committee r Public Schools Week. Highlight of the week will be the Chamber's annual Education-Business iy (Thursday, April 25), when businessmen visit schools to "bone up" on newest teaching ethods and content.*

Chamber Directors Vote Support For Anti-Sunday-Selling Measure

State Senate Bill 845, which, if passed, would make it a misdemeanor for any erson to sell "non-essential articles" in "specified areas of the state" on Sundays, as been voted support by the Chamber board of directors, according to Harry A. ee, Chamber president.

Board action followed the recommendation of the San Francisco Retail Mer- iants Association, of which Jack Podesta of odesta & Baldocchi is president.

The Senate bill, authored by Senators)seph Rattigan (Santa Rosa) and Hugh M. urns (Fresno), would affect the Sunday iles of clothing, accessories, furniture, ap- liances, televisions, radios, cameras, jewelry, itomobiles, and other goods not considered isential to public health and safety.

Not affected by the proposed law would be rugs, gasoline and automobile supplies, food, :al estate, newspapers, souvenirs and novel- es and items used primarily for recreational urposes sold in recreational areas.

The three objectives primarily sought in ie bill, according to the Retail Merchants ssociation, are:

• "To secure for hundreds of thousands of alifornians employed in retailing and allied elds the privilege of home life, friendly as-

sociation and community participation;

• "To prevent thousands of small shop- keepers and large merchants from being driven into Sunday business slavery;

• "To protect the state and its communi- ties from the moral, social and economic damage caused by Sunday selling."

The Rattigan-Burns Bill also is supported by the California Retailers Association, the Retail Dry Goods Association and the San Francisco Council of District Merchants As- sociations.

Coordinating the campaign for passage of the measure is the Californians Against Com- mercializing Sunday Committee of which Ernest L. Molloy, president of Macy's, is area chairman. Area Three, of which the Bay Area is a part.

Walter 'The Great' On KFRC Radio Program

Prospects of the San Francisco Giants in 1962 will be discussed by Walter (The Great) Mails, former major league and Pacific Coast League pitch- ing star, on the San Francisco Progress Report program of the Chamber over KFRC Sunday at 9:45 p.m.

Moderator is G. L. Fox, executive vice president of the Chamber.

S. F. Giants—

(Continued from page one)

$493 million dollars turned over during the '62 season as a financial result of all 86 home games — including 81 regular season games, one playoff game and four series games.

"It is obvious that increased attendance is of great benefit to the local economy," said G. L. Fox, executive vice president of the San Francisco Chamber of Commerce.

"The Chamber, with the cooperation of all Northern California chambers of commerce, has done its best to deepen interest in the Giants since their arrival here in 1958.

"It also is significant that 50 per cent of the fans were from out of town last year, contrasted with 20 per cent the previous year.

"The Giants have obviously entrenched themselves in the minds of all northern Cali- fornians as a great ball club.

"The San Francisco Chamber, keenly aware of the intercounty and intercom- munity cooperation which exists be- tween the city and all northern Cali- fornia communities on all economic levels, is happy that the local and re- gional economies, as well as the coffers of the Giants, have been enriched.

"What is good for the Giants is good for the San Francisco Bay Area. What is good for the Area is good for the Giants."

Invest-in-America

(Continued from page one)

Council Investment Bankers Association (Cal- ifornia Group), the San Francisco Real Estate Board and the San Francisco Life Under- writers Association.

Odlin, a native of Washington, has spent his entire banking career in that state after matriculating at Princeton, the University of Washington, and the University of Toulouse, France.

He is a director of several northwestern in- dustries, president of he Washington State Historical Society and a National Associate of the Boys' Club of America.

Ted Lewy to Exhibit His Paintings on the Continent

San Francisco landscape artist Ted Lewy preparing to exhibit his "America the eautiful" gallery of 26 paintings in Euro- ran cities this spring as part of the United tates Travel Service "Visit USA Program." Reginald H. Biggs, Chairman of the Board, alifornia Century Stores (The White louse), which recently i id an exhibition of ewy's work, said. "There is something in- escribable about Ted Lewy's paintings which iake them most appealing.

"They are not photographic, not impres-

sionistic, yet they are rugged, colorful and create a desire to visit the scene painted. We are arranging to have the paintings exhibited in stores throughout Britain and the Conti- nent, it is most fitting that Secretary of Com- merce Luther Hodges joined with the USTS in the exhibit with the full cooperation of Trans World Airlines."

Oil and water color paintings depicting such attractions as the Golden Gate Bridge, Redwood Empire, Grand Canyon and New England, comprise the exhibit. In conjunc-

tion with Trans World Airlines' overseas of- fices, the USTS will present the exhibit in England, France, Germany, Switzerland, Italy, Greece and Spain.

Lewy also recently was lauded by Mayor George Christopher for having "depicted a wide and colorful variety of San Francisco scenes" and for having brought "further re- nown to San Francisco" by his original oil paintings and water colors.

By JOE HAUGHEY

WALTER J. BROWN, former publicity manager for the Chamber, has been named head of the newly created public relations department of the State Chamber here. New department supplants former publicity and magazine services headed by Will Williams, who has resigned to take a new post in Los Angeles....

SEVEN BAY AREA COLLEGES have entered the campus competition in the Furniture Fashions Exposition in Brooks Hall, May 11 to 19. Schools are Stanford, San Jose State, College of Marin, Oakland City College, College of San Mateo, California College of Arts and Crafts and Rudolph Schaeffer School of Design....

BAY AREA AIR POLLUTION CONTROL directors have endorsed federal aid for air pollution control....

MAYORALTY CANDIDATES, Supervisor Harold Dobbs and Congressman John F. Shelley, have joined Committee for Rapid Transit Now, committee officials announced....

TRANS WORLD AIRLINES increases its nonstop San Francisco-to-Europe schedules to four a week by June 3. Elapsed flying time on nonstop trips to Paris is 10 hours, 55 minutes....

E. MICHAEL COSTELLO has been appointed to designer staff of Albers-Gruen Associates, Inc., according to chief designer Bert Franklin....

THREE ADDITIONAL FLOORS in the Western Merchandise Mart will be redecorated before Summer Market, July 22-26. New floors make total of seven to be redecorated. Remaining three will be designed and completed at a later date....

CALIFORNIA SAFETY CONGRESS and Exhibits has been set for the Jack Tar Hotel, May 1 and 2. Congress is sponsored by the San Francisco Chapter, National Safety Council....

J. D. ZELLERBACH, chairman of the board of Crown Zellerbach, has been named chairman of 1963 National Library Week, to be observed here April 21-27....

KRON-TV's "ON CAMPUS" show will feature panel discussion of new book, The Teaching of Anthropology, Sunday (April 14) at 2:30 p.m....

MONDAY, APRIL 29, is date set for the door-to-door drive of American Cancer Society, according to Cancer Crusade chairman O. Cort Majors, who said advance contributors are upgrading their gifts this year....

WELLS FARGO BANK president Ransom M. Cook announced after-tax earnings for first three months of this year were up 17 per cent over the comparable period of 1962. On per-share basis, earnings returned 88 cents as compared with 75 cents in 1962....

WORLD AFFAIRS COUNCIL's schedule of April lectures and addresses: April 16, Gerald Clark, associate editor, Montreal Star, "The Latin-American Tragedy—and Ours"; April 18, Satellites in Communications, a movie; April 20, a panel discussion of France, Germany and European Unity; and April 23, Gunnar Myrdal, Swedish economist, subject to be announced....

QANTAS AIRWAYS will commemorate issue of Coros Islands postage stamps on June 11 with specially designed flight covers for American philatelists. Applications at 350 Post Street will close May 10....

GEORGE H. MAHONEY of W. R. Grace & Co. has been named chairman of the San Francisco Area World Trade Association subcommittee on trade relations with the Americas. The subcommittee works closely with representatives of other American nations who are assigned to San Francisco, and with U. S. government and chamber of commerce officials....

PREMIERE EPISODE of "Sam Benedict" series, seen locally on KRON-TV, has been nominated for American Bar Association's 1963 Gavel Awards. Winners will be named at ABA's Chicago convention, Aug. 12-14....

PROBLEMS AND TECHNIQUES of communication by businessmen will be analyzed in two seminars of the University of San Francisco Management Development Center. One series, "Making the Most of Meetings," began yesterday (Thursday); a 10-week series, "Building Effective Managerial Communication," begins Monday, April 15....

KPIX (CHANNEL 5) has made its library of Encyclopedia Britannica educational films available to educational station KQED. General Manager Louis S. Simon announced the move; the films were accepted by KQED general manager James Day....

SPECIAL DISCOUNT RATES for groups of 15 or more have been announced for some dates in the season of the San Francisco Ballet. Rates apply to Wednesday and Thursday evening performances April 17, 18, 24 and 25, and May 1 and 2, and Sunday matinees April 21 and 28....

NEGOTIATIONS for construction of a $25 million atomic reactor plant at Fayetteville, Arkansas, are under way, according to J. Robert Welsh, president of Southwest Atomic Energy Associates, group of 15 investor-owned utility companies in the south and southwest....

PAUL MASSON Wines has announced Music at the Vineyard Series for 1963. Music of the Baroque is scheduled Saturday and Sunday, June 15 and 16; Sonatas and Trios of Brahms, July 27 and 28; and a Chamber Choir and Brass Instruments Ensemble August 24 and 25....

HAROLD B. GODWIN, vice president of Bakke Steamship Company for the past eight years, has been appointed northern California director of sales for States Steamship Company, according to States vice president R. G. Jubitz, Jr....

PAUL E. HOOVER, board chairman of Crocker-Anglo National Bank, announced all-time highs in loans and capital accounts for first three months of the year. Net operating income, after taxes, showed increase of 8.9 per cent....

PAN AMERICAN AIRWAYS has scheduled two "Yacht Race Special" flights for trans-Pacific yacht races in July. Passengers will be able to talk with boat of their choice as yachts near, or round, the Koko Head finish line....

S. FURMAN, president of Paradise Park Marina, Inc., Tiburon, announced construction plans for new yacht center and country club at Paradise Cove. New facilities will berth 215 boats....

SUMITOMO BANK opened its San Jose branch at 515 North First St. on March 25. Mayor Robert Welch presided at ribbon-cutting and opening ceremonies....

Large Manufacturers' Directory Available

The 1963 edition of the Large Manufacturers Directory for the Bay Region's 13 counties is still available, though it is selling rapidly, Chamber general manager Sidney H. Keil said this week.

Copies of the directory are available—at $1 each to Chamber members, $3 to non-members—at the Chamber, 333 Pine Street, EXbrook 2-4511, extension 85.

SAN FRANCISCO'S Sandra Church, who co-stars with Marlon Brando in the film "The Ugly American," recently visited the Chamber publicity offices. Prior to her work with Brando in her first movie, she appeared in the Broadway musical "Gypsy," in which she replaced Ethel Merman in the leading role portraying Gypsy Rose Lee. "The Ugly American" will open April 26 at the St. Francis Theatre.

UNIVERSITY OF SAN FRANCISCO Alumni Association will stage its 82nd annual banquet and class reunions at the Fairmont Hotel Wednesday (April 17). Class reunions will be held in the Venetian Room at 5:30 p.m., the banquet in the Grand Ballroom at 7 p.m. Pierre Salinger, an ex-USF'er, will be the speaker....

PAINTINGS of Margaret D'Hamer and Helen Dunham will be on display at the Bolles Gallery, 729 Sansome Street, through April 26 (Mondays through Fridays from 10 a.m. to 6 p.m.)....

G. L. FOX (l.), executive vice president of the Chamber, received the key to Atlantic City from Ada Taylor, vice president of sales of the Claridge Hotel, who recently was voted "Hotel Salesman of the Year." Miss Taylor, former chairman of the women's division of the Atlantic City Chamber, presented keys to Chamber and governmental officials while touring the west coast last week to promote tourism for Atlantic City. Miss Taylor emphasized that U. S. Highway 40, which ends in San Francisco, originates at Black Horse Pike in Atlantic City and "constitutes a direct although long-distance tie between the two cities."

'hamber 'Plant-a-Tree Week' Sees 'ome 5,000 Trees Planted in S.F.

Some 5,000 trees were planted as a result of Plant-a-Tree Week, which ended iday, according to Brian Fewer of the Department of Public Works, co-spons of the event with the Chamber and San Francisco Beautiful.

The week, highlighting a three-year continuing campaign on the part of the amber and the Department of Public Works, "caused a deluge of inquiries and applications for tree-planting." Fewer said.

JANE NIKOLS *of Novato will hold a "one-woman" revue highlighting the Sunday Salon concert of April 21 at 2 p.m. in the Crystal Ballroom of the Marines Memorial Building. Formerly with the S. F. and L. A. Civic Light Opera Company, she will present "Musicals in Miniature" — taking her audience on a conducted tour of several celebrated Broadway productions.*

"The assistance of downtown business and financial organizations and firms has exerted a great influence on the program," he continued. "We now feel that the ultimate goal of 350,000 street tree plantings, which at one time looked like an impossibility, will be achieved within the next seven years.

"Considering that these plantings have been done largely by individual citizens, neighborhood associations, and business firms on a voluntary, pay-for-it-yourself basis, the achievement thus far is extremely remarkable."

Among the larger projects in business districts and neighborhoods were:

• Crocker-Anglo National Bank, Dean Witter & Co., and Post Street Merchants—35 to 50 trees at Post and Montgomery;

• Mrs. Lawrence Blair and Mrs. George Wolff, Jr., 70 Victorian Box trees in the two-block Jordan Street area;

• Walter Landor Associates, 15 trees at One Jackson Place (Battery between Jackson and

Pacific);

• William Marquis, 15 Victorian Box trees. Strillings Avenue (off Monterey Boulevard);

• Mrs. Helen Brooks, Merced Heights, 15 New Zealand Christmas trees, 300 block of Ramsell street;

• W. H. Clark, 10 ficus trees in front of three Russian Hill apartment buildings;

• The Recorder Publishing Co. and San Francisco Daily Commercial News, 12 Acacias, South Van Ness avenue;

• The Whitcomb, 18 laurel figs;

• 2900 Pierce street, 15 Victorian Box trees.

PERVISOR HAROLD S. DOBBS *joined celsior District leaders Mrs. Clare Chonopis l Angelo Bosso (r), president of the Excelsior siness Men's Association, in observing the amber Plant-a-Tree Week. They planted the t of 30 flowering Bottle Brush trees along 4400-4600 blocks of Mission street. The proj- was organized by camera shop proprietor lter Jebe.*

Calendar

New Chamber Members

Wayne Laemmle   T. D. Brown   Jack W. Aufricht   Thomas Fong   John J. Goodwin, Jr.

MEMBERS NEW TO THE CHAMBER ROSTER include (above, l. to r.) Wayne Laemmle, Bay Area sales representative, *Pacific Northern Airlines, Inc.*, Sir Francis Drake Hotel; T. D. Brown, programming manager, *Encyclopedia Britannica,* 444 Market Street; Jack W. Aufricht, district manager, *Unitours of San Francisco, Inc.*, 323 Geary Street; Thomas Fong, part owner and general manager, *Royal Pacific Motel,* 661 Broadway; John J. Goodwin, Jr., executive vice president, *City Savings & Loan Association,* 2521 Mission Street.

BAY SECTION BUSINESS
PUBLISHED BY THE
SAN FRANCISCO CHAMBER OF COMMERCE

HARRY A. LEE, President
G. L. FOX, Executive Vice President
M. A HOGAN, Secretary
JOSEPH I. HAUGHEY, Editor
CHARLES McHGAN, Associate Editor

ublished semi-monthly, and owned by the San Francisco
hamber of Commerce a non- ofit organisation, at 333
ine St., San Francisco "one C ounty of San Francisco,
atifornia. Telephone hXland. 2-!.11. (Non-member sub-
cription, $5.00 a year.) Labread as Second Class matter
pril 26, 1944, at the Post Office at an Francisco, Cali-
rnia, under the Act of March 3, 1879.
Circulation: 7 00

BAY REGION BUSINESS

SAN FRANCISCO CHAMBER OF COMMERCE

Business Heart of San Francisco

VOLUME 20 • NUMBER 8 • APRIL 26, 1963

"ABOVE STANDARD"—Site clearance for the new Standard Oil Company of California office building on the south side of Market street opposite the Sansome street intersection will begin early next month. The new skyscraper will rise over 300 feet—22 stories plus a penthouse—with provisions to be made for a helicopter stop on its roof. The building, to be completed in 1965, will gross 326,000 square feet and accommodate about 1,500 employees. Architects are Hertzka and Knowles, AIA, of San Francisco.

Transportation Forum To Be Held May 16 In Jack Tar Hotel

The Chamber's Transportation Department, the Transportation Association of America and 32 local and regional civic and transportation organizations will sponsor a Pacific Coast Transportation Institute at the Jack Tar Hotel, Thursday, May 16.

Dr. George P. Baker, Dean and Professor of Transportation at the Harvard Graduate School of Business Administration and chairman of the association's board, will be the principal speaker.

Charles C. Miller, manager of the Chamber department, said the theme of the institute will be "Gearing Transportation for a Dynamic America."

D. Clair Sutherland, senior vice president of the Bank of America and vice president of the Chamber, is general chairman of the Institute.

Subjects to be discussed at the Institute will include: "Moving People and Goods in 1975"; "Significant Transport Labor Problems," and "Cracking Down on Bootleg Trucking."

Chamber Moves to Coordinate South-o'-Market Development

(Publicity on the development of the South-o'-Market area received front page, eight-column banner treatment from all the local daily newspapers. Among the articles written was this excellent treatment of the subject by Charles F. Ayres, Associate Editor of the Daily Commercial News.)

By Charles F. Ayres, Associate Editor
San Francisco Daily Commercial News

The San Francisco Chamber of Commerce yesterday hopefully assumed the role of "coordinator" in anticipated efforts to redevelop the South of Market area.

The action was taken following an open discussion by six persons who were joined by quite a few others in the audience in room 200 of the Chamber building in which the potentials, the problems, current construction, planning and long-range thinking all were explored.

The event was chaired by Randell Larson, chairman of the Chamber's redevelopment coordination committee, and was staged with the cooperation of the capital improvement and land use section (Norman Impelman, chairman) and the industrial development section (Ralph W. Seely, chairman).

'Coordinated Effort'

The Chamber's role, Larson suggested at the outset, should probably be the effecting of a coordinated effort, avoidance of overlapping efforts, and "at all times to see that private enterprise has its proper place in the development area."

Ernest Locher, assistant vice president, United California Bank, disclosed that his bank already has applied for authority to put a branch in the area, has its eye on a site somewhere in the area bounded by Bryant, Brannan, Fifth and Sixth streets, and is ready to go as soon as authority is received.

The banker, expressing strong faith in the comeback potential of the area, noted that larger lots at reasonable prices should be made available to attract new business and payroll.

'North-o'-Market'

Impelman, who is an investment and real estate broker, offered the somewhat differing view that "the north of Market area" must be considered in overall planning. In this area, he reminded, "thousands and thousands of units of housing for single people are fast depleting in value" and eventually must be replaced if a readily available labor force is to be assured industry which might enter the South of Market area.

He suggested that the South of Market area in the Haight-Guerrero region might eventually prove a good project area for housing for single persons making up new industry's work force.

Arnold H. Cassady, general commercial engineer, Pacific Telephone and Telegraph Co., whose company is building a new, $15 million Bay Area headquarters building on Folsom

THROUGH THE LOOKING GLASS — *The shape of things to come is mirrored in the windows of Bank of America's newest San Francisco branch which opened for business last month. Located opposite the site of the Hilton Hotel, which is scheduled for completion late this year, the Ellis-Taylor office is the bank's 56th branch in San Francisco. Reflecting the renascence of an area once known as San Francisco's "Uptown Tenderloin," the branch and the Hilton Hotel are two of several new construction projects begun recently.*

between Second and Third streets, had no difficulty in expressing his employer's faith in the area. The new headquarters, he said, are expected "to become the nucleus of a well-planned development in the surrounding area."

Here's how panelists viewed the problem:

John S. Bolles, architect, representing "a group of entrepreneurs" interested in commercial development in the heart of the area and

(Continued on page four)

Blessings of S. F. Bay Area
Counted in Economic Survey

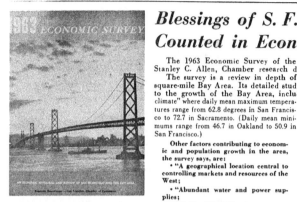

The 1963 Economic Survey of the Chamber is now available, according to Stanley C. Allen, Chamber research department manager.

The survey is a review in depth of the economy of the nine-county, 6,989 square-mile Bay Area. Its detailed study is based on all factors which contribute to the growth of the Bay Area, including the "moderate, Mediterranean-type climate" where daily mean maximum temperatures range from 62.8 degrees in Francisco to 72.7 in Sacramento. (Daily mean minimums range from 46.7 in Oakland to 50.9 in San Francisco.)

Other factors contributing to economic and population growth in the area, the survey says, are:

• "A geographical location central to controlling markets and resources of the West;

• "Abundant water and power supplies;

• "Highly skilled labor force;

• "Presence of at least 20 colleges and universities, including two of the world's greatest; and over five hundred research facilities of industry, schools, government and private institutions;

• "One of the world's finest harbors, with deep water ports inland as far as Sacramento and Stockton;

• "A constant influx of new residents, and

• "Nearly one thousand new or expanded manufacturing industry projects annually."

In some areas covered by the survey, a 13-county Bay Region definition is used, adding Sacramento, San Joaquin, Yolo and Santa Cruz counties to the basic counties under consideration which include San Francisco, San Mateo, Santa Clara, Alameda, Contra Costa, Marin, Sonoma, Napa and Solano counties.

In the expanded 13-county region, 962 manufacturing projects were announced in 1961. They had a total valuation of $170,378,-000.

Bay Area retail sales increased 29.7 per cent between 1950 and 1960, the survey said. Wholesale sales increased 39.1 per cent in the same period and salaries were increased by 62.5 per cent.

Barton Associates Open Worldwide Placement Agency

Lon Barton Associates, Inc., an affiliate of the worldwide executive and enginering placement and procurement organization, Cadillac Associates, Inc., has opened an office in San Francisco, Suite 1080 of the new Equitable Building, 120 Montgomery Street, as a result of the San Francisco Chamber of Commerce headquarters city campaign. Ray C. Pruitt, who has spent many years in the personnel management field, including three years with New Orleans agency and three years with Lon Barton Associates of Los Angeles, will head the San Francisco office as general manager. Explaining the opening of the San Francisco affiliate, Barton said: "Opening of his San Francisco office will permit us to offer executive placement and recruiting service to a much greater number of people in the Bay Area and in the Pacific Northwest."

Trek to Vallejo Set For Intercity Section

The inter-city section of the Chamber and other Chamber members will visit Vallejo's Mare Island Naval Shipyard and the Napa Valley as guests of the Chamber's Great Golden Fleet.

F. T. Garesche, Standard Oil Company of California, chairman of the section, said that boats for the trip will leave San Francisco Yacht Harbor or Sausalito Harbor at 8:30 a.m., Friday, May 3.

Guests will participate in a tour and no-host refreshments and luncheon at Mare Island, where they will meet officials of the yard and directors of the Vallejo Chamber.

A tour of the Hans Kornell winery and a no-host barbecue stack dinner with civic leaders of the Napa Valley are on the agenda, Garesche said.

Guests will return to San Francisco by bus. Cost of the tour will be about $10, not including return bus transportation.

Chamber Tree-Selling Project Huge Success, 5,000 Fruit Trees Go

Some 5,000 flowering fruit trees — donated by the California Nursery Company of Freemont to the Chamber street tree-planting program — were sold at a bargain rate of 25 cents each last weekend at the City Hall plaza and Kezar Pavilion parking lot.

The trees, distributed from huge vans through the cooperation of the Chamber, the Department of Public Works, San Francisco Beautiful, Recreation and Park Commission, and the San Francisco Police Department, were sold out by 1 p.m. Friday.

Average cost of such trees, if purchased from a nursery, is about $5 each, according to George C. Roeding, Jr., president of California Nursery.

During the past four years, the Chamber, the Department of Public Works, and San Francisco Beautiful have seen some 30,000 trees planted throughout the central business district and the city's outlying neighborhoods — including a record 5,000 for the recent Plant-a-Tree Week. Ultimate goal of the continuing campaign is some 350,000 plantings.

Section chairmen of San Francisco Beautiful manned the vans under the direction of William R. Graves of Richfield Corporation, chairman of the event.

THE CHAMBER street, highway and bridge section recently hosted the State Highway Commission and staff members of the State Division of Highways at a luncheon in the Del Webb Towne-House. Left to right are Leonard Mosias, architect and chairman of the section; San Francisco Supervisor Peter Tamaras; Chief Administrative Officer Sherman P. Duckel; and C. L. Fox, executive vice president of the Chamber.

By Joe Haughey

)URTEEN GERRY HIMALAYAN TENTS :re contributed to current American expedi- n climbing Mt. Everest. Other paraphernalia · the dangerous journey was contributed by rry Mountain Sports, Inc., with Bay Area tlet at 315 Sutter Street. Mrs. Mary King, :merly of Roos Brothers and Abercrombie d Fitch, is manager of the San Francisco re. . . .

ESTERN AIRLINES brought three "Vacation »rth" representatives to the Bay Area this :ek. They were Carol Hall, former Seattle afair queen and skiing champion, Helen :rry of Vancouver, B. C., and Susan Koslovsky Anchorage, Alaska. . . . .

)BERT E. HARRIS, promotion manager of :BS, has been named vice president of the n Francisco Bay Area Publicity Club. He ll also serve as chairman of committee for st annual awards competition for best PR mpaigns of the year by club members. . . . 3FO has issued new LP album, "The Giants in the Pennant," with Giants sportscasters, ass Hodges and Lon Simmons. Accrued royal- :s will go to a recognized charity. . . .

ALIFORNIA FINANCIAL CORPORATION nounced earnings of 17.1 cents per share for ar's first quarter, compared with 20.6 cents r same period in 1962. President John J. :ters noted that the decrease reflects an in- ease in federal taxes on income from $78,000 uring the first quarter of 1962 to $163,100 for e quarter just ended. . . .

RS. JOHN O. AHERN, immediate past presi- nt of the League of Women Voters of San ancisco, was elected executive vice president the League of Women Voters of California the league's annual state convention. . . .

AW DAY will be saluted on KRON (Channel tomorrow (Saturday) with a panel discussion »m 2-2:30 p.m. on "Jury on Trial." Attorney nelists include Ben K. Lerer, Isabel Greiner, hn W. Herron, Bruce Walkup, John B. tes and Wallace E. Sedgwick. . . .

CK FOISIE, S. F. Chronicle aviation writer, s named winner of the Aviation/Space riters Association's top award for 1963. . . .

RAPER COMPANIES, developers of shopping iters, announced development of a new cen- at Los Banos. President Jerome C. Drapr, , said new center brings number of com- mity and regional shopping centers developed the firm to six in northern California. . . .

NIOR GRAND NATIONAL Livestock Ex- »ition announced payment of top prices for ck sold by young farmers. Henry's Fashion staurant and Duchess Catering of Oakland :h paid $1.20 a pound for champion lambs »e:l by Lanini Sharon, 13, Salinas, and Leslie mmel, Bakersfield. Concoran Chamber paid 10 a pound for a hog raised by Burnes Mc- inch, Corcoran (Kings County), and Oliver's staurant, South San Francisco paid $1.10 a und for a steer raised by Jim Sanders, 13, Gilroy. . . .

FEWAY STORES announced record highs 1963 initial period. Sales increased by 5.1 ' cent, net income by 36 per cent over com- :able period in 1962. Net income amounted to cents per common share, compared with 50 its per share in 1962. . . .

E. W. (STACE) CAREY, president, Fibreboard Paper Products Corporation and former Cham- ber director, announced five and half per cent increase in sales for first quarter of 1963. Sales total for the period was $26,783,000, compared with $25,371,000 for same period in 1962. . . . ROBERT P. LUTHY, formerly of the Federal Reserve Bank, has been appointed chief auditor for the Sumitomo Bank of California, according to president Makoto Sasaki. . . .

MOTEL MANAGERS' TRAINING SCHOOL announced completion of its "start-up" period for its northern California branch at 2525 Van Ness Ave. School, headquartered in Los Angeles, was founded in 1950 by Mrs. Kay Venuto. . . . WAYNE L. HORVITZ, Director of Industrial Relations for Matson Navigation Co., has been elected a vice president of the line, according to Matson president Stanley Powell, Jr. · · · · STANLEY E. BOYANICH, president and gen- eral manager of Dairy Industry, Inc., has been named general manager of new organization, Key Industrial Associates. Key Industrial will service food, brewery and bakery fields with specialty processing equipment and supplies. . . . UNIVERSITY EXTENSION of University of California announced lecture series on "Alcohol- Drugs-the Mind-and Society" at three locations: Children's Theater, Palo Alto, S. F. Extension Center, 55 Laguna Street, and 145 Dwinelle, the Berkeley campus. Palo Alto series of six lectures will be presented Mondays at 8 p.m., beginning May 13; S. F. lectures will begin at 8 p.m., Tuesday, May 14; and Berkeley talks will start at 8 p.m. Wednesday, May 15. Series costs $12; single admissions, $2.25. . . .

JAPAN AIR LINES reported a 35 per cent in- crease in Orient-bound passengers over last year, an increase of almost 100 per cent over 1960. . . . CALIFORNIA FIRE PREVENTION Commit- tee meetings to plan 1963 activities have been set for San Francisco and Los Angeles. Local meeting will be held in the Pacific Telephone Auditorium, 26th floor, 140 New Montgomery street, Tuesday from 9:20 a.m. until noon. Chamber staff members Randle P. Shields and Harold V. Starr will represent the Chamber at the meeting. . . .

NATIONAL AIRLINES PRESIDENT L. B. Maytag, Jr., reported record earnings for the January-March period. Maytag said net profit for National during first three quarters of its business year was $2.94 per share, compared with $1.72 for same period in 1962. . . . PUBLIC UTILITIES COMMISSION of San Francisco yesterday received bids for construc- tion of San Antonio Dam in southern Alameda County. Plans and specifications were approved on January 29. . . .

CUTTY SARK'S Porthole Window Display, with its illusion of sea spray, won the Light and Motion class in the Point of Purchase Ad- vertising Institute's annual Western Regional competition. Display was planned by Honig- Cooper & Harrington, San Francisco advertising firm. . . .

BROADCASTERS PROMOTION ASSN. has set its convention for San Francisco, Nov. 17-20. Planning committee includes Joe Constantino, KTVU; George Rodman, KGO-TV; Dick Rob- ertson, KRON-TV; Bob Nashick, KPIX; Bob Harris, KCBS; Ron Wren, KGO; Bill Sweeney, KFRC; Don Allen, NBC-TV (Los Angeles); Tony Bachman, KXTV (Sacramento); Louise Z. Jorjorian, KSFO; and Jack Armstrong, TV Guide. . . .

S. F. Quotes

"Until my arrival in San Fran- cisco I had thought that Naples was the most beautiful city in the world. Now I know it is San Francisco."

—Valentin P. Katayev
(Russian novelist)

HARVEY'S WAGON WHEEL *Resort Hotel- Casino, which opened April 3 to the general public, is a gleaming tower rising 11 stories over Lake Tahoe at South Shore. Along with 200 rooms and 10 luxurious suites, this first luxury high-rise resort hotel at the lake features three fine restaurants, continuing entertainment—and a full casino.*

Linsky Resignation Effective May 6th

Resignation of Benjamin Linsky as Bay Area Air Pollution Control Officer becomes effective on May 6, according to Clarence D. Erickson, chairman of the District board.

Linsky was lauded by Erickson for his role "in establishment of the initial technical standards upon which the District's Regula- tions No. 1 and No. 2 were dependent."

Currently on terminal leave, Linsky, a vet- eran engineer in administrative and safety ftelds, is seeking employment opportunities in Bay Area industry.

Youth Symphony to Appear on KPIX-TV

The California Youth Symphony Orchestra will appear on KPIX (Channel 5) from 5:30 to 6:30 p.m. Sunday, May 5, in its drive for funds to finance a San Francisco-Osaka "Sister City" cultural exchange trip through Japan this summer.

Soprano Mary Costa and the San Francisco Symphony Orchestra have appeared with the youth organization in the past month to aid in the drive for $35,000 — still needed to finance the tour to be made at the invitation of the Cultural Commission of Japan.

Subsequent television appearances will be made by the orchestra, according to Aaron Edwards, KSFO newscaster, one of the spon- sors of the orchestra which has a membership of 104 young musicians, aged 11 to 18, from 30 senior and junior high schools in the Bay Area.

Contributions toward completion of the sum- mer excursion may be made to the California Youth Symphony Association, P. O. Box 1441, Palo Alto.

New Chamber Members

Hugo J. Odetto   Russel J. De Salvo   Silverino Silvestre   Mrs. Patricia Mackay   Mrs. Agnes Jenkins

MEMBERS NEW TO THE CHAMBER ROSTER include (above, l. to r.) Hugo J. Odetto, Western Region sales manager, *Parker Pen Company*, 278 Post St.; Russel J. De Salvo, owner, *De Salvo Travel*, 12 Geary St.; Severino Silvestre, owner, *Silbraz International*, 1489 Folsom St.; Mrs. Patricia Mackay, executive supervisor, *Welcome Wagon International*; Mrs. Agnes Jenkins, San Francisco Supervisor, *Welcome Wagon International*, Welcome Wagon Bldg., 209 Post St.

Chamber Heads Attend U.S. Chamber Conclave

President Harry A. Lee and four other Chamber officials will attend the 51st annual meeting of the United States Chamber in Washington, Sunday through Wednesday.

Accompanying Lee to the meeting on "Freedom and Economic Growth Through Voluntary Action" will be vice president William J. Bird, directors Ross Barrett and Robert W. Walker, and executive vice president, G. L. Fox.

Some 4,000 business and professional men and women are expected to attend the annual conclave, representing more than 3,800 local, state and regional chambers and trade and professional associations.

Calendar

April 29—INVEST-IN-AMERICA LUNCHEON, Garden Court, Sheraton-Palace, noon.
May 1—WORLD TRADE ASSN. LUNCHEON, World Trade Club, noon.
May 1—FRENCH COMMERCIAL CONSUL MEETING, Room 200, 4 p.m.
May 2—BD. OF DIRECTORS MEETING, Room 1, Cnm...

Casey Named Head Of Regional Problem

Attorney Thomas F. Casey, Jr., has been named chairman of the Regional Problems Section of the Chamber civic development committee, according to Harold V. Starr, manager of the civic development department.

The problems with which the Regional Problems Section is concerned are rapid transit, regional planning, a study of Bay Area transportation, recreation and parks and beaches, and the Association of Bay Area Governments.

T. F. Casey

Most pressing problem at this moment, Starr said, is advancement of the rapid transit program approved by voters in last November's elections. Rapid transit plans have been temporarily stymied by taxpayers' suits in Contra Costa County.

MARKET STREET

(Continued from page one)

already in possession of some parcels of land there (Fourth and Minna streets apparently the focal point):

In his opinion, the area can provide light industrial and commercial accommodation running up to 10,000 square feet in building, rising about 12 stores at rentals lower than obtainable now in downtown areas.

'Grant Center'

Bolles' group has a "Grant Center" development in mind, with pedestrian malls, which would close off some now existing narrow streets, pass over Howard and Folsom streets and blend in rail (Southern Pacific) facilities in such a manner as to provide quick service to San Francisco International Airport (for example).

Frank Gomez, industrial realtor: Gomez attributed some loss of former industry in the area (which moved down the Peninsula or to East Bay communities) to freeway development, but laid a great deal of the blame on what he called an "offensive" land price of $3 to $4 a square foot for industrial land in the area.

And a "literally cruel and fantastically high" tax burden, Gomez maintained, will have to be somehow eased if the area is to realize its true potential to attract high dollar value enterprise offering greater payroll, hence a boost in the community's economy.

He foresees a conversion from heavy industry to light industry and commercial use in a transition designed to keep the desirable industry that remains in the South of Market area and, hopefully, "to create the conditions to invite others to come and live with us."

Sports Arena Opposed

Comparing the "relatively free wheeling possibilities" of a redeveloped South of Market with the more restricted uses of the city's downtown and general business area, Cassady said, "We look forward to many new (industrial) neighbors."

Charles L. Conlan, San Francisco lithographer, asked for a study of the tax rate as compared with other communities, warned against establishing a "sports arena" type operation in the area.

BAY REGION BUSINESS

SAN FRANCISCO CHAMBER OF COMMERCE

VOLUME 20 • NUMBER 9 • MAY 10, 1963

R. A. Peterson to Address World Trade Week Lunch

DEEP INTO SAN FRANCISCO'S PAST

. . . Balclutha points up rich heritage

World Trade and Travel Week through the Golden Gate — an annual 1½ billion dollar industry, will be celebrated May 19 through May 25, according to Lester Goodman, president of the San Francisco Area World Trade Association.

Highlight of the 36th annual observance of the event will be a luncheon Tuesday, May 21, in the Peacock Court of the Hotel Mark Hopkins at which Rudolph A. Peterson, vice chairman of the board of directors of the Bank of America NT & SA, will discuss "A Commercial Banker Looks at World Trade." The luncheon, sponsored by the Chamber and the San Francisco Area World Trade Association, will officially honor representatives of 52 nations comprising the local consular corps. Chairman of this event is Anona Pickard of the American President Lines.

Typifying the great interest of the Chamber in world trade was the late and great Henry F. Grady, president of the American President Lines in 1941 and president of the Chamber in 1945. Largely because of him, the Chamber world trade department has gained worldwide recognition for its labors in the field of world trade.

Many of the earlier Chamber presidents were seafarers and world traders. Frederick W. Macondray (president of the Chamber in *(Continued on page four)*

(Continued on page four)

General McKee to Speak At Armed Forces Luncheon

General William Fulton McKee, Vice Chief of Staff, United States Air Force, will discuss "Vital National Defense Developments"—a first-hand, up-to-the-minute report—at the Armed Forces Day luncheon Friday, May 17, 12:15 p.m., at the San Francisco Commercial Club.

Sponsors include the Chamber and the San Francisco Commercial Club in cooperation with the Air Force Association (San Francisco Squadron), Association of the United States Army (San Francisco Chapter), Navy League of the United States (San Francisco Council), and Reserve Officers Association of the United States (Department of California).

Harry A. Lee, president of the Chamber, will preside. Chairman is Richard C. Ham. Colonel, USAR. and chairman of the Chamber Armed Forces section.

General McKee

General McKee graduated from West Point and was commissioned a Second Lieutenant in the Coast Artillery in 1929. He has served, with distinction, in the Canal Zone, the Pacific and Europe.

He was named a four-star general in 1961. and, in July of the following year, he became Vice Chief of Staff of the Air Force in Washington.

Chamber is Now 113 Years Young

The San Francisco Chamber of Commerce—oldest Chamber in the West—celebrated its 113th birthday Thursday.

The same day the Chamber was officially organized also was the day the city's civil government was first formed—according to Colville's directory of 1856.

"Instituted before California achieved statehood, the Chamber has been closely connected with civic welfare and the expansion and development of commerce, industry and business in San Francisco almost since the inception of San Francisco's history," Harry A. Lee. Chamber president, noted.

Sam Brannan

The first recorded interest in forming the Chamber appeared in a notice in the San Francisco *Alta California*, in August of 1849, announcing a meeting at the old schoolhouse on what is now Portsmouth Plaza. One of the first men who formed the *(Turn to page 2)*

(Turn to page 2)

SAN FRANCISCO'S *own Pierre Salinger, Press Secretary to President Kennedy, received the Ambassador Extraordinary Award of the Chamber on April 17 from Ross Barrett, President of Foster and Kleiser, Division of Metromedia. The award, for national achievement reflecting so highly on his native city, was presented at a press conference at the University of San Francisco, from where Salinger was graduated in 1947. Barrett is a director of the Chamber.*

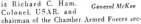
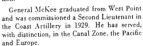

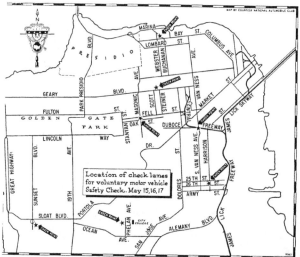

SHOWN ABOVE are check points for conduct of the Chamber's annual voluntary vehicle safety check campaign, May 15, 16 and 17. Chamber coordinates program which involves civic, police, military, transportation and industrial groups, and national safety clubs and councils. Campaign for 1962 saw San Francisco winning the Excellence Award for cities of more than 300,000 in population. —Drawing courtesy of National Automobile Club

Goal of 100,000 Is Set for '63 Car Checkdown

Goal of this year's voluntary vehicle safet' check, to be conducted on a citywide basi May 15-17, will be no less than 100,00 vehicles, according to Clifford M. Luster, div sion plant safety supervisor of the Pacifi Telephone and Telegraph Company and ger eral chairman of the event.

Check lanes will be located on Bay Stree between Webster and Buchanan; Geary Boule vard between Scott and Steiner Streets; Ma sonic Avenue between Oak and Fell Streets Golden Gate Park Panhandle; Sunset Circle end of Sunset Boulevard off Sloat Boulevard Balboa Reservoir on Phelan Avenue; Harr son Street between 25th and 26th Streets; an underneath the skyway at 13th Street an South Van Ness Avenue.

Last year, the Chamber, which spearheade the drive through its traffic safety and contro section, won the award of excellence for citie of more than 300,000 population throughout the nation. The award was based on the num ber of vehicles (100,000) passing throug check lanes and the public presentation o the campaign. In 1961 the San Francisco can paign won the overall Certificate of Exce lence, topping all other cities, large and smal

This year more than 175,000 folders, detai ing the location of seven check lanes, wer distributed by the Chamber to public, paro chial and private schools, the motor vehicle license bureau, traffic courts, local, state an federal governmental agencies, all branches o the military services, automobile dealers, truc fleet operators, service stations and insuranc companies.

'Pens Dipped, Ledgers Flipped'
Fireman's Fund Now 100 Years Old

Fireman's Fund Insurance Company, which celebrated its centennial May 6, began doing business in the old Government House at Sansome and Washington Streets with "pens dipping and ledgers flipping" in three dark rooms above a dingy staircase.

This year Fireman's Fund reached its biggest milestone by affiliating with the American Insurance Company to rise to a position of major importance in the property-casualty insurance world with combined assets of $1 billion.

During the past century millions of customers from all over the country have trod the path to the agents of Fireman's Fund—whose home office remains to this day in San Francisco.

In contrast to its first transaction—the insuring of a thousand five-gallon kegs of Boston syrup for $1,200 — the company now writes a multitude of multimillion-dollar coverages as well as coverage for the ordinary citizen's property.

One of the oldest trademarks of the company, then the Home Fire and Marine Insurance Company, was a picture of a painting of a full-rigged ship (see cut) by San Francisco marine artist W. A. Coulter.

The W. F. Babcock

The ship, named after W. F. Babcock, president of the Chamber five times (1874-76 and 1880-83), also was used as a design for a 21-cent stamp.

Among those attending the centennial ceremonies at the home office, 3333 California Street, last Monday were Fred H. Merrell, president of the company, Mayor George Christopher, James F. Crafts, chairman of the board, Fireman's Fund Insurance Company, stockholders and others.

CHAMBER BIRTHDAY
(Continued from page one)

Chamber was Samuel Brannan, leader of th 1846 Mormon immigration to San Francisc who started the city's first newspaper, th California Star.

Later, at a meeting in the Merchants' E change Building, May 9, 1850, William Hoo er, city treasurer and collector in 1846, wh led a sweeping reform to "purify City Ha from partisan trickery," (according to the hi torian Bancroft) was named the first Chambe president.

One of the greatest of a great line of Chan ber presidents was William Tell Coleman, th "Lion of the Vigilantes" who headed the Vig lance Committees of 1851, 1856 and 1877— described as "the most heroic figure in Cal fornia history" by Rockwell D. Hunt in h California's Stately Hall of Fame.

Josiah Royce, one of America's greate philosophers, noted the role played by th Chamber in stabilizing law and order in Sa Francisco in his book, California:

"Businessmen chose to enlist their servic in the cause of good order by choosing th only alternative—they avoided mob law, pu and simply, only by organizing the most r markable of all popular tribunals, the Vig lance Committee, whereby was effected th unique historical occurrence — a Busines man's Revolution."

By Joe Haughey

EDWARD C. SEQUEIRA, general manager of the Sir Francis Drake Hotel and a Chamber director, has been named assistant to the president of Western International Hotels, according to Edward E. Carlson, president of the hotel management firm. Sequeira will be headquartered at the St. Francis Hotel where he will handle public relations and promotional activities under Carlson's direction. Joseph Mogush, general manager of the Bayshore Inn in Vancouver, will become general manager of the Sir Francis Drake Hotel May 15. . . .

SUPERVISION PROBLEMS from the viewpoint of management, the educator and the labor relations expert will be the main topic of the Supervisors' Forum, at the 10th annual spring conference in the Claremont Hotel, Berkeley, Saturday, May 11. Conference is sponsored by the University Extension of UC. . . .

EICHLER HOMES announced record earnings for year's first quarter. Unaudited reports showed earnings gain of 93 per cent over same period of 1962. . . .

THE INTRIGUE will exhibit statuary—replicas of famous Greek and Roman plaques and statuary—at the Furniture Fashions Exhibition at Brooks Hall, May 11-19. . . .

HARRY A. LEE, president of the Chamber, and four other Chamber officials attended the United States Chamber of Commerce meeting in Washington last week. Accompanying Lee were William J. Bird, western vice president of John Hancock Mutual Life Insurance Company and vice president of the Chamber; Ross Barrett, president of Foster & Kleiser, a Chamber director; Robert W. Walker, vice president-executive representative, The Atchison, Topeka & Santa Fe Railway System, also a Chamber director; and G. L. Fox, executive vice president of the Chamber. The meeting was attended by some 4,000 business and professional men and women representing more than 3,800 local, state and regional chambers and trade and professional associations. . . .

THE A. B. BOYD Company, with head offices in San Francisco and branch offices in Seattle, Portland and Los Angeles, has announced that George Vosper, chairman of the Chamber manufacturers' committee, will be in charge of sales in the S. F. territory. . . .

WESTERN AIRLINES has inaugurated jet-powered Lockheed Electra II service on flights linking Los Angeles, San Diego and Mexico City. . . .

His Heart 'Belongs In San Francisco'

Last week the Chamber received this telegram from Syracuse, N. Y.:

"Please return my heart airmail special delivery. Thank you.

"Tony Bennett."

SFO HELICOPTER Airlines, Inc., has opened a downtown general sales and services office at 421 Powell street off Union Square. Roger Hall, vice president sales and services, is in charge of the facility. The airline offers 80 jet flights daily and expects to expand operations to Marin, Contra Costa and Santa Clara counties. A NEW exhibit, "Jacques Lipchitz: a Retrospective Selected by the Artist," presents 143 works by the internationally-known sculptor at the San Francisco Museum of Art through June 2. Organized by the UCLA Art Council, the exhibit includes 28 drawings, spanning the years 1914-1962, in a variety of media. . . .

ANONA PICKARD, manager of the American President Lines World Trade Center office, has been named chairman of the World Trade and Travel Week luncheon committee, according to J. T. Buckley, general chairman of the event. The luncheon will be held on May 21 at the Hotel Mark Hopkins. Buckley also named William A. Muriale of the Bank of America as Treasurer and George H. Mahoney of W. R. Grace and Co. as finance chairman. . . .

WILLIAM HURST of the Bank of America has been appointed deputy chairman of the subcommittee on trade relations with the Americas of the San Francisco Area World Trade Association, Lester L. Goodman, Association president, has announced. . . .

USF's Management Development Center will stage a one-day program for Executives' Wives Only on Saturday, May 25. Day begins at 8:45 a.m. . . .

MISS SISTER CITY envoy to Osaka is 17-year-old Ellen Margaret McGinty, daughter of Mr. and Mrs. James M. McGinty. An honor student at Mercy High School, she departs on Sister City visit June 14 via Japan Air Lines. . . .

DAMON RAIKE, realtors, leased building at 283 Clementina St. to sculptor Aristides Demetrios, who is currently busy with two projects —Sacramento County Courthouse and White Memorial Fountain at Stanford. . . .

HIRO IMAMURA, young University of California pianist, will perform Beethoven's Concerto for Piano and Orchestra No. 3 in C Minor, Opus 37, with the San Francisco Symphony Wednesday and Thursday, May 15 and 16, at 8:30 p.m., and at 2:15 p.m. Friday, May 17. . . .

HANS U. GERSON of William Gladstone Merchant & Associates announces imminent completion of working drawings and specifications for the Palace of Fine Arts. Gerson's firm is working on project with Welton Becket and Associates. . . .

ROBERT W. BURNETT has been appointed chief appraiser of Security Savings and Loan Association, according to board chairman John J. Peters. . . .

BERTOLT BRECHT'S Caucasian Chalk Circle opens May 10 as final production of year at San Francisco State College. It will play in the Main Theatre, May 10, 11, 15, 16, 17 and 18 at 8:30 p.m.

CAPTAIN JOHN W. DOLAN, JR. has been named new commander of the San Francisco Naval Shipyard, relieving Rear Admiral Charles A. Curtze who goes to Washington as Deputy Chief, Bureau of Ships. . . .

CONGRESSMAN JOHN F. SHELLEY announced plans for construction of a new and enlarged pier at Naval Shipyard to replace Pier A, destroyed by fire last November. . . .

SHIRLEY FONG, 1963 Miss Chinatown USA, will conduct a Queen's Orient-Around the World tour beginning June 29. Tour was organized by Jeanette's Travel Service. . . .

THE "CRYSTAL TOWER" apartment building was recently opened with a champagne preview cocktail party by Dimitri M. Barton, President of the Barton Development Company. This 84 unit, ultra modern, 14 story apartment building is one of the few average rentview apartment buildings recently built near the downtown area. Located on Russian Hill, the "Crystal Tower" offers one and two bedroom apartments from $155 to $340 per month. Built by Peter Kiewit & Sons at a cost of over $2,500,000, the reinforced concrete tower offers quiet, unsurpassed Bay views and modern rentals. Handled by Robert Little Co., EX 2-1457.

SAN FRANCISCO SYMPHONY, conducted by Enrique Jorda, will present final Los Altos Hills Symphony in Foothill College gymnasium, Saturday, May 18, 8:15 p.m. . . .

FOSTER AND KLEISER, Division of Metromedia, moves its executive offices to the Bethlehem building in downtown San Francisco and its northern California regional operating headquarters to Oakland within next 90 days. Announcement was made by F&K president and Chamber director Ross Barrett. . . .

ALBERS-GRUEN ASSOCIATES will redesign the entire first floor of Reno's Riverside Hotel. Bert Franklin will supervise the project for Albers-Bruen, named by Hotel Gazette magazine as one of top 20 interior design firms in nation last year. . . .

WALTER E. VAN DER WAAG, president and chief executive officer, Meadow Brook National Bank, Jamaica, N. Y., told financial analysts at the Bohemian Club that rising costs of time and savings deposits and increased operating costs are two most challenging problems facing American banks. . . .

JOHN L. HOGG, president, San Francisco Building Trades Council, will be guest of honor at a testimonial dinner sponsored by City of Hope Sunday, May 19, at Fairmont Hotel. . . .

STANDARD OIL OF CALIFORNIA first quarter net income reported at $81,901,000, increase of seven per cent over same period of 1962. . . .

PACIFIC GAS AND ELECTRIC COMPANY president, Norman R. Sutherland, said firm will apply to California Public Utilities Commission for permission to expand Moss Landing Power Plant into largest kilowatt producer west of the Mississippi. . . .

New Chamber Members

Wm. H. Trzcinka   *Arthur Formichelli*   *Hans U. Gerson*   *Mary King*   *Harry Shifs*

MEMBERS NEW TO THE CHAMBER ROSTER include (l. to r.) William H. Trzcinka, President, *Nadisco, Inc.,* 1495 Custer Ave.; Arthur Formichelli, partner, *Leonard, Dole and Formichelli,* attorneys, Mills Tower, 220 Bush St.; Hans U. Gerson, *William G. Merchant and Associates,* architects, 57 Post St.; Mary King, *Gerry Mountain Sports,* 315 Sutter St.; Harry Shifs, president, *Fillmore Merchants Development, Inc.,* 1565 Fillmore St.

WORLD TRADE WEEK
(Continued from page one)

1856-57), spent 25 years on the China coast, collected hides with Richard H. Dana, and fostered the tea importing business in San Francisco in 1847. Macondray, who "studied navigation by the binnacle light," could be called the "Father of World Trade in San Francisco." Daniel Gibb, president of the Chamber through 1859, led the famous Bulkhead Bill fight against greedy private interests

to insure the waterfront for the people of San Francisco for all time.

There were other "seadogs" among the Chamber presidents: George C. Perkins (1879-1891), later a U. S. Senator and a Governor of California, built the first six steam whaling vessels on the coast and was a pioneer in the Alaska canning industry; Horace Davis was a seafarer before starting a flour company which later became the Sperry Flour Company of which he served as president for 18 years; others were founders of mighty shipping concerns — among them, Captain William A. Merry, Captain William H. Marston, Captain William Matson and Wallace McKinney Alexander, the "Sugar King." Captain Robert Dollar, founder of the Dollar Steamship Lines, forerunner of the American President Lines, was a Chamber director.

Calendar

May 14—AGRICULTURAL COMMITTEE LUNCHEON, Crystal Room, Fairmont Hotel, 12 noon.
May 14—WORLD TRADE ASSOCIATION MEETING, Room 200, 4 p.m.
May 14—MEMBERSHIP ORIENTATION MEETING, John Hancock Bldg., 3rd Floor, Signature Room, 10:30 a.m.
May 15—RETAIL MERCHANTS ASSN. BOARD OF DIRECTORS MEETING, Bohemian Club, 8 a.m.
May 15—WORLD TRADE LUNCHEON, World Trade Club.

Ambitious Slate Set Up For New Members Program

Eleven orientation and assimilation membership meetings have been set up for the balance of the year, according to Herbert H. Harmon, manager of the Chamber membership relations department.

The "koffee-klatches" — a series of highly informative meetings relating to the nature, functions and scope of the Chamber and its significance to the business community—will be held Tuesdays, 10:30 a.m., in the Signature Room of the John Hancock Building on May 14 and 18, June 11 and 25, July 9 and 23, August 6 and 20, September 17, October 15 and November 12.

The first meeting of the '63 series, held April 24, involved an analysis of Chamber services, activities and projects for the information of new and regular members and a display of new Chamber literature, statistical reports, folders, brochures and directories. G. L. Fox, Chamber executive vice president, was the speaker.

Fox pointed out that the series of membership meetings is "designed to make membership investment in the Chamber as useful and beneficial as possible."

Business Directory Issued by Chamber

More than 200 San Francisco business, professional and labor organizations are listed in a revised business organization directory issued by the Chamber research department, according to department manager Stanley C. Allen.

BAY REGION BUSINESS

SAN FRANCISCO CHAMBER OF COMMERCE

VOLUME 20 • NUMBER 10 • MAY 24, 1963

James C. Hagerty to Address S.F. Advertising Club

James C. Hagerty, vice president in charge of news, special events and public affairs of the American Broadcasting Company—and former White House Press Secretary—will be the guest speaker at the 60th anniversary luncheon of the San Francisco Advertising Club Wednesday (May 29), 12:15 p.m., at the San Francisco Commercial Club.

Hagerty will discuss "Advertising's Role in the Economy of the Future."

Sponsors are the San Francisco Advertising Club, Commercial Club and the Chamber.

Harry A. Lee, Chamber president, will preside. Chairman of the day will be King Harris, president of the San Francisco Advertising Club.

Hagerty, former *New York Times* political reporter and Press Secretary to Dwight D. Eisenhower, was appointed to his present position in 1961. He was named Press Secretary to Thomas E. Dewey in 1943.

Also appearing at the luncheon will be Jules Bergman, precocious and youthful science editor of ABC. Bergman was appointed to his post by Hagerty in 1961. He joined the ABC as a newswriters in 1955. He is author of *90 Seconds to Space*

Jules Bergman

—*The Story of X-15*. He has also contributed to *Science World, Reader's Digest, Air Force, Space Digest* and *The New York Times*.

Reservations, $3.50 each, can be made or tickets purchased at the Chamber.

FORMER WHITE HOUSE PRESS SECRETARY
Ad Clubbers to hear "Ike's" former aide . . .

Dr. Louis G. Conlan Is Speaker At "Salute To Scholarship" Luncheon

Dr. Louis G. Conlan, president, City College of San Francisco, will discuss "Grades, Goals and Business Gains" at a "Salute to Scholarship" luncheon Wednesday noon, June 5, at the Del Webb TowneHouse.

The luncheon is sponsored by the Chamber Education committee of which John G. Levison, its vice chairman, is chairman of the day.

Harry A. Lee, president of the Chamber, will preside.

"This luncheon, now an annual event, is held as an encouragement of youth's best efforts in the world of education," Levison said. "Valedictorians of San Francisco's public, parochial and private high schools will be guests of honor at the luncheon.

"It is fitting that Dr. Conlan, a grid immortal at St. Mary's College, should address this team of all-star scholars."

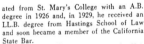
Dr. Conlan

Doctor Conlan joined the City College faculty in 1935 as instructor in business law and as head of the physical education department. In 1949 he assumed the presidency. He gradu-

ated from St. Mary's College with an A.B. degree in 1926 and, in 1929, he received an LL.B. degree from Hastings School of Law and soon became a member of the California State Bar.

He earned his M.A. degree from the University of California in 1946 and a Doctorate of Education in 1950.

Doctor Conlan served in the U. S. Navy during World War II as Commanding Officer of Navy V-12 Unit and the Medical V-12 Unit concurrently.

From 1925 until 1929 he was head football and basketball coach at Commerce High School in San Francisco. For many years he was an official of the Pacific Coast Football Conference.

Reservations, $3.50 each, can be made at the Chamber.

Seely Chairman of Industrial Committee

Ralph W. Seely, vice president of sales, Columbia-Geneva Steel Division, United States Steel, has been named chairman of the industrial committee of the Chamber, according to industrial department manager H. C. (Bud) Marsh.

Seely, active in the steel industry in California for almost 20 years, has held his present position since 1955.

Married, and the father of three children, Seely is a member of the American Society of Mechanical Engineers, Phi Gamma Delta, the California Club of Los Angeles, the Annandale Country Club in Pasadena, the Duquesne Club of Pittsburgh and the Burlingame Country Club in Hillsborough.

Ralph W. Seely

The Chamber committee he heads is concerned with the industrial development of the Bay Area, and with the development of San Francisco as an Executive Headquarters City for firms with main offices in the East and Midwest.

By Joe Haughey

"THE TREASURES OF VERSAILLES," on exhibit at the California Palace of the Legion of Honor from today through July 7, will be the topic of a special report beginning at 1:30 p.m. Sunday on KPIX, Channel 5. Films and photographs, supplied by the French Government Tourist Office, will be utilized to depict the story of Versailles. The exhibit itself, insured for $2,700,000, is, however, for historical and patriotic reasons, considered close to priceless. It consists of 102 paintings, 24 drawings, 20 pieces of sculpture, 28 items of furniture and objets d'art, eight tapestries and two carpets....

THE BUSINESS COMMUNICATIONS CENTER is sponsoring three parallel classes on Principles of Business Correspondence in June, to be repeated in July, August and September. All classes will be held in the Crystal Ballroom of the Marines Memorial Building, 609 Sutter St. Series A will be held from 7 to 9 p.m. on Mondays, Series B during the same hours on Tuesdays, and Series C from 2 to 4 p.m. on Wednesdays. The program will be conducted by Waldo J. Marra, founder and general director of the center....

"I AM WITH YOU," the most extensive religious-historical documentary ever filmed for television, will be broadcast on the Catholic Hour on four successive Sundays at 8:30 a.m., starting Sunday, on KRON-TV, Channel 4. The series is dedicated to Pope John XXIII. The history of the Catholic Church and its Ecumenical Councils will be the subject matter....

THE FIRST ANNUAL ERNIE FORD Amateur/Celebrity Invitational Golf Tournament tees off Friday at the California Golf Club, South San Francisco. Golfing stars, including Harvie Ward, Vern Callison, Ron Cerrudo, Bob Roos, Tom Culligan III, Tom Dixon, Bob Cardinal, Bill Higgins, Dr. Bob Knutson and Jim Asbell, will be matching skills in the 18-hole event. Playing celebrities will include Ernie Ford, George Gobel, Phil Harris, Buddy Greco, Jack Carter, Alex Dreier, Tom Harmon, Jim Lange, Lon Simmons, Vin Scully, Jerry Doggett and others....

SYDNEY G. WORTHINGTON, San Francisco division manager for Pacific Telephone and chairman of the legislative and national affairs section of the Chamber, has been named chairman of the commerce and industry division of the United Bay Area Crusade. Worthington will supervise efforts to raise more than $1,250,000 during the October drive, according to campaign chairman John R. Beckett....

CONGRESSMAN WILLIAM S. MAILLIARD, California's Sixth District (San Francisco), receives the second biennial distinguished service award of the Americans for Constitutional Action at a reception in his honor by the ACA national board of trustees tonight in Washington....

COMMANDER JOHN F. FAGAN, JR., commandant of U. S. Naval Nuclear Power School Mare Island, won Navy's Legion of Merit award "for outstanding performance of duty" while he was commanding officer of nuclear sub, USS Shark....

BRIG. GEN. JAMES W. COUTTS, USA (ret.), general manager of the San Francisco Retail Dry Goods Assn., will be the keynote speaker tomorrow during a one-day program for the wives of business executives at the University of San Francisco Management Development Center. He will speak on "The Importance of the Executive Wife." Other sessions include "The Wife as an Individual," featuring San Francisco Examiner columnist Anita Day Hubbard, and "Social Graces and Obligations," led by recreation director Kit Whitman of the Awahnee Hotel in Yosemite National Park....

MUSIC AT THE VINEYARDS will open its 1963 series with a program, "Music of the Baroque," Saturday, June 15, followed by a repeat performance on Sunday, June 16. This marks the sixth year of this unique series of concerts held at the Paul Masson Mountain Winery near Saratoga....

EXECUTIVES' SECRETARIES, INC., a national organization with 41 units, is presently holding its 16th annual convention on Nob Hill at the Mark Hopkins and the Fairmont Hotel. Today's events include an Enchanted City Tour, a bus tour of the city, a coffee break in Golden Gate Park's Hall of Flowers, and a Maritime Dinner tonight in the Fairmont's Grand Ballroom. There'll be a general session in the Fairmont's Terrace Room tomorrow morning, with Blanche Jones, of Houston, national president, presiding, culminated by election of national officers and directors. President of the hosting San Francisco chapter is Eileen Lynch....

GOLDEN GATE NATIONAL BANK will be listed as an associate member of the Pacific Coast Stock Exchange, effective June 1, according to Jacob Shemano, the bank's president. Joachim R. Raede has been appointed manager of the stock trading department, Shemano said. The bank created the department to function under its Exchange membership....

UNIVERSITY OF SAN FRANCISCO's board of regents has selected Dr. Vincent P. Wright, 49, as new dean of the College of Business Administration after a year-long search of major U. S. business schools, according to the Very Rev. Charles W. Dullea, S.J., university president. Dr. Wright has been dean of the Boston College Graduate School of Business Administration since 1956. His USF appointment becomes effective July 1....

"THE NEW MATHEMATICS," considered a revolutionary advance in the teaching of the science, will be taught during the new summer school session at Lincoln University, 2518 Jackson Street, by internationally famed mathematician and physicist Chul Mo Kim, Ph.D.C. Although a law school since 1919, Lincoln University recently inaugurated liberal arts courses. Registration for summer classes will take place at the university June 19-21....

Fly through your shopping—use the Yellow Pages

THINK YOU'RE SEEING DOUBLE? You're wrong. You're seeing triple. But don't worry, your eyes are all right—it's a triple exposure of the latest in a series of animated spectaculars rendered by Foster & Kleiser artists for the Pacific Telephone Company. The canine genie rocks cheerfully on a magic carpet made from the Yellow Pages. Created by art director Bob Watkins of Batten, Barton, Durstine and Osborn, the animated doggie currently floats through the air with the greatest of ease along the S. F. Skyway.

NEW POST FOR NEW ZEALAND CONSUL GENERAL—R. L. G. Challis, New Zealand's former Consul General in San Francisco for the western United States, is shown with Japan Air Lines Hostess Yuriko Nakatsukasa before boarding a JAL Jet Courier at San Francisco International Airport en route to his new assignment as Commissioner for New Zealand in Singapore.

BALLET CELESTE dedicated a special program Sunday at the Lamplighters' Harding Theater to the people of the Philippines. The occasion was presentation of a new work, "Mindanao Suite," choreographed by the company's first dancer, Benjamin Reyes-Villanueva. Reyes is a citizen of the Philippines and was chosen "dancer of the year" in Manila in 1951. Guests of the ballet company at the performance were the Philippine Consulate staff and their business associates....

MYRON M. CHRISTY, executive vice president of the Western Pacific Railroad Co., San Francisco, spoke yesterday at a luncheon during the 34th annual meeting of the Association of Interstate Commerce Commission Practitioners in the Statler-Hilton Hotel, Los Angeles. His topic was "Closing the Transportation Gap." Other Bay Area participants at the meeting, which continues today, are William M. Bennett, commissioner, California Public Utilities Commission, San Francisco; and Karl M. Ruppenthal, director of Stanford University's Transportation Management Program....

JAPAN TRADE CENTER announced Camera Show, June 13-18, and a November exhibit of Japanese-manufactured dental equipment....

KPIX (CHANNEL 5) received George Foster Peabody Award for Distinguished Achievement and Meritorious Public Service for its San Francisco Pageant series....

APPOINTMENT of James L. Tolley as manager of San Francisco General Motors public relations was announced by Anthony De Lorenzo, vice president in charge of public relations staff....

SHELDON MACHLIN sculpture exhibit will continue showing at Bolles Gallery, 729 Sansome, through May 24....

SCHLITZ BEER staged ceremonies marking production of Schlitz in 12-ounce cans for first time in San Francisco. Overseeing the production were T. J. Woods, manager of Pacific Plants; V. A. Sariotti, assistant manager, San Francisco plant; and R. N. Wagner, office manager....

KRON-TV (Channel 4) will telecast the 1964 Olympic Games in Tokyo. Games open October 10, 1964, and will be seen here under exclusive arrangements worked out by NBC-TV....

KTVU (Channel 2) announced appointment of chief engineer Robert E. Arne to post of vice president of San Francisco-Oakland Television, Inc....

CHICKEN DELIGHT of California has leased the 5,000-square-foot warehouse and office building at 1655 Jerrold Street, according to Damon Raike and Company, realtors....

BREAKFAST, INTERNATIONAL STYLE, was served to Mayor George Christopher to note World Trade and Travel Week—ending tonight with the International Ball at the Jack Tar Hotel. Serving the Mayor was Angie Touloume, Queen of World Trade Week and a student at City College of San Francisco.

International Ball Climaxes Trade Week

As a climax to World Trade and Travel Week, overseas students in the Bay Area will be guests of honor at the 16th annual International Ball, sponsored by the Junior World Trade Association, tomorrow night in the Grand Ballroom of the Jack Tar Hotel.

There will be dancing from nine p.m. until one a.m. and entertainment will be provided by overseas students from San Francisco State College. Ronald Hostetter is chairman of the Ball.

Blocki to Address Transport Banquet

Robert A. Blocki, president of the National Transportation Fraternity, will discuss "Your National Fraternity" Tuesday (May 28) at a dinner meeting of the San Francisco Chapter No. 48 of Delta Nu Alpha, NTF at Engler's Restaurant, 20 - 10th Street.

Officials of the local chapter for 1963-64 will be installed: Don Chisholm, president; Don Griffith, first vice-president; Robert Ryan, second vice-president; Ben Roth, director; Ray Vinick, secretary; and Jim Cooper, treasurer.

Retiring after heading the local Delta Nu Alpha organization during a highly successful year (1962-63) is Charles Miller, manager of the Chamber transportation department.

Wilson is Appointed Aviation Chairman

Edwin M. Wilson, vice president of Thompkins and Company, insurance brokers, has been appointed chairman of the Chamber aviation section.

A veteran of World War II, Pacific theatre, Wilson holds three Distinguished Flying Crosses and three Air Medals. He is a task force captain with the Navy's Ready Reserve.

Wilson operates his own Piper Comanche on business trips throughout the state.

Progressogram No. 57

$1½ Billion Industry

San Francisco—Gateway to World Trade

San Francisco, strategically located on a 456-square-mile landlocked harbor, is widely recognized as the leading international trade center on the Pacific Coast and the key to the vast western United States market.

The San Francisco Customs District handles imports and exports in excess of $1.3 billion a year, the Chamber reports.

Surrounding San Francisco Bay is a 10,817-square-mile area known as the 13-county Bay Region. With a population of nearly 5 million it is the richest, most diversified and most significant market in the western United States, and one of the most important in the nation.

Approximately 2,500 San Francisco firms are engaged in international trade. The firms deal in virtually all commodities and all markets.

Thousands of industrial and agricultural products produced in the Bay Area and northern California are distributed to markets all over the world.

About 85 per cent of San Francisco's exports fall into the classifications of (1) food products, (2) chemicals and pharmaceuticals, and (3) industrial and electrical machinery and equipment. In specific commodities, raw cotton leads, machinery, petroleum products, dried fruit, rice, grains, iron and steel, canned fruit, automobiles, trucks and parts, and iron ore are also important export items.

The bulk of the city's imports are foodstuffs and basic raw materials to service American industry. Coffee leads, with raw wool, nonferrous ores, copra, newsprint paper and other major import items following. Crude petroleum, jute and burlap, crude rubber, inedible animal products and, finally, fresh and canned fish are among our essential imports.

San Francisco is headquarters for 52 foreign government consulates with whom the Chamber cooperates. San Francisco is also the district and regional headquarters for many federal agencies of the United States and the headquarters for some of the largest corporations in the nation.

The Port of San Francisco is a hundred-million-dollar public utility which meets every possible shipping requirement. It also encompasses an 18-mile stretch of ship berthing space, 229 acres of covered and open wharf areas, and a total of 43 piers. Here the largest ships in the world are accommodated.

The port's general cargo piers are mostly of the one-story finger type, ranging in length from 500 to 1,300 feet, and in width from 15 to 300 feet—each side capable, in most cases, of berthing two vessels, and in every instance providing railroad spur tracks along the aprons.

More than 100 shipping lines regularly pass through the Golden Gate and more than 200 steamship companies have offices or agencies here. Five international shipping companies have their home office in San Francisco. In 1961, more than 10 million short tons of foreign imports and exports were handled by San Francisco Bay's ports and harbors.

The city itself is mature and urbane, a cultural and educational center famed for gracious living. Since practically every race in the world is represented in its approximately 775,000 population, San Francisco has an international flavor unique in the United States.

Concentrated in San Francisco alone are tremendous regional supply bases and production and management headquarters for big commercial enterprises. World-wide operations are conducted from hundreds of business management headquarters in the city.

San Francisco is served directly by four Class I railroads operating more than 27,000 miles of lines, more than 100 common carrier truck lines and bus lines radiating to all points of the nation.

Reprints available at the Chamber Research Dept., 333 Pine St.

Sacramento Valley Days Set for June

Sacramento Valley Days will be held June 13 and 14 by the Chamber intercity section, according to F. T. Garesche, chairman.

General chairman for the event is Paul Bissinger, 1950 president of the Chamber.

Committee chairmen for Sacramento Valley Days are: Frank Crossman, Santa Fe Railroad, baseball chairman; Irving Danielson, Bank of California, finance chairman; Dan E. London, managing director of the St. Francis Hotel, 1960 Chamber president and Commodore of the Great Golden Fleet; Ivan Branson, Morning Glory Caterers, and Ian Russell, Wells Fargo Bank, hospitality chairmen; and Perry Spackman, Southern Pacific Company, transportation.

SAFETY CHECK CLICKS! *Harold V. Starr, manager of the Civic Department of the Chamber, reported yesterday that results of the Chamber-sponsored sixth annual voluntary motor vehicle safety check are expected to reach 100,000 vehicles checked during the three day campaign, May 15-17. Shown above at kickoff ceremonies for the event in front of City Hall are, left to right: Starr; Sergeant Paul Stephens, U. S. Marine Corps; Cort Edmunston, Auto Industries Highway Safety Committee; Gale Hiett (Miss San Francisco); Clifford Luster (division plant safety director, Pacific Telephone), chairman of the Safety Check; Roy E. Matison (Federated Metals Division, American Smelting and Refining Co.), chairman of the traffic safety and control section; Lucille Lando (S. F. Progress columnist), Hi-Board Council coordinator; Gregory Heine (Greyhound Corp.), chairman of the kickoff committee; Lewis R. Hall (American Society of Safety Engineers), lane supervisor, and Walter Lunsford, regional representative for the Auto Industries Highway Safety Committee.*

S. F. Quotes—

"I've traveled all over the world only to discover that San Francisco is the finest city I've ever been in."

—GEN. WILLIAM FULTON McKEE
Vice Chief of Staff, USAF

CALENDAR

May 28 — Membership Orientation Meeting — John Hancock Bldg., 255 California Street, 3rd Floor, Signature Room, 10:30 a.m.

May 29 — Joint Chamber of Commerce and Advertising Club Luncheon — Commercial Club, 465 California Street, 12:15 p.m. Speakers: James Hagerty, "Advertising's Role in the Economy of the Future," and Jules Bergman.

June 5 — Salute to Scholarship Luncheon — Golden Gate Room, Del Webb's TowneHouse, 12 noon. Speaker: Dr. Louis G. Conlan, "Grades, Goals and Business Gains."

June 6 — Special Group Meeting — Mr. Paul Bissinger, Room 200, 11 a.m.

June 6 — Board of Directors Meeting — Room 1, Commercial Club, 12 noon.

June 6 — Industrial Development Committee —Torino's, 12 noon.

Weekend Radio Programming

Chamber radio programs for the weekend ahead are:

SAN FRANCISCO IN THE SIXTIES—KNBR, 8:05 p.m., Saturday, May 25—"World Trade Week—Assessed"—Lester Goodman, president, San Francisco Area World Trade Association; James P. Wilson, manager, world trade department, San Francisco Chamber, and Howard R. Stephenson, assistant manager, chamber world trade department.

CONFERENCE CALL—KFRC, 8 p.m., Sunday, May 26—"San Francisco's Stake in the Future of Air Cargo"—Belford Brown, manager, San Francisco International Airport; William B. Wright, district sales manager, Flying Tiger Line, and George Ryan, vice president (traffic), Airborne Freight Corp.

SAN FRANCISCO PROGRESS REPORT — KFRC, 9:45 p.m., Sunday, May 26 — "Experience Unlimited" — George LaBar, director of the "Experience Unlimited" program of the California State Employment Service.

Civic-Improvement Directory Published

A Civic and Improvement Organization Directory has been updated and published by the Chamber research department, according to Stanley C. Allen, department manager.

The 10-page listing is available free to the public.

formed by Mayor George Christopher.

C. C. Walker, former chairman of the San Francisco Chamber of Commerce practical politics committee and former vice president of General Electric, has been named chairman of the mayor's committee.

"The prime purpose of the mayor's citizens committee is to encourage all public and private organizations to fly our national flag every day — and especially during Flag Week," Walker said.

"Many fraternal, civic and business organizations are planning to have a special Flag Day program during the week."

The citizens' committee for Flag Week is comprised of:

AIRLINES—Sterling R. Newman, sales manager, United Air Lines, Inc.
AUTOMOBILE COMPANIES—Edwin S. Moore, executive vice president, California State Automobile Association.
BANKS — Alvin F. Derre, vice president, Crocker-Anglo National Bank.
BUSINESS AND TRADE ORGANIZATIONS—G. L. Fox, executive vice president, San Francisco Chamber of Commerce.
GOVERNMENT PROPERTIES — Sherman P. Duckel, administrator, City and County of San Francisco.
HOTELS—Edward C. Sequeira, assistant to the president, Western International Hotels.
INSURANCE COMPANIES—Stuart D. Menist, vice president, Fireman's Fund Insurance Company.
OFFICE BUILDINGS — Ralph J. Nartzik, manager, the Russ Building.
OIL COMPANIES—Robert M. Douglas, regional manager, Standard Oil of California.
PRIVATE SCHOOLS AND COLLEGES—Clarence A. Phillips, president, Heald's Business College.
PUBLIC SCHOOLS—Melvin T. Petersen, assistant superintendent, senior high schools.
PUBLIC RELATIONS — Philip G. Laskey, vice president, Westinghouse Broadcasting (KPIX).
RETAILERS — Vernon A. Libby, executive vice president, Better Business Bureau.
TRANSPORTATION — Gene E. Holmes, president, The Gray Line, Inc.
UTILITIES—Harry A. Lee, division manager, the Pacific Gas and Electric Company.
FRATERNAL ORGANIZATIONS — Theodore T. Mumby, exalted ruler, B.P.O. Elks, Lodge No. 3.
VETERANS ORGANIZATIONS — Robert M. Kehoe, past commander, Amvets.

Junior Chamber Ends Seat Belt Campaign

The Junior Chamber climaxes a week-long drive for the sale and installation of seat belts to motorists tomorrow and Sunday.

Three clinics will be operated by the Junior Chamber this weekend between 9 a.m. and 5 p.m. each day.

Jaycee clinics will be located at the Civic Center, Auto Park, Grove at Van Ness Avenue, the Panhandle and San Francisco State College.

BAY REGION BUSINESS
PUBLISHED BY THE
SAN FRANCISCO CHAMBER OF COMMERCE

HARRY A. LEE, President
G. L. FOX, Executive Vice President
M. A. HOGAN, Secretary
JOSEPH C. HAUGHEY, Editor

Published semi-monthly and owned by the San Francisco Chamber of Commerce, a non-profit organization, at 333 ... ., San Francisco, Zone 4, County of San Francisco, California. Telephone 1-3 break 2-4511. (Non-member subscription, $5.00 a year.) Entered as Second Class matter ... 26, 1911, at the Post Office at San Francisco, California, under the Act of March 3, 1879.

Circulation: 7,500

BAY REGION BUSINESS

SAN FRANCISCO CHAMBER OF COMMERCE

VOLUME 20 • NUMBER 11 • JUNE 14, 1963

Full Calendar of Events Climaxes
Sacramento Valley Days Festivity

Valley Days — saluting the great Sacramento Valley — in this, its 14th year, reaches its climax today.

The event is sponsored by the San Francisco business community and coordinated by the Chamber intercity section, of which F. T. Garesche is chairman.

On today's agenda is a $600 million construction tour of San Francisco followed by a tour of the San Francisco Naval Shipyard.

Paul Bissinger, general chairman of this year's Valley Days and 1950 Chamber president, will address some 200 businessmen, ranchers, growers and civic leaders at a luncheon at the Naval Shipyard at 12:30 p.m. A cruise on San Francisco Bay by the Great Golden Fleet, of which Dan E. London, Managing Director of the St. Francis Hotel, is Commodore, is scheduled this afternoon.

Paul Bissinger

Yesterday's events included a "welcome breakfast" at the St. Francis Hotel, industrial tours, and the San Francisco Giants-Chicago Cubs baseball game at Candlestick Park, followed by a reception at the World Trade Club for guests and their wives.

"San Francisco—the Gateway to the potentially vast market of the Pacific Basin, and its northern California neighbors, particularly in the great Sacramento Valley — have common goals of a very compelling nature," Bissinger pointed out. "And each year, for that reason, Valley Days is becoming an event of increasing significance.

"Thus Valley Days, signalling a declaration of interdependence between San Francisco and its neighboring communities and counties, is an important element in the shape of things to come."

Charles Ayres New Publicity Department Assistant Manager

Charles F. Ayres, associate editor of the *San Francisco Daily Commercial News* and a veteran newspaper reporter, has been appointed assistant manager of the Chamber publicity department, according to G. L. Fox, executive vice president.

Purpose of the Chamber publicity department, of which Joseph I. Haughey is manager, is to publicize the City and County of San Francisco and its economic and cultural development on local, national and international levels for the benefit of local business, and to keep the public informed of the multiple aims, actions and goals of the Chamber itself.

Charles F. Ayres

Ayres was associate editor of the *Daily Commercial News* for the past three years. He also operated the night city desk of the *San Francisco Call-Bulletin* prior to its merger with the *San Francisco News* in 1959. He began his career with the *San Francisco Chronicle* in 1943, has worked on the *San Francisco Examiner* sports desk, and was Sunday editor of the *Rockford* (Illinois) *Morning Star*.

"THE SKY *is no longer the limit" is the slogan of parachutist Kaz Ostrom, "the Viking of the Sky," who has recently joined the Chamber. All of which points up the fact that the Chamber membership drive is reaching new altitudes these days. (New members' panel, page three).*

Civic Improvement List Is Published

An updated Civic & Improvement Organization Directory has been published by the Chamber research department.

The 10-page listing is available to the public, free.

Re-Enactment of 65-35 Bill Urged by Chamber

Legislation now before Congress to continue the present 65-35 percentage split of repair and conversion work between Navy and private enterprise shipyards has been voted unanimous support by the board of directors of the Chamber.

Action of the Chamber board resulted after a recommendation of the Chamber shipbuilding and ship repair committee, of which William B. Swan, manager, San Francisco marine and defense facilities sales, General Electric Company, is chairman.

In seeking Chamber support of "definite re-enactment" of the bill, Swan urged that the action of the Chamber board "be immediately brought to the attention of the defense appropriations subcommittee, the Secretary of the Navy, each California congressman and others concerned."

"It is fully agreed by the Chamber shipbuilding and ship repair committee that the San Francisco Naval Shipyard is a much needed factor in the local economy," Swan continued.

"However, private and commercial yards are not getting their fair share of naval ship repair work as provided for in the 65-35 formula. Nevertheless, the committee feels that the re-enactment of the provision would help to ensure an equitable distribution of naval ship repair work among local private yards, which it has been proved are capable of doing such repair work more economically than the Navy."

By Joe Haughey

CALIFORNIA YOUTH SYMPHONY will perform Antonin Dvorak's Symphony No. 5 ("From the New World") and the overture to Carl Maria Von Weber's opera, "Der Freishutz" tomorrow (Saturday) from 1:30 to 2:30 p.m. on KPIX, Channel 5. The 104 young musicians under the direction of Aaron Sten are preparing for a 30-day tour of Japan in July in which they will perform 14 concerts in 10 cities. . . . GALERIE DE TOURS, 559 Sutter Street, currently exhibits a one-man show of oils by Shi Pratini, and a wood sculpture show by Robert Kingsbury. It will continue until July 7. . . . AMERICAN ARBITRATION ASSOCIATION announces the appointment of Donald Watson, president of Weyerhaeuser Steamship Co., San Francisco, to its national panel of arbitrators. He will be available to serve in disputes over the performance of commercial contracts. . . . THE DAILY COMMERCIAL NEWS announces the appointment of J. Frank Beaman, widely known newspaperman, as its new editor. Beaman succeeds Mary T. Fortney, who resigned to take a position with the S. F. Examiner. Beaman's appointment was announced by George G. McDonald, president of the Recorder Printing and Publishing Co., of which the DCN is a subsidiary. . . . NATIONAL DEFENSE TRANSPORTATION Association's San Francisco Bay Area chapter is sponsoring a full dress study by nationally known experts of land, sea and air containerized shipments during the afternoon and evening at the Presidio on June 27. . . . GAIL REID, Seattle Seafair's "Golden Girl," will visit San Francisco and the Bay Area tomorrow, Sunday, Monday and Tuesday to invite "one and all" to attend the festival August 2-12. The "one girl tourism task force" will arrive tomorrow, 5:48 p.m., via Western Air Lines. She will meet Mayor George Christopher Monday morning to invite him to be the guest of Seattle Mayor Gordon S. Clinton at a Mayor's Day Seafair Sunday, August 11—feature of the day will be a $25,000 Seafair Purse Trophy Race for unlimited hydroplanes on Lake Washington. . . . WILLIAM N. COTHRAN has been named director of KRON-TV's new Department of News and Documentary Programs. For the past six years he has been news director. . . .

THE SAN FRANCISCO *Hilton Hotel will be officially dedicated Monday, June 24, at 11:30 a.m. at the Ellis-Taylor Streets side of the site. When completed, the hotel will rise 18 stories and contain 1,200 rooms. To the left is the proposed 22-story Hilton office building.*

"SAN FRANCISCO DETECTIVE," an unprecedented "inside view" of actual police work in San Francisco, will be presented Sunday (June 16) on the Du Pont Show of the Week (KRON-TV, Channel 4, 10 p.m.). The central figure of "San Francisco Detective" is 42-year-old Inspector George Asdrubale, homicide. An NBC film crew rode with Asdrubale and his partners for weeks, filming every facet of his work. . . . PACIFIC COAST SECURITIES CO. has leased offices on the ninth floor of the John Hancock Building, according to Damon Raike & Co., commercial and industrial real estate brokers. Pacific Coast, nationwide investment banking house, was established in 1947. Its old address: 240 Montgomery Street. . . . SAN FRANCISCO SYMPHONY Association fund drive had reached 82 per cent of its $272,-000 goal as of May 31, according to J. D. Zellerbach, president of the orchestra's governing body. The remaining $50,000, Zellerbach noted, is vitally needed to meet the deficit of the season just ended and to provide a firm fiscal basis for the forthcoming season, which will introduce Joseph Krips as permanent conductor. . . . HANDLERY HOTELS Corporation has begun construction on a new 10-story, 93-room Handlery Motor Inn in the 200 block on O'Farrell Street, a block from Union Square. Architect is Mario Gaidano and the contractor, Barrett Construction Co. The $2 million inn is the 14th Handlery Hotel in California. . . . THE ACTOR'S WORKSHOP is presenting a summer festival of the most popular plays of the season just concluded. Each revival, with original cast, is being presented in straight runs on Wednesdays through Sundays, but Saturday matinees will be continued only until June 22. The first of the series, ending with a matinee tomorrow (June 15), is Shakespeare's "Twelfth Night." On Wednesday, June 19, the second of the series, "Galileo," begins a three-week run. "The Balcony" starts July 10 for four weeks. All performances are at Marines Memorial Theater. . . . RED CHIMNEY Restaurant in Stonestown is now under the management of the world famous Cliff House, according to C. C. Carrigg, operating manager of the owner corporation. Carrigg said Cliff House credit cards now will be good at both locations. . . . S. F. GENERAL AGENTS AND MANAGERS Association (life insurance) has elected John O'Brien Cullen, general manager here for New York Life, president, succeeding W. D. Oberholtzer. Other new officers: Arthur P. Carroll, CLU, Equitable Life Assurance Society manager, vice president; Jack A. Martinelli, CLU, New England Mutual Life manager, secretary-treasurer; and directors—John A. Lester, CLU, manager for Metropolitan Life, and Ellison C. Grayson, Home Life manager. . . . "PORT OF CALL, San Francisco," a new documentary film produced by the San Francisco Port Authority, is now available nationally for free showings to trade and shipping groups. Prints of the 16-mm, 20-minute sound-and-color film can be obtained from film centers of Modern Talking Picture Service in major cities of the country, including San Francisco. . . . GOLDEN GATE NATIONAL BANK will hold formal opening of its new Day and Night Branch, 999 Market Street (at Sixth) on Monday (June 17) at 10 a.m., according to Jacob Shemano, the bank's founder-president. It's the third branch opened by the new bank, just two years after the bank itself opened for business. Executive offices are at 130 Montgomery Street and the second branch is at 2539 Mission. . . . A MIDSUMMER WATER CARNIVAL features the gala grand opening at Steele Park, Lake Berryessa, in Napa County. Steele Park is billed as "California's newest and most modern year-around recreation community." The grand opening festivities will be held July 18-21. . . .

SITE CLEARANCE *is scheduled to begin in August for this new 43-story Wells Fargo Building—the tallest in the U. S. west of Dallas and the largest commercial office building in San Francisco. Dillingham Corporation, owners and developers, plan completion by early 1966.*

BALLET '63 offers a varied program tonight (June 14) at the San Francisco Ballet School Theatre, 378 Eighteenth Avenue. The program—Opus I, Prokofiev Waltzes, Dance Variations and Ebony Concerto—will be repeated tomorrow night and Sunday afternoon. Ballet '63 consists of performances by artists from the San Francisco Ballet. Critics raved last year about Ballet '62. Performances are at 8:30 Friday and Saturday evenings and 3 p.m. Sundays. Among new ballets and previous hits to be staged here are Bach Concerto and Cocktail Party as well as those named above. Dance stars appearing include Jocelyn Vollmar, Terry Orr, Thatcher Clarke and Robert Gladstein. . . . .

SIXTIETH ANNIVERSARY EXHIBIT of the U. S. Department of Commerce opens June 24 in the History Room of the Wells Fargo Bank, 30 Montgomery Street, and will continue to July 3, according to Philip M. Creighton, Commerce Department director here. An opening ceremony at 9:30 a.m. on Monday, June 24, will feature brief talks by Mayor George Christopher; Ransom M. Cook, president of Wells Fargo Bank; George F. Hansen, vice president of the S. F. Chamber, and Creighton. . . .

BERT W. COYLE has been elected a vice president of National Union Insurance Companies, Pittsburgh, Pa. He will continue as head of the company's Pacific Coast department with headquarters in San Francisco. . . .

(Continued on page four)

List of S. F. Books Available at Library Issued by Research

The Chamber research department has updated its list of books about San Francisco available at the city's public library, according to Stanley C. Allen, research manager.

"Debonair Scoundrel"

The list, compiled alphabetically by the name of the author, contains some 112 titles ranging from Mary Ellen Bamford's opus of 1899, *Ti: A Story of San Francisco Chinatown*, to the 1962 work about Abe Rueff, *A Debonair Scoundrel*, by Lately Thomas.

The subject matter ranges through a colorful gamut. Obtainable at the San Francisco Public Library are such intriguing works as F. W. Aitken's on-the-scene report, *A History of the Earthquake and Fire in San Francisco*, published in 1906, and later titles, such as Richard H. Dillon's *Shanghaiing Days* (1961) and *The Hatchet Men* (1962).

The San Francisco Giants get their turn at the literary bat in Charles Einstein's *A Flag for San Francisco*. The city's pro football team is the subject of Dan McGuire's 1960 effort, *San Francisco 49ers*.

Those seeking to know the 'Forty-niners of an earlier era will find them in Archer Butler Hulbert's 1949 book, *'Forty-niners, the Chronicle of the California Trail*.

Real 'Cool' in S.F. This Summer

THE SHIPSTADS & JOHNSON ICE FOLLIES, *opening their 1963 series at Winterland on Wednesday (June 19), has become another San Francisco tradition of seasonal festivity. And while the Follies obviously brighten up the city's entertainment front, less evident to the public is the fact that such sparkling shows mean good business for San Francisco. It is estimated that approximately 250,000 tourists from Idaho, Oregon, Nevada, Washington and California will attend the show this year—pouring an estimated $200 million into the city's financial coffers. The Ice Follies, family entertainment in the finest sense, involves presently 250 employees and has played to nearly 58 million spectators since 1939.*

Chamber Takes a Look at Monorail

Monorail rapid transit in San Francisco and San Mateo counties will be discussed at a joint meeting of the mass transit and regional problems sections of the Chamber civic development committee Tuesday, 10:30 a.m. (June 18) in room 200 of the Chamber building.

Edward Haas of Haas & Haynie and Attorney Edward Keil of Keil & Connolly will present the monorail rapid transit proposal.

Comments will be made on the following bills: SB 344—Collier; SB 748—West Bay Transit; and SB 371—Bay Area Transportation Study Commission.

Chamber Publishes Steamship Directory

Some 170 steamship companies with offices or agencies in San Francisco are listed in a steamship directory just issued by the Chamber transportation department, according to Charles C. Miller, manager.

Seventy-nine companies listed in the 69-page directory call at the Port of San Francisco and serve an estimated 279 world ports.

The *San Francisco Steamship Directory* can be obtained free by Chamber members by calling the transportation department—EXbrook 2-4511, ext. 58.

PAUL R. HANDLERY, *vice president of Handlery Hotels, tries to paint pretty Karen Jensen into the picture of the new 93-room, 10-story Handlery Motor Inn, a block from San Francisco's Union Square, as Karen pitches in to officially begin construction work.*

Kaz Ostrom   Ernest L. Buchanan   James L. Morse   Paul Golz   Grant A. Robbins

MEMBERS NEW TO THE CHAMBER ROSTER include (above, l. to r.) Kaz Ostrom, "the Viking of the Sky," professional parachutist, Concord; Ernest L. Buchanan, manager, *State Life Insurance Co.*, 400 Montgomery St.; James L. Morse, owner, *Morse Bros. Painting & Waterproofing*, 1339 Folsom St.; Paul Golz, executive vice president, *FC Housing Company, Inc.*, 593 Market St.; and Grant A. Robbins, *Grant Robbins & Associates*, Flood Building, 870 Market St.

Calendar

June 17—Agricultural Subcommittee on Water Policy—Commercial Club, 12 noon.

June 17—San Francisco Council of District Merchants' Associations—Room 200, 8 p.m.

June 18—Joint Meeting of Regional Problems and Mass Transit—Room 200, 10:30 a.m.

June 18—Transportation Conference—Room 200, 12:30 p.m.

June 20—Board of Directors Meeting—Commercial Club, 12 noon.

June 20—U. S. World Trade Fair Luncheon—World Trade Club, 12 noon.

June 25—Membership Orientation Meeting—John Hancock Building, Signature Room, 255 California, 10:45 a.m.

BUSINESS BEACON

(Continued from page two)

A "BOUTONNIERE For Boys Day"—a flower sale to augment income for recreational activities for the San Francisco Boys Club—will be held throughout the city Tuesday, June 25. More than 500 youngsters will be flower salesmen seeking to sell 50,000 blossoms to men and women alike for 25 cents each. . . .

HOWARD G. VESPER, president of Standard Oil Company of California Western Operations, Inc., will receive the honorary degree of doctor of laws tonight at the Golden Gate College commencement exercises in the Veterans War Memorial Building. . . .

S. F. PUBLIC LIBRARY'S 1962 Scrapbook has been given a special award in the annual John Cotton Dana Publicity Awards Contest for "the initiation of a publicity program as part of a design to effect the renaissance of a library system and its adaptation to the cultural and educational needs of its community." . . .

ROY N. BUELL, assistant general commercial manager of Pacific Telephone & Telegraph Co., retired on May 31 after a career of nearly 40 years with the company. A member of the Chamber, he is also a director and past president of the Down Town Association; director and past president of the San Francisco Better Business Bureau; vice president and board member of the San Francisco chapter of the National Safety Council; a director of the San Francisco Convention and Visitors Bureau; board member of the Redwood Empire Association; former board member of the San Francisco Council, Navy League of the United States; former director and active member of the Press and Union League Club; a director of the San Francisco Council of the Boy Scouts of America; and a trustee of the Saints and Sinners Milk Fund. . . .

THE SAN FRANCISCO PAGEANT, a 20-page, multicolored brochure honoring KPIX's San Francisco Pageant series for winning the George Foster Peabody Award, has been mailed to some 2000 Bay Area educators, religious leaders, government officials, advertising agencies and other "opinion makers," according to KPIX promotion manager Bob Nashick. The series is produced by the KPIX program department and is sponsored by Home Mutual Savings and Loan Association. . . .

Directories Available At Chamber Offices

The *Large Manufacturing Directory* and the *Electronics Directory* are available in the Chamber business and trade section, according to Sidney H. Keil, general manager.

The manufacturers directory can be purchased for $1 each by Chamber members and for $3 each by non-members.

The electronics directory sells for $1. Both can be obtained by telephoning the Chamber, EXbrook 2-4511, ext. 56.

San Franciscana

Stern Grove — 'Nature's Music Box'

Within San Francisco's city confines there are 63 spectacular acres of forest and field known as Sigmund Stern Grove. A green and wooded ravine, today this retreat, just steps away from the city's bustle, is truly a picnickers' Eden — lost to the busy world of affairs among towering Eucalyptus trees planted more than 100 years ago by the land's first homesteader, George Greene, a New England horticulturist who came around the Horn in 1847.

An original gift to the people of San Francisco (12 acres) by Mrs. Sigmund Stern in 1931, as a memorial to her husband, it was enlarged by further acquisitions over the years. Today the Grove, together with adjoining Pine Lake land, totals 63 acres.

Sigmund Stern Grove becomes especially festive during the summer months when the Stern Grove Festival Association annually stages a series of rich and varied Sunday afternoon concerts—ranging from hit Broadway musicals and band concerts through operetta, opera, symphony and ballet—often with world renowned artists.

ACRES OF VERDANT FORESTS WITHIN THE CITY
. . . and San Franciscans pile up like pine-cones

This midsummer music festival has become a unique San Francisco "habit" which attracts an average attendance of 15,000 persons at a single Sunday concert. There are a number of compelling reasons for its popularity —the performances are uniformly excellent, the natural amphitheater, formed by ravine and towering trees, enhances the music, and—there is no charge.

Verdant Stern Grove, with its tradition of family fun and musical excellence, has been variously called "Nature's Music Box" *(San Francisco News,* July, 1952), "Music's Summer Capital" *(San Francisco Chronicle,* July, 1948), and "a spot which, perhaps among all others, is most San Francisco in its appearance, history and culture" (KCBS broadcast script, July, 1953).

And, indeed, there is quite a bit of San Francisco history enshrined in the Grove—beginning with the trees planted there by the Greenes, and also the Trocadero Inn. The Trocadero, a gabled, gingerbread dream, is used for recreational purposes during winter months. Bullet marks are neatly preserved, in its front door and hall stairs. One story has it that they were made by a jealous lover during the 1890's, when it was a popular resort. Another attributes them to the time the colorful, if infamous, "city boss," Abe Ruef, hid out at the Troc in 1907 when his political machine was smashed.

In modern times, the area has become a green and flowering musical countryside peacefully embraced in the arms of a great city.

Reprints available at the Chamber Research Dept., 333 Pine St.

BAY REGION BUSINESS

SAN FRANCISCO CHAMBER OF COMMERCE

VOLUME 20 • NUMBER 12 • JUNE 28, 1963

Flying Becomes More Fantastic

OVERNIGHT *cargo jet service to the Far East has been launched by Pan American Airways. The Clipper-type cargo ship (right) carries twice as much cargo twice as fast as the older piston-type cargo plane. Each of Pan Am's Boeing 707-321C cargo jets has a carrying capacity of 40 tons.*

5 PALLETS
(30 tons freight)

109 TROOPS

DELIVERY *of 40 Boeing-727 jetliners now in production for United Air Lines will begin this fall and service from San Francisco to Los Angeles, Reno and Sacramento will begin early next spring. The unusual tri-engine jet cruises at 550-600 miles an hour and is capable of carrying 92 passengers in a one-class configuration.*

WORLD TRADE FAIR SET HERE
* * * * *
Chamber Sponsors International Event

San Francisco will host the seventh United States World Trade Fair September 10-20 of next year under the auspices of the City and County of San Francisco and the San Francisco Chamber of Commerce. Cooperating in this major event will be the state of California and the United States Government, including the Departments of State, Commerce and Treasury.

Purpose of the U.S. World Trade Fair—the first time it is being held outside of New York City—is "to create an international market on the West Coast of the United States for the exhibition, promotion and volume sale of products and services to the American trade and public in order to foster world trade and tourism," according to William J. Wilkin, director of the Trade Fair San Francisco Office.

"The Chamber, under G. L. Fox, executive vice president, and James P. Wilson, manager of its world trade department, played a key role in making the U.S. World Trade Fair San Francisco showing a reality," he added.

The Civic Auditorium - Brooks Hall complex — now undergoing a $7½ million renovation program—will be the scene of the Trade Fair. When it is completed, San Francisco will have one of the most modern and best-equipped exposition halls in the United States. Completely air-conditioned, the facility will have a total area of about 250,000 square feet.

The U. S. World Trade Fair is the only exposition in North America ever admitted to the *Union des Foires Internationales,* governing body of the world's foremost international fairs.

"Thus San Francisco will host North America's counterpart of the great trade fairs of the world," Wilkin commented.

Anti-Chamber Bill Draws No Applause From This Corner

The board of directors of the Chamber voted unequivocal opposition to Assembly Bill 2571, which would prohibit city and county legislative bodies from contracting with private organizations for community promotional and advertising work, according to G. L. Fox, Chamber executive vice president.

The bill would add a section to the Government Code and prohibit a county board of supervisors or city council from contracting with a chamber of commerce or board of trade to advertise the county or city, and prohibit use of public money for advertising by such organizations.

"Persons throughout the world recognize chambers of commerce as the authentic sources of information about the communities in which they are located," Fox commented. "Consequently, they perform many semi-public services."

Fox emphasized that "the proposed legislation would be contrary to another long-standing policy of the Chamber whereby it has favored vesting all possible authority at the level of government closest to the people.

"In other words," he explained, "if a city or county desires to participate in advertising through private organizations, the local legislative body should have the authority to make its own decisions and not be subject to dictation by the state."

SCHOOL DISTRICT TAX BILL REJECTED BY CHAMBER

The Chamber has announced this week its opposition to a number of school allocation bills in the State Legislature which would equalize state taxes among school districts by taking from "rich" industrial districts and giving to "poor" districts.

Under definition of the bills, it was noted by G. L. Fox, Chamber executive vice president, high-income residential areas, such as Hillsborough, Atherton and Orinda, would be "poor" districts because "virtually no industry exists in these communities to provide school tax revenues."

Conversely, highly industrialized districts wherein average incomes may be low would be classified as "rich."

"While San Francisco would not be affected, because there is only one school district in this county, the Chamber board of directors took a stand on the side of simple justice," Fox explained.

These school allocation bills (the main ones are A.B. 1000 and A.B. 888) would pool the total assessed value of a county among the school districts within that county just as if the physical locations of the industrial plants were evenly distributed.

BUSINESS BEACON

By Joe Haughey

VILLIAM H. MARRIOTT has been named vice president of Guaranty Printing & Lithograph Co., affiliated with Pisani Printing Co., publishers of "Attraction Publications," a group of nine opera, symphony, ballet and concert magazines. Marriott, a veteran of the publishing field, was est known locally as the publisher of the *San Francisco Daily Commercial News*. . . .

AN FRANCISCO CHAPTER, American Society of Chartered Life Underwriters, has elected Leo H. Evart, Mutual of New York, president or the 1963-64 year. Other new officers: Douglas Emery, Phoenix Mutual Life, vice president; William R. Bills, Union Central Life, secretary; Leo A. Gansmiller, Connecticut Mutual Life, treasurer; and directors — George O. Braden, Nationwide Life; Jane A. Howell, John Hancock Mutual Life; David A. Kamp, New England Mutual Life; and Nicholas J. Toth, Equitable Life Society. . . .

U.S.F. ANNOUNCES two San Francisco civic and business leaders have been named to the board of regents. They are Jack H. How, former S. F. Chamber president and general partner, Edward R. Bacon Co., and Roger D. Lapham, Jr., president of Alexander, Sexton & Carr, insurance brokers. . . .

BETTY JOHNSON HAMILTON, noted for her decorative design work and line drawings, announces reestablishment of her art service at McCormick St. (GRaystone 4-5206). She recently won top honors in the annual San Francisco art directors' and artists' competitions and has had a show of her opera sketches at Gump's. . . .

BUSINESS TRAVELERS INTERNATIONALE announces a new cash plan, "reversing the trend oward credit cards," has been placed in operation in California. The plan features an immediate 5 per cent discount on purchases at selected top-flight restaurants, as well as motels, hotels, auto leasing agencies and other businesses serving the traveling executive and salesman. Sidney G. Head, president of the Western Division of BTI (and a member of the S. F. Chamber), notes BTI identification cards and directories are free to all S. F. Chamber members. . . .

OWEN SPANN, outstanding Bay Area radio personality, has joined KGO-Radio and emcees a new midday show from 11:30 a.m. to 3 p.m., Mondays through Saturdays. Each day the show originates from a well-known San Francisco luncheon spot (moving to suburbia on Saturday) and highlights a visit with a guest celebrity. . . .

CALIFORNIA YOUTH SYMPHONY, under the direction of Aaron Sten, makes its only San Francisco appearance at Stern Grove Sunday (June 30), at 2 p.m. Admission is free. The 104 young musicians (11-18) will make a 30-day tour of Japan in July. . . .

EICHLER HOMES announces new management appointments. Founder Joseph L. Eichler steps up from president to chairman of the board, Edward P. Eichler becomes president, and Richard L. Eichler, as senior vice president and treasurer, will be in charge of financial matters. Three new vice presidents are Neil Crawford, Eugene H. Longuevan and Donald E. Kimball. George Newell has been named president of the company's wholly owned subsidiary, the Concrete and Supply Co. . . .

"SAN FRANCISCO STORY," KNBR's Sunday morning (10:05) feature written by Samuel Dickson and narrated by Budd Heyde, has been given the "Silver Spindle" (first prize) award of the San Francisco Bay Area Publicity Club for "service to the community" and for "outstanding presentation." . . .

S. F. BAY AREA RAPID TRANSIT District has named William A. Bugge, director of highways for the State of Washington, to direct the design and construction of the Bay Area's 75-mile rapid transit system. . . .

PAN AMERICAN AIRWAYS this month (June 17) began first scheduled jet freighter service with Boeing 707-321C all-cargo Jet Clippers. Pan Am will provide 12 jet freighter flights each week between the United States and Europe, and six between the U. S. and the Orient. . . .

A DINNER CONFERENCE honoring Lt. Gen. Walter K. Wilson, Jr., Chief, U. S. Army Corps of Engineers, will be staged by the California State Chamber of Commerce Monday night (July 1) at the El Dorado Hotel in Sacramento. State Chamber president Milton Teague will preside. . . .

"INTERACTION OF COLOR: A Presentation of Paintings and the Color Theory of Josef Albers" is showing at the San Francisco Museum of Art through July 14. Organized by Yale University Press, the exhibition is comprised of paintings which have been included in a special book on the work of the 75-year-old artist-teacher. . . .

GOVERNOR EDMUND G. BROWN this month signed a bill creating a San Francisco Bay Area Transportation Study Commission. The bill, S.B. 371, by Senator J. Eugene McAteer of San Francisco, creates a 37-member commission of Bay Area officials, state legislators, transportation officials and laymen to develop a master plan for the area's freeways, bridges, transit systems and air and seaport facilities. . . .

STUART (SCOOPY) SMITH has moved into the KSFO sports department as production assistant, general manager William D. Shaw announced. . . .

WESTERN GREYHOUND LINES announced completion of plans for its 1963 program of escorted tours for northern Californians this summer. . . .

"TECHNOLOGY and the Community" was discussed by G. L. Fox, executive vice president of the Chamber, at a meeting of the Golden Gate chapter of the California Society of Professional Engineers Wednesday night at Maximos. . . .

WEARIN' O' THE GREEN — *S&H Green Stamps, that is. The Sperry & Hutchinson Co. Western Headquarters office at 1446-1452 Market Street was honored last week by the Market Street Development Project for remodeling of offices and frontage, including the greenery of new trees out front. At open house celebrating the occasion are (l. to r. above) Richard M. Oddie, Bank of America assistant vice president; Mrs. George Christopher; G. L. Fox, S. F. Chamber executive vice president; Mayor Christopher; and John G. Beinert, Western vice president, S&H. Oddie presented a citation to S&H in the name of the development group.*

CALIFORNIA'S OLDEST fact-finding agency, the Division of Labor Statistics and Research, is honored this week for 80 years of service in measuring the state's social and economic progress. Established in 1883 on a wave of concern over the plight of "the working class," the agency has chronicled the spectacular growth of both population and the labor force in the state during the 80 years. Population climbed from less than a million to more than 17 million, the labor force from less than one-half million to more than 6½ million. The 80th anniversary of the oldest division of the California Department of Industrial Relations was duly noted this week during the Interstate Conference on Labor Statistics ending today in the Bellevue Hotel, San Francisco. . . .

PROPOSED MERGER of Crocker-Anglo National Bank and the Citizens National Bank of Los Angeles has been approved by shareholders of both banks. Merger, forming Crocker-Citizens National Bank which would serve more than a million depositors, awaits approval of the Comptroller of Currency. . . .

(Continued on page four)

New Chamber Members

MEMBERS NEW TO THE CHAMBER ROSTER include (above, l. to r.): Richard B. Loomis, branch office owner, *Motel Managers Training School of Northern California*, 2525 Van Ness Ave.; Robert L. Jacobs, area director, *Partake Associates*, 315 Montgomery St.; Virginia Green, president, *Architectural Models, Inc.*, 361 Brannan St.; Charles S. Hobbs, vice president, *Broadway-Hale Stores, Inc.*, 601 California St.; and E. A. Lusch, president of both *A. B. Boyd Co.*, 1235 Howard St., and *Nelson Adams Co.*, South San Francisco.

CONTACT CLUB *at John Hancock Building. Left to right (seated): Art Hirsch, Standard Oil; Ron Johanson, Standard Oil; Hank White, PG&E; Beverly Lee, Citizens Federal Savings & Loan; J.W. Boundy, Wilbur-Ellis Co.; Charles Fracchia, Paine, Webber, Jackson & Curtis; Jerry Brown, Joseph Magnin & Co.*

Second row (seated): Jack Parkerson, Neptune World Wide Moving; John Pfeil, BBD&O; Ernie Jensen, Bank of America; Al Groeper, Equitable Life Assurance Society of America; Jim Lewis, Industrial Indemnity Co.; George Prevot, Metropolitan Life Insurance Co.

Standing (l. to r.): Allan Hirsch, Harry Cramer and Walter Maxwell, Chamber; Bill Siden, PG&E; William J. Bird, John Hancock Mutual Life Insurance Co.; Chris Christensen, KPIX; Terry Flynn, Marsh & McLennan-Cosgrove & Co.; Vince O'Brien, The Morris Plan Co. of Calif.; G. L. Fox, Chamber; E. L. (Tex) Stewart, Standard Oil Company of California; Tom Maloney, Metropolitan Life; Jim Bailey, Kraft Foods; Lee Porter, Standard Oil; Earle L. Hawkins, Chamber; Joe Young, PT&T, and Herbert H. Harmon, Chamber.

1963 Contact Club Formed; Members Convene Wednesday

Formation of the 1963 "Contact Club" to solicit memberships in the Chamber has been announced by Chamber officials.

Herbert H. Harmon, manager of the Chamber membership department, noted the first regular meeting of the 1963 "Contact Club" will be held Wednesday, 10 a.m., in the John Hancock Building's third floor Signature Room.

The "club" is comprised of young executives who will be carrying the Chamber message to the business community, it was explained by William J. Bird, western vice president of John Hancock Mutual Life Insurance Company and chairman of the Chamber membership committee.

The image of the Chamber as "an organization of men and women who know the wisdom of working together ... to build the commercial, industrial and civic factors of the community in order to enhance the total economy" will be vigorously promoted, Bird said.

Both Bird and Harmon said the club's rolls are by no means closed and invited executives "young in spirit—25 to 60" to join the 1963 "Contact Club."

Sales aids are provided by means of frequent club meetings, they noted, and incentives include trophies, cash awards, luncheons, parties and trips.

"Project Missionaire"
Program for Retired Citizens in High Gear

Successful retirement for senior citizens—a problem for companies as well as employees—is a continuing difficulty for all concerned in our complex society.

San Francisco's Mission district, experimenting with formulas to solve these complexities—"Project Missionaire"—is pioneering in this field. Financed through a grant from the San Francisco Foundation—"Project Missionaire," in its first year of existence, placed more than 100 men and women over the age of 50 in interesting and personally-rewarding community service jobs.

Sponsors claim retired men and women, and others who will be retiring within the next few years, are finding the project "appealing and irresistible." They note the "Project Missionaire" is "a radical departure from the usual volunteer placement program of community health and welfare agencies" and, that it has attracted the interest of company personnel departments, medical directors and top management throughout San Francisco.

A "streamlined" formula of screening and placement is the key to its success. The emphasis is on an individual's skill and interests, with regard to the fact that there must be no excessive demand on the retiree's time, energy and resources.

Interested individuals are encouraged to contact a representative at the company where they work or at the Project's main office, 362 Capp Street.

The personal interview is always arranged at the convenience of the applicant.

Because this is a program that attempts to provide the retired person with meaningful and rewarding activity and to make available to the community a pool of skilled manpower (often measured as "mindpower")—the emphasis is on the applicant's free choice. Thus, each selects the day and hours and frequency of assignment. Assignments vary from a few hours a month up to as much as five hours every working day. The jobs themselves (and there are 200 to choose from) vary from the semi-skilled and technical to policy-making and consultive assignments.

The program is sponsored by the United Community Fund, along with other civic groups.

TRANSPORTATION MEN INSTALL—*San Francisco chapter (Number 48) of Delta Nu Alpha, Transportation Fraternity (at a dinner meeting at Engler's Restaurant) recently installed officers for 1963-64 year. Installing officer was Robert Blocki, national president from Chicago. Left to right (seated) are: Don Chisholm (Rock Island Lines), president; Blocki; Charles C. Miller (Chamber transportation manager), immediate past president. Standing: Robert Ryan (Owens-Illinois Glass), first vice president; James M. Cooper (Chamber transportation department), treasurer; and Ray Vinick (Oregon-Nevada-California Fast Freight), secretary.*

be scheduled for Chicago, Washington, D. C., Seattle and Denver. One Chicago flight will provide through service to Cleveland. . . .

IGNACIO VALLESPIR has been appointed new district Sales Manager for Iberia Air Lines of Spain. . . .

ASSETS, GOODWILL and name of Container Laboratories of California have been purchased by a group of investors including W. Buckingham Little. . . .

P&O ORIENT LINES has announced a summer cross-country campout of 60 teenagers. It will be followed by trip to Hawaii on POSH liner *Orsova* and return on *Oriana*. . . .

A FIRST IN AMERICA—*The Kuo-Wah Restaurant, 950 Grant Avenue, held a "Chinese-American Bierstube" last week. "Tyrolean" Chinese-Americans included (l. to r.) Al Gee, secretary, Chinese Optimist Club; Fred Dong, first vice president, Chinatown Optimist Club; Helen Lew (attired as a Tyrolean maid); and Philip Chai, president of the Chinese Lions Club.*

Calendar

July 3—World Trade Luncheon—World Trade Club, 12 noon.

July 9 — Membership Orientation Meeting — John Hancock Bldg., 255 California St., Signature Room, 10:45 a.m.

July 10 — Festival of France Meeting — Room 200, 11 a.m.

July 10 — World Trade Luncheon — World Trade Club, 12 noon.

July 11 — Executive Committee Meeting — Room 200, 11 a.m.

---

dant song of a wandering minstrel whose handiwork in the late 1890s was warmly rewarded by the Park Commission in 1910. Hagiwara was given supervision over the concession (first known as the Japanese Village) and his children continued its operation until 1942 when wartime relocation of Japanese families ended the "dynasty."

The Tea Garden saw its birth in 1893, a feature of the famous California Mid-Winter Exposition which opened in January, 1894. The exposition was an effort to facilitate a business revival after 18 of the city's banks closed during a nationwide depression. One of the exposition's backers was Australian George Turner Marsh, who had opened America's first art goods store in the arcade of the old Palace Hotel in 1873.

The Japanese Village was created with the advice of Marsh's good friend, San Francisco's great, creative park superintendent, John McLaren.

The Tea Garden is entered through a tall, arched gateway comprised of hundreds of hand-carved pieces of wood. Its famous rock garden has been created primarily of stones shipped directly from Japan. Each stone has a symbolic meaning, representing an imaginary mountain or similar object of nature.

Shortly after the end of World War II, Japan sent a peace lantern to San Francisco. This lantern now graces the Tea Garden.

Among the many other features are a moon bridge, a model Japanese dwelling, a gigantic bronze Buddha (said to be the largest ever to leave the Orient), a multiple-tiered temple and picturesque gateways. In the area formerly occupied by the homes of the Hagiwara family is a broad terrace overlooking a sunken garden with a series of pools and a lush planting of dwarf maples, azaleas and conifers against a backdrop of bamboo.

The variety of plants includes Japanese cherries, specimens of the famed Magnolia Campbellii and a very old Magnolia Soulangeana which flowers heavily. There also are many varieties of Chinese rhododendrons, azaleas, maples, bamboos, pines and other conifers. Contributing boldly to the scene are specimens of the Aralia Sieboldii and Papyrifera.

The shrubs and trees are especially pruned. Even the mature 40-foot pines have been carefully thinned and pruned. Every single branchlet—of which there are many thousands—has been individually hand pruned. Adding to this zigzag pattern of Oriental gardening are trimmed hedges of evergreen bamboo.

The garden combines the concepts of a landscape style popular during the Muromachi Era 5,000 or so years ago and of the Impressionist School (1534-1565).

*Reprinted from Bay Region Business, official publication, San Francisco Chamber of Commerce

---

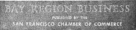

BAY REGION BUSINESS
PUBLISHED BY THE
SAN FRANCISCO CHAMBER OF COMMERCE

HARRY A. LEE, President
G. L. FOX, Executive Vice President
S. A. HOGAN, Secretary
JOSEPH I. HAUGHEY, Editor
CHARLES F. AYRES, Associate Editor

Published semi-monthly and owned by the San Francisco Chamber of Commerce, a non-profit organisation, at 333 Pine St., San Francisco, Zone 4, County of San Francisco, California. Telephone EXbrook 2-4511. (Non-member subscription, $5.00 a year.) Entered as Second Class matter April 26, 1944, at the Post Office at San Francisco, California, under the Act of March 3, 1879.

Circulation: 7,500

BAY REGION BUSINESS

SAN FRANCISCO CHAMBER OF COMMERCE

VOLUME 20 • NUMBER 13 • JULY 12, 1963

THE MORRIS PLANT—*The Morris Plan of California is the latest business on Market street to add a touch of greenery to the city's famed thoroughfare. As Brian Fewer (l.), supervisor of the tree division of the city's department of public works, looks on approvingly, Ralph N. Larson, Morris Plan president (at right), and Harry T. Hicks, assistant vice president, complete the planting of one of a group of laurel fig trees in front of company offices at 715 Market street. It's all part of the Market Street Improvement Project and the tree planting program of the Chamber.*

'Wanna Make a Speech?'

Members who are interested in filling public speaking engagements for the Chamber on topics of major concern to the city are invited to volunteer their services.

Are you interested? Contact Harold V. Starr, manager of the civic development department — EXbrook 2-4511, ext. 74.

EDITORIAL

DON'T Cut Your Nose Off to Spite Your Face

The proposal to split the San Francisco-Oakland Metropolitan Area is decidedly and uncontrovertably against the basic welfare of the entire Bay Area community.

Cutting in twain the unity of the Bay Area's central six counties would be as disastrous as it would have been if Solomon had actually carried out his threat to slice in half the Biblical baby.

The San Francisco-Oakland Metropolitan Area (the counties of Alameda, Contra Costa, San Francisco, San Mateo, Marin and Solano) now ranks sixth nationally in economic wealth; to set up a separate metropolitan area comprised of the counties of Alameda and Contra Costa with Solano going it alone in opposition to the counties of San Francisco, San Mateo and Marin, would be to relegate the San Francisco metropolitan area to 14th, the proposed East Bay Area to 16th. The result: a plummeting of the market strength and economic prestige of both.

Based upon the undeniable fact that the San Francisco Bay Area's counties are economically and geographically interdependent, the business community of San Francisco recognizes the imperative need to preserve its existing unity.

The San Francisco-Oakland Metropolitan Area is the economic hub around which revolves the spokes comprising northern California's 48 counties. Major manufacturing and branch operations of northern California in general and the San Francisco Bay Region in particular are directed out of San Francisco headquarter offices, the city also being one of the nation's most financial centers.

If the Bay Area is to continue to progress dynamically, the bonds of economic unity should be tightened and strengthened—not loosened and untied.

Response to Survey Running High

Response to the Chamber survey questionnaire regarding the development of the South of Market area has been running "surprisingly close to 20 per cent," according to Randle P. Shields, manager, public affairs department.

With more than 3,800 questionnaires mailed out two weeks ago, the number of returns by mail has exceeded 700, Shields said.

The questionnaire was directed to property owners and business operators, seeking their viewpoints on future development of the area for commercial and industrial use by a steer-ing committee of the Chamber including attorney Randell Larson, chairman of the redevelopment coordinating committee; developer Norman Impelman, chairman of the capital improvement and land use section; steel executive Ralph W. Seely, chairman of the industrial development committee; and two past Chamber presidents, Thomas J. Mellon, Wesix Electric Heater Company, and Dwight L. Merrimon, E. S. Merriman & Sons.

Statistical results, now being compiled by The Pacific Gas and Electric Company, will be

(Continued on page four)

Two New Directors Elected to The Chamber Board

Two new directors have joined the Chamber board. They are Paul E. Hazelrig, president of Kilpatrick's Bakeries, and John Paul Garling, Jr., vice president and director of Macy's California.

Educated in business and administration at the University of Georgia and a former Army Air Force major, Hazelrig has been in the baking business 26 years. He is an active member of San Francisco Rotary, Bay Counties Peace Officers Association, San Mateo Elks Club and San Francisco Olympic Club.

Garling, who is also a director of the Valley Fair and the Sterling Furniture Company, is a Navy veteran of World War II. He began his business career with R. H. Macy & Company, New York, in 1931.

He served on the labor-management committee, Western Region, U. S. Defense Manpower Administration, from 1950 to 1953, is a former chairman of the Governor's Safety Conference, a director of the Governmental Research Council of San Mateo County and of the Kiwanis Club of San Francisco.

John P. Garling, Jr.

Paul E. Hazelrig

BUSINESS BEACON

By Joe Haughey

GALE COOK, veteran San Francisco newsman, has been named city editor of the *San Francisco Examiner*, according to Ed J. Dooley, editor. Cook, 44, a native San Franciscan and 1940 Stanford graduate, has been a staff member of the *Examiner* since 1947. . . .

SONOMA COUNTY FAIR planners promise bone-jarring rodeo events," rare bird displays and many other fascinating features at the fair in Santa Rosa July 17-27. . . .

CHINATOWN, San Francisco's, that is, recently received an editorial kudo from one of its own native newspapers, *Young China*, founded in 1910 by Dr. Sun Yat Sen, father of the Chinese republic. A special edition of *Young China*, planned as a boost for tourism, features a message from the president of the Chinese Chamber of Commerce, Dr. T. Kong Lee. Artist Dong Kingman has illustrated the cover of the publication, an English-language supplement. . . .

ACTOR'S WORKSHOP stage production of Jean Genet's "The Balcony" is currently offered in the Marines Theater, Sutter & Mason Sts., nightly Wednesdays through Sundays, and will continue until Aug. 3. . . .

COLOR LINE, the first program in an upcoming public affairs series on KPIX, Channel 5, will be shown from 1:30 to 2 p.m., Sunday (July 14). This first program considers organized Negro groups in the Bay Area. . . .

THE UNUSUAL WORK of Gertrud and Otto Natzler, internationally known potters, is currently on exhibit at the San Francisco Museum of Art, Civic Center. The exhibit will continue to Aug. 18. . . .

COL. ALBERTO E. MERRILL, of Los Gatos, has been elected chairman of the board of directors of the Bay Area Air Pollution Control District. Kenneth G. Cheatham, of San Leandro, was elected vice chairman, and Dr. Charles W. Aby, of San Rafael, secretary. Sidney D. Herker, Redwood City, was appointed to the district board to replace the late Lester B. Morgan of Burlingame. . . .

WORKS OF EIGHT California figurative artists are on display at Bolles Gallery, 729 Sansome St., through July 19. John S. Bolles, the gallery's owner, lists the artists as William H. Brown, Joe Clark, Clayton Pinkerton and Elizabeth McClelland (all of northern California), Ben Bishop and Joan Savo (of the Monterey Bay Area), and Morris Broderson and Frederick Wight (of Los Angeles). . . .

NATIONAL WINE WEEK will be observed Oct. 19-26, according to the Wine Advisory Board and the Wine Institute, joint sponsors of the annual tribute to California wines. A national wine queen will reign during the week. . . .

HO'S INTERNATIONAL Cuisine Restaurant has been opened at 45 Turk St., near Market, site of the former Bay City Grill. The operating proprietor is Harry Ho. . . .

SCHOOL ENROLLMENTS in America, surging along at high tide in the '50s will slow down substantially during the balance of the '60s, according to a Stanford University expert. As a result, the outlook for adequate financing of education is bright, Roger A. Freeman, senior staff member of Stanford's Hoover Institute, believes. Only a national economic turndown could adversely affect the picture, he said. . . .

"CHARGE-A-CAB," a new taxicab credit system, is announced by San Francisco-Oakland Cab Co. (Yellow Cab). "Yellow Cab will be able to offer convenient, ride now-pay later service to many more companies than was previously possible," according to Granville L. Harris, vice president and general manager. The new system uses IBM card vouchers. . . .

KRON-TV (CHANNEL 4) is recipient of the first award ever made by the California Attorney General's office to any news medium. Attorney General Stanley Mosk presented a certificate of commendation to Harold P. See, general manager of Channel 4, honoring "Junkie," a two-part documentary on the Assignment Four series. Bob Anderson, writer-producer, cameramen Al Kihn and John Hines, director Vern Louden and film editor Nancy Williams all received letters of commendation. . . .

UNIT-HAUL, a new R E A system of rail-sea-highway shipment containers said to provide "significant economic, operational and shipper-service advantages," was initially displayed during the recent containerization seminar of the Bay Area chapter, National Defense Transportation Association. First rail-highway hauls under the new system link 60 Bay Area communities with Chicago and New York. . . .

HEADQUARTERS for the Seventh U. S. World Trade Fair—to be held in this city Sept. 10-20, 1964—have been opened at 681 Market Street (mailing zone 5), according to Charles Snitow, which the Chamber is interested—bounded by Market street to Valencia to 16th street to the bay and back to the Embarcadero—includes the $100 million "Grant Center" proposal of GALERIE DE TOURS has mounted the first West Coast showing of the paintings of Raymond A. Whyte, called by Edwin Dickinson "a poet who paints with the ability and technique to communicate his thoughts in an individual and beautiful manner." The one-man show at the gallery, 559 Sutter Street, runs from today (July 12) to August 4. . . .

JAPAN'S CANON CAMERA CO. has come up with an auto-focus camera that not only sets the focus automatically but also sets the exposure and shutter speed and completes the winding operation all by itself. This new 35mm camera, an almost completely automated instrument, suggests the future course of the camera manufacturing industry in Japan. . . .

PACIFIC TELEPHONE'S San Francisco exchange reports daily calls have increased 17 per cent during the past five years. Daily calls last year averaged 2,890,000, compared with 2,472,000 in 1957. During the same period the number of telephones increased 14 per cent from 519,000 to 592,000. . . .

A PACIFIC CRUISE that logs more miles than an around-the-world voyage is announced for this fall by Ambassador Tours of San Francisco. The 52-day circle Pacific cruise, with stops at 11 ports in the South Pacific and the Orient, leaves San Francisco on September 19 aboard the P&O Orient liner *Oronsay*. . . .

SUMMER SHAKESPEARE Festival, the second annual, will present in the Hall of Flowers, Golden Gate Park, on three subsequent Sundays (July 21 and 28, and Aug. 4) three of the bard's works. On each date, all three plays, performed by the Arena Theater of San Francisco, will be presented, each rotating in time: 2 p.m., 5 p.m., 8 p.m. . . .

NUCLEAR ENGINEERING Company, which disposes of the nation's private nuclear industry's atomic wastes, has sold its decontamination laundry at Pleasanton, according to Terry D. Hufft, Nuclear president. The laundry, started six years ago, was disposed of so the company could devote its full energies and capital to its principal business — land burial of radioactive waste materials — Nuclear has moved its headquarters to Cowell, Calif. . . .

BAY VIEW FEDERAL *Savings and Loan* dedicated its new $4½-million headquarters building at 22nd and Mission Streets last month (June 19). George F. Hansen, *vice president of the S. F. Chamber, made a dedicatory address at the civic affair. Hansen is shown (l.) above with Mayor George Christopher and Elwood L. Hansen, president of Bay View.*

AN EXHIBIT of trees which flourish in San Francisco's varied climate was shown when the Sperry and Hutchinson Company (S & H Green Stamps) dedicated its $100,000 modernization program last week. The exhibit was sponsored by the Department of Public Works of the City and County of San Francisco and the Chamber in conjunction with their year-around tree-planting program. Dedicatory ceremonies of the S & H Green Stamps Building at 1452 Market Street marked another step in the development of Market Street, a key Chamber project. . . .

LYONS-MAGNUS, INC., 111-year-old San Francisco firm, has named S. F. attorney Frank Sloss to the board of directors. Sloss, member of the law firm of Sloss & Eliot, also serves on the boards of the Emporium-Capwell Co. and Livingston Bros. . . .

NEW LAKESIDE VACATION community will be opened on south shore of Lake Berryessa this summer. Project is financed by group of Bay Area businessmen. . . .

P. D. ELDRED has been elected national president of the Order of Military Wine Tasters. He is a lieutenant colonel in the U. S. Army reserve and a veteran AP writer and editor. . . .

KAISER STEEL CORPORATION reported a net loss of $1.4 million, or 66 cents per share of common stock, after provision for dividends on preferred and preference stocks, according to Jack L. Ashby, president. . . .

HILTON TOURS, Vallejo, has arranged a tour from the west coast through the Caribbean to England, followed by a conducted tour through the Continent. Trip has been arranged with co-operation of P&O Orient Lines. . . .

FRANK N. GROSSMAN, formerly traveling representative for Santa Fe Lines' public relations department of San Francisco, has been appointed special representative here. . . .

A PROPOSAL to work toward establishment of a Wine Capitol Building in San Francisco—to serve the $700 million California wine industry —won the approval of the state's wine growers at their recent annual membership meeting here. . . .

SOLAR ECLIPSE can mean permanent eye damage to the unwary who stare at the darkened sun through sunglasses, smoked glass, or exposed photographic film, the National Society for the Prevention of Blindness warns. North America's next solar eclipse will occur on July 20. A simple eclipse viewer can be created from a piece of cardboard: punch a round hole in the cardboard so the sun's rays are focused through the tiny hole onto another cardboard or similar white surface. An image of the eclipsed sun also can be projected through a telescope or binoculars on a white screen. . . .

ONE-MAN SHOWS of the recent oils of Robert Watson and works of Giancarlo Erizzo are currently on display at Maxwell Galleries, 551 Sutter street. Both will continue through July 27. . . .

(Continued on page four)

First Half Bank Figures Paint Bright San Francisco Picture

San Francisco's banks toted up the results this past week for the first half of 963 and the aggregate of totals maintained the bright picture of a strong and eadily growing economy.

Whether it was the world's largest — Bank of America — or one of the city's ewest—Golden Gate National Bank—the conclusions all ran to the sunny side of te street. The figures varied, of course, acording to the size of the institution, but they ll tended to similar interpretation—the econmy of San Francisco is a thing of dynamic tality.

Nine reporting banks tallied net earnings for the period for a grand total of $73,463,696—ranging all the way from the big Bank of America's $42,559,398 to the new Golden Gate National's $223,199.

The nine banks covered in this report are ank of America, Bank of California, Crockernglo, First Western, Golden Gate, Hibernia, acific National, United California, and Wells argo.

All nine banks reported significant increases deposits. Their total count in the column as $21,824,472,506 approximately. The cuulative gain over the total a year earlier was ist about $1,724,930,396, a shade under a ealthy 8 per cent growth ratio.

The general details were the same for loans, hich increased better than 12 per cent for the ine in the aggregate, from $12,046,064,363 at te end of June, 1962, to $13,714,375,499 as of ine 30, 1963.

Bank of America's outstanding loans as of June 30 this year reached $7,857,853. Bank of California total for loans and discounts was $432,282,947. Pacific National Bank scored it $114,074,111. United California Bank reported $1,619,-)8.208 in loans. The Hibernia Bank's figure: l37,894,769. Wells Fargo's loan volume imbed to $1,876,431,665.

Crocker-Anglo loans, less reserves, stood at l,299,027,883. First Western's loan total was l57,129,000.

Golden Gate National Bank, barely two :ars old at the half, saw loan volume rise in year from $11,184,325 to $20,603,163—a hopping increase of almost 46 per cent.

S. F. Bridge Murals Available at Chamber

Large and small four-color photomurals of the San Francisco-Oakland Bay Bridge—with the city in the backdrop — are available in the publicity department of the Chamber.

The large mural, 58 inches by 38 inches, sells for $4; the small mural, 29 inches by 21 inches, for $1.

Both are suitable for framing.

HAROLD (TWO-GUN) STARR, *managing director of the Retail Merchants Assn., "went Hollywood" recently at the annual meeting of the Council of Western Retail Associations. With Starr in this Wild West scene is actress Cherie Foster. A film, "How Movies Are Made," was shown to the group. No contract was offered to Starr, but he reports that next year's conference will be held in San Francisco and that he was elected to the CWRA board of directors.*

San Franciscana
Reliving the Lusty Days Out West

During the 1860's, James Wales Miller saved a $30,000 payroll shipment from bandits and his grateful employer—Wells, Fargo & Co.—awarded him a fine watch encased in two pounds of Nevada silver. Miller wore it proudly for the rest of his life, pocketed and attached to his belt by a two-pound silver chain.

The watch and chain, along with a splendid example of the wagonmaker's art—a Wells, Fargo Concord stagecoach—are two examples of memorabilia displayed in abundance in the Wells Fargo Bank History Room at the bank's head office, 420 Montgomery St.

The History Room, directed and maintained by a charming and highly competent curator, Irene Simpson, is open to the public on every banking day from 10 a.m. to 3 p.m., and also by appointment during other business hours.

Both the researching historian and the pleasure-seeking tourist find much of high-quality and interest in this high ceilinged room which displays documents, posters, firearms, buttons, badges, artifacts and other items of early San Francisco and the pioneer West.

The name, Wells, Fargo, of course, summons up many, romantic, often violent, images for the "wild west" afficionado." Names occur—such as Black Bart. During the 1870s and '80s, Bart terrorized the stagecoach trails throughout the Mother Lode country and all the way to San Francisco. The Wells Fargo museum displays many reward posters, "left handed" tributes to the highwaymen who haunted transport between the mines in the old days.

Black Bart, committed at least 28 successful robberies. He stands as a swashbuckling symbol for old western badmen.

Prominent in the Wells Fargo History Room's permanent display are many samples of gold in all its raw forms, an array of ore, nuggets and gold dust that has its own special fascination.

One measures the glitter of gold with the eye (and is sometimes fooled), but its worth is weighed. In the Wells Fargo display is a set of scales so accurate, it is claimed, "it can weigh a pencil mark on a piece of paper."

A library of reference works is maintained for the scholar, who can really steep himself in his subject here where many of his references are the actual documents or iconography of the times.

The Wells Fargo History Room is a wonderful world of discovery for young and old seeking rich and new experiences in their tours of the city.

(Reprints Available, Chamber Publicity Department)

Black Bart

OSHIYUKI FUKUSHIMA, *president of Nipn Express Co., Ltd., had his sunflower, the >mpany flower symbol, adjust 'd by Miss Mayo Uyemura at a recent reception held in the siting executive's honor at the Sheraton-Palace otel. Looking on are Toshio Yamanaka, Japan >nsul General in San Franiesco (left), and ikeshi Nagaoka, vice president and general ianager of Nippon Express, U.S.A., located here.*

FLOATING HOMES—*Houseboats are not new to Sausalito, but luxury floating homes, like the one above, are giving houseboat dwelling a new look. Thus the manufacturer, Nathaniel Bliss, president, Pacific Floating Homes, Inc., can truly boast he's introduced "a new way of life" for San Francisco Bay Area residents.*

BUSINESS BEACON

(Continued from page two)

EIGHT MEMBERS of the San Francisco Symphony Orchestra have retired under the orchestra's retirement program, Symphony officials announced. The retired include Ferenc Molnar, principal violist; Boris Blinder, principal cellist, and Ralph Murray, principal tubist. Others are Harold Wright, second violinist; Karl Hesse and Herman Reinberg, cellists; Victor Kress, trumpet, and Joseph Sinai, percussionist....

SAN FRANCISCO ATTORNEY John E. Benson is the new president of the University of San Francisco Alumni Association. Other new officers: first vice president — Joseph J. Allen, deputy executive director, S. F. Housing Authority; second vice president — Marvin E. Cardoza, vice president, Bank of America; third vice president — Dr. Louis F. Batmale, City College of San Francisco; and secretary-treasurer — John H. Cronin, secretary-treasurer of Van Ness Dodge, Inc....

Radio Programs

LEST WE WAX WORDY *at Madame Tussaud's Royal London Wax Museum, suffice it to say President Franklin Delano Roosevelt (l.), and Winston Churchill are listening seriously to the suggestions of the "man in the middle." The man in the middle waxed wordier than the others in the wax works at Fisherman's Wharf. He's Charles F. Ayres, assistant manager of the Chamber's publicity department. He lectured his two companions at some length during the pictured chat. They've yet to make any comment.*

South of Market—

(Continued from page one)

made known to the public when completed.

In addition to the 3,805 who were sent questionnaires, a special letter with the questionnaire was mailed to some 100 bankers and industrial developers outside the area.

The questionnaire seeks "plus factors" and "guide lines" from the current business occupants of the area and from leaders outside the area.

Chamber Will Renew Pleas for Continuing Freeway Construction

Freeway construction in San Francisco at total estimated cost of $45,350,000 will b recommended by the Chamber when the Cal fornia Highway Commission meets to con sider the 1964-65 highway budget in August.

"Although the board of supervisors' resolu tion of January, 1959, which halted majo freeway construction in the city, has not bee changed, the San Francisco Chamber main tains a continued interest in a freeway pro gram for San Francisco," G. L. Fox, executiv vice president of the Chamber, explained.

The chamber's board of directors approve recommended items for presentation to th state body which were prepared by the stree highway and bridge section of the chamber' civic development committee.

Included in the proposals are: extension c the Southern Freeway from end of presentl budgeted project at Army street 3.4 miles t Howard street; and completion of rout studies for proposed Hunters Point Freewa (Bayshore Freeway near south county line t junction with Southern Freeway extensio near Islais Creek channel).

The proposed Southern Freeway extensio carries a price tag of $45 million.

Other Chamber-supported items are lanc scaping of 1.1 miles of Southern Freewa ($100,000); revised signing on James Lic Memorial Freeway ($250,000), and the con pletion of negotiations respecting Richardso avenue approach to Golden Gate Bridge, a well as studies for widening. These and th preceding items are not in conflict with th supervisors' policy.

The Chamber recommendations to the hig way commission will include this statemen "The chamber takes the position that it i necessary to have a well-integrated freewa system in the City and County of San Fran cisco, and strongly urge that the state procee with studies as soon as practical on rout connecting the Junipero Serra Freeway to th Central Freeway and the Golden Gate Bridge.

Chairman of the Chamber's civic develop ment committee is Edward C. Sequeira, assis ant to the president, Western Internationa Hotels (St. Francis Hotel). The street, hig way and bridge section chairman is Leonard S Mosias, San Francisco architect.

BAY REGION BUSINESS
PUBLISHED BY THE
SAN FRANCISCO CHAMBER OF COMMERCE

HARRY A. LEE, President
G. L. FOX, Executive Vice President
S. A. HOGAN, Secretary
JOSEPH I. HAUGHEY, Editor
CHARLES F. AYRES, Associate Editor

Published semi-monthly and owned by the San Francisco Chamber of Commerce, a non-profit organization, at 333 Pine St., San Francisco, Zone 4, County of San Francisco, California. Telephone EXbrook 2-4511. (Non-member subscription, $5.00 a year.) Entered as Second Class matter April 26, 1944, at the Post Office at San Francisco, California, under the Act of March 3, 1879.
Circulation: 7,500

BAY REGION BUSINESS

SAN FRANCISCO CHAMBER OF COMMERCE

VOLUME 20 • NUMBER 14 • JULY 26, 1963

BRIAN FEWER
"Trees, t:ees, everywhere ..."

Brian Fewer Is Named Chairman of Chamber Tree Planting Section

Brian Fewer, supervisor of street tree planting for the San Francisco Department of Public Works, has been named chairman of the landscape and tree planting section of the Chamber, according to Harry A. Lee, president.

Fewer will guide a program with which he has been closely identified since its inception four years ago and which has resulted in the planting of more than 35,000 trees on a voluntary citizen's basis throughout the city, Lee noted. It is a program in which the Chamber and the Department of Public Works have closely cooperated.

"Purpose of the landscape and tree planting section of the Chamber is not only to encourage private citizens, merchants and

Record Building Permits In S. F. During First Half of the Year

Building permits in San Francisco reached $90 million in valuation for the first half of this year, an all-time high for any six-month period in the history of the city, according to the Chamber research department.

Total construction authorized during the period was nearly 50 per cent higher than the same period last year with a total of 7,431 building permits issued for the first six months of 1963.

In types of permits issued those for new non-residential buildings led with a total valuation of nearly $43 million — a whopping 256 per cent increase over the $12 million for the first six months last year. Included were the Wells Fargo Building at Market, Montgomery and Sutter streets — 43 stories, $20 million (Dillingham Corporation, developer) and the $11 million, 12-floor Pacific Telephone and Telegraph Company building, now under construction at 666 Folsom street in the heart of the South-of-Market area.

Although the value of residential permits slipped 22.3 per cent from the $32 million of mid-year, 1962, nearly $25 million was authorized for 1,731 new dwelling units during the first half of this year. Of these permits, 252 were for single family housing, 84 for two-family units and 1,395 for multi-unit apartment buildings.

The total number of 1,731 dwelling units authorized was 19.8 per cent below the 2,158 units for the same period last year. Largest single permit issued was for the Gough-O'Farrell community housing project in the Western Addition — 103 units with a valulation of $2.3 million.

Permits for additions and alterations amounted to $21,602,000, a 38.6 per cent increase in value over the similar period last year.

commercial interests in the value of the program, but, perhaps, even more importantly, to make the individual builder and developer cognizant of the fact that greenery enhances buildings, whether they be office buildings, high-rise apartments or housing projects," Fewer said.

The new tree planting chairman of the

Chamber stressed that "the ultimate goal of the program is 350,000 trees throughout the city which will not only add immeasurably to the aesthetic charm of San Francisco but also will have the practical effects of enhancing property values, protecting the citizens against smog and acting as a natural air-

(Turn to page four)

Study of 19th Avenue Traffic Urged by the Chamber

Increasingly heavy traffic congestion on 19th avenue has prompted the Chamber board of directors to officially request an intensified study of the situation by city officials.

Action of the directors resulted from a recommendation of the Chamber street, highway and bridge section of which Leonard S. Mosias, architect, is chairman.

The study, Mosias said, should take in 19th avenue from Lake street to Junipero Serra boulevard with an aim to relieve congestion "as quickly as feasible, with the concomitant improvement of traffic flow and reduction of accidents."

The Chamber developed the following facts to support the request for city study:

• 40,000 vehicles a day travel over 19th ave.

• accidents reported on the thoroughfare totaled 500 in one year.

• during peak hours, 2600 cars an hour travel the route.

• because of heavy congestion, travel speed during peak periods slows down to five or six miles an hour, and it often takes as much as 4½ minutes to go through signals set to change on a 30-mile-per-hour cycle.

• The area is the second most heavily traveled in the city and also has the second heaviest accident rates (Market street is first). One out of 40 accidents in San Francisco occurs on 19th avenue.

BUSINESS BEACON

By Joe Haughey

SAN FRANCISCO BAY AREA is featured in the July issue of *Clipper Cargo Horizons*, a Pan American Airways publication distributed in more than 80 lands of the world. Lead article in the pocket-size magazine (circulation 120,000) states: "San Francisco, historic U. S. gateway to the markets of the world, is keeping pace with the jet age growth of international trade." . . .

SACRAMENTO-YOLO PORT District Commission this month dedicated its new deepwater Port of Sacramento, keynoting with the theme, "Sacramento Joins the Sea in '63" and the claim, "preferred service to all but preferential treatment to none." . . .

THE GODKIN LECTURES, a series by Clark Kerr, president of the University of California, are being presented on Saturdays from 11:30 a.m. to 12:30 p.m. in the "on campus" spot, KRON-TV, Channel 4. Subject matter of the three addresses, originally delivered at Harvard University, is "The Role of the University of the Future." The final two will be presented on KRON-TV tomorrow (July 27) and on August 3. . . .

M. H. DE YOUNG MEMORIAL Museum board of trustees has selected Jack Richard McGregor as museum director. McGregor is at present administrative assistant at the Metropolitan Museum of Art in New York City. He takes his new post on Sept. 1. . . .

WESTERN GREYHOUND Lines this month announce plans to build a $9 million, multi-story terminal building on the present Seventh Street site between Market and Mission. Frederick W. Ackerman, chairman of the board of Greyhound Corp., announced the directors had ratified the plan. . . .

PG&E PRESIDENT Robert H. Gerdes announced this month the appointment of Frederick W. Mielke, Jr., as assistant to the president of the big utility concern. Mielke has been an attorney in the PG&E law department since 1951. . . .

HARVEY J. WEXLER, director of international services for the Air Transport Association at Washington (D. C.), joined Slick Airways division as vice president there earlier this month, according to Delos W. Beutzel, president of the Slick Corporation. . . .

SPORTSCASTERS Chick Hearn and Lee Giroux have been named to call the action for the live KTVU telecast of the twelfth annual North-South Shrine Football Classic, to be played Aug. 1 in Los Angeles Memorial Coliseum, according to Channel 2 sports director Bill Perry. . . .

HYATT CORP. OF AMERICA currently is distributing a new, full color brochure on its 25 hotels and motels in the country. . . .

EVERETT BROWN, F. A. I. D., head of Everett Brown & Associates, San Francisco and New York, recently was elected chairman of the board of governors of the American Institute of Interior Designers. . . .

"GOD OF THE ANDES, Treasure of Peru." a special exhibition of 513 gold objects, will have its west coast premier at the M. H. de Young Memorial Museum here beginning August 29. . . .

SECURITY SAVINGS and Loan reports savings increased 31.7 per cent as of June 30 over the same date a year earlier, totalling $123,968,054. Loans reached $132,308,348 in value, a 31.3 per cent rise. . . .

"BULLET TRAIN" super-express, developed by Japanese engineers for the new Tokaido Line between Tokyo and Osaka (San Francisco's sister city"), is expected to be carrying passengers between Japan's two largest cities at regular speeds of 107 mph when the line opens next year, according to the summer issue of *Trade with Japan*, quarterly bulletin issued by the Japan Trade Center here. . . .

NATIONAL AIRLINES completed the first year of its "Triangle Fares" on June 30, enjoying "phenomenal success," according to J. Dan Brock, vice president, traffic and sales. "Triangle Fares" offer a westerner heading east stopover in a Florida resort for a small extra fee. . . .

A RECORD $600 BILLION gross national product is still possible in 1964 "if appropriate measures are taken now," according to Henry Ford II, chairman of the board of Ford Motor Company. Ford stressed "the long-range importance of a tax cut now." He argued that "an increase of only one-half of one per cent annually in the growth rate over the past six years would have virtually assured us a gross national product of $600 billion in 1963." . . .

A TAX EXEMPT common trust fund, providing for investment in securities free from federal income tax, was approved this month by the board of directors of Wells Fargo Bank, it is reported by Harold G. King, vice president and senior trust officer. . . .

HYATT CORPORATION of America board of directors has elected Donald N. Pritzker president, succeeding Jay A. Pritzker, who remains as chairman of the board. A new, fifth member of the board also was elected—Joseph Blumenfeld of San Francisco. The board also elected Donald N. Pritzker as treasurer, Hugo M. Friend, Jr., as vice president and secretary, Joseph J. Amoroso as vice president, and Victor L. Harvey as assistant secretary and assistant treasurer. . . .

JOSEPH G. KENNEDY, 46, formerly San Francisco's deputy public defender and a leader of the Negro community here, was named to the S. F. Municipal Court by Governor Edmund G. Brown. Kennedy succeeded Judge William A. O'Brien, who was elevated to the Superior Court. . . .

BAY AREA RIGHTS to Tennessee Williams' New York hit, "Night of the Iguana," have been obtained by the San Francisco Actor's Workshop for production in the 1963-64 subscription series. The Williams play will replace a previously scheduled revival of Arthur Miller's "Death of a Salesman," it was announced. . . .

PODESTA BALDOCCHI'S far-ranging modernization program, inaugurated a little over a year ago through the efforts of Jack Podesta, president of the Retail Merchants Association here, receives full feature treatment in a recent (June 29) issue of *Business Week*. Title: "The Florist Who Has a Business Diploma" (that's Jack). . . .

C. JOHN MORENO, veteran Peninsula and San Francisco banker, has been elected assistant vice president of Golden Gate National Bank and assigned as a lending officer to the 130 Montgomery Street office, according to Jacob Shemano, president. . . .

J. MAX MOORE *(l.), local industrialist, i sworn in as a supervisor of the City and Count of San Francisco by Superior Judge John I Molinari as Mayor George Christopher looks on Moore, who was appointed to succeed Superviso James Leo Halley, is executive vice president o Moore Manufacturing, Inc., a division of Quake Pacific Rubber Co.*

ROSS BARRETT, president of Foster & Klei er, Division of Metromedia, Inc., announces th following sales department changes: Charles F Hardison, vice president in charge of sales i Southern California, becomes general sales man ager; J. Dean Jacobs is appointed vice presiden and sales manager for northern California an returns to San Francisco after a year's stay i Seattle as the northwest regional sales manage Jacobs succeeds Paul Hanson, who is transferre to the headquarters office as vice president i charge of F&K's new program of market devel opment. . . .

CALIFORNIA LIVING magazine, a new quar terly publication, makes its bow this fall with colorful Christmas issue—starting with a con trolled circulation of more than 850,000, accord ing to the president of the company, Edwar Andersen. . . .

COL. J. E. JOHNSTON, commander of the Sa Francisco Procurement District, announces yea end contracts totaled $5,339,972 and brought th amount of new U. S. Army defense busines competitively awarded to western science an industry in fiscal 1963 to "some $110 million. Col. Johnson anticipates the District will admi ister $155 million in contracts during the fisc year which began July 1. . . .

MIDSUMMER MUSIC Festival will present th Lamplighters' production of Gilbert and Sulli van's production of Gilbert and Sullivan's "Mi kado" on the outdoor stage at Stern Grove, 19t avenue and Sloat boulevard, Sunday (July 28 at 2 p.m. This will be the seventh performanc in the festival's 25th anniversary season. A always, admission is free. . . .

CALIFORNIA'S 225 industrial parks and fa tors advantageous to manufacturing in this stat are highlights of the current issue of *Californi* official magazine of the State Chamber of Com merce. . . .

U. S. COMMERCE DEPARTMENT has re leased a booklet, "Do You Know Your Econom ic ABC's?", explaining in simple terms the gro national product which mirrors the Nation' economy. Single copies are available at 20 cent each. Individual orders of 100 copies or mor are filled at 15 cents a copy. . . .

"TWO PAINTERS and a Sculptor" is the titl of an exhibit currently at the Bolles Gallery 729 Sansome street. The painters are Hugh Cu tis and Paul Pernish, the sculptor Robert Broth erton. . . .

San Francisco Business Activity For May In 14.2 Per Cent Climb

Business activity in San Francisco for the month of May rose 14.2 per cent above the same month of last year, according to the Chamber research department.

The May business activity index was 135.5 compared to 118.5 for May a year ago, based on the 1957-59 average of 100.

Of the four factors which comprise the Chamber business activity index, bank debits showed a significant increase of 6.5 per cent over last year—$6,460,619,000 compared to $5,955,895,000 for May of 1962. Department store sales rose 2.8 per cent, electric energy sales were up 9.9 per cent. Freight car loadings increased by 5.8 per cent.

In Oakland, bank debits were up 5.4 per cent from $949,837,000 in May of 1962 to $1,011,387,000 for the same month this year. Department store sales slipped 0.6 per cent.

San Jose's bank debits increased from $568,-93,000 to $594,898,000, a 4.6 per cent rise. Department store sales rose 10.3 per cent.

The value of construction permits issued during May for the nine-county San Francisco Bay Area (counties of San Francisco, Alameda, Contra Costa, Marin, San Mateo, Solano, Napa, Santa Clara and Sonoma) set a record high of $155.7 million. The valuation of residential building was $81.4 million, an increase of 25 per cent over May of last year. The total valuation for May of $155.7 million was an increase of 56 per cent over $99.6 million registered in May of last year.

Permits were issued in the nine counties for 4,256 new dwelling units. Of these, 2,752 were for single family dwellings, 202 for duplexes and 4,302 for multi-family units. Santa Clara County, as usual, led with 2,618 permits for new dwelling units.

Total employment during May in the six-county San Francisco-Oakland Metropolitan Area (counties of San Francisco, Alameda, Contra Costa, Marin, San Mateo and Solano) totaled 1,199,600—an increase of 30,200 over May of last year. Unemployed persons numbered 67,200 or 5.3 per cent of the total labor force.

An estimated 278,000 persons were employed in the San Jose labor market (Santa Clara County), up 18,000 from May of 1962. There were 17,800 unemployed, six per cent of the labor force.

MERCHANTS HONOR MAYOR—Mayor George Christopher (l.) receives a plaque from the San Francisco Council of District Merchants Associations at a recent luncheon at the Michael Catering Co. headquarters. The presentation was made by Matthew J. Boxer, chairman of the council's mayor's committee. The council has met with the mayor four times a year since his election in 1955.

Edwin Wilson Named Aviation Chairman

The new chairman of the Chamber's 52-man aviation section is Edwin M. Wilson, vice president of Thompkins & Co. Wilson succeeds George Rhodes, aviation editor of the San Francisco News Call Bulletin.

The new vice chairman is A. P. Fioretti, manager, defense programs, S. F. district, General Electric Co.

Rhodes remains a member of the committee.

Supervisors Approve Of World Trade Fair

The San Francisco Board of Supervisors has endorsed the observance Sept. 10-20, 1964, of the seventh annual World Trade Fair in this city.

A resolution passed by the legislative body adds its endorsements to Mayor (George) Christopher's statements, and do hereby assure the foreign governments and industry leaders, the San Francisco Chamber of Commerce" and other cooperating groups "of the board's full support and appropriate assistance...."

Agriculture Committee Chairman Appointed

Carl L. Garrison, general manager, Porter Estate Co., this week was reappointed chairman of the Chamber's agricultural committee. Garrison's right hand man will be William Hunt Conrad, public relations representative of Kern County Land Co., who was named vice chairman.

Your Chamber On The Air

Are you keeping informed on civic affairs? One of the best ways to do so is to listen to your Chamber-sponsored and Chamber-conducted radio shows. Did you know the Chamber stages three public service radio programs every week of the year?

It's suggested you find the time to catch one of the following shows; all are provocative and each will help you gain a better balance to your perspective of the local scene:

At 8:05 p.m. every Saturday, San Francisco in the Sixties may be heard on KNBR (680 on the AM radio dial). At 9 p.m. on Sundays, the show, Conference Call, is heard on KFRC (610 on the dial), and the program San Francisco Report occurs on the same station 45 minutes later.

All three shows are moderated by G. L. Fox, your Chamber's executive vice president, and all present issues of the day discussed by leaders of the community.

Since the first of the year, San Francisco in the Sixties has delved into such subjects as population explosion, municipal railway fares, overcrowding at Juvenile Hall, the problem of school dropouts, Governor Brown's tax program, California's textbook program, the state's wilderness, the cost of administering charities, community renewal, student employment and many other vital topics.

Among community leaders who have appeared on this KNBR Saturday night show are Thomas F. Strycula, chief probation officer in San Francisco; James R. McCarthy, San Francisco planning director; Lt. Dante Andreotti, of the San Francisco Police Department, and Robert Holt, manager of the California Tomato Growers' Association, to mention just a few.

KFRC's 30-minute Conference Call has in the period examined such vital questions as delinquency and the increasing defiance of police authority, private property assessment methods, the delta water projects, automation and the labor force, charities, racial tensions, South of Market development, bay planning, the state apprenticeship program, and topics of similar weight.

Panelists have included Assessor Russell Wolden; Cyril Magnin, president of the S. F. Port Authority; Examiner sportswriter Prescott Sullivan; Chief of Police Thomas Cahill; Charles Hanna, chief of the State Division of Apprenticeship Standards, and many other leaders.

San Francisco Progress Report, a 15-minute Sunday nighter on KFRC, has looked at such programs as Big Brother Week, our fire department, the Golden Gateway, Invest in America Week, litter control, the Stern Grove story, and many other topics.

Speakers on this show have included such personalities as the Most Rev. Joseph T. McGucken, Catholic Archbishop of San Francisco; Supervisor Roger Boas; Aziz Ahmed, Pakistan Ambassador to the U. S.; Philip M. Creighton, director of the local office of the U. S. Department of Commerce, and others.

Top issues of the day discussed by leaders in their respective fields, that's the format for Chamber radio shows.

Brian Fewer Is Named Chairman of Chamber Tree Planting Section

(Continued from page one)

reshening agency."

Fewer noted that San Francisco experienced its most successful "Plant-a-Tree Week" this year with more than 5.000 trees planted during that time. "The event was well-publicized by the Chamber." he said. "and its effect has lasted over the months. Our office is continually receiving applications for planting and is deluged with requests for tree information."

The chairman's optimism was reflected throughout the Chamber executive staff. It was recalled by G. L. Fox. executive vice president. and by Sidney H. Keil. Chamber general manager. that the last big tree promotion (April) also resulted in the sale of 5,000 flowering fruit trees in the matter of hours. "reflecting the keen interest that has developed throughout the city in the Chamber campaign."

Myron S. Tatarian, director of the city's Department of Public Works. noted that "few programs for community betterment have had such a popular response" and that his office has received many inquiries from other cities throughout the United States about the program.

"Individual home-owners in the city's outlying areas and commercial and industrial interests in the central district can reap many benefits by planting trees," he continued.

"In addition to enhancing homes and businesses, a carefully and fully planned voluntary tree planting campaign is a sure-fire method to avoid the encroachment of the concrete jungle."

A tree planting booklet, describing the trees most suitable to San Francisco's various districts with their differing climates, is available free at the Chamber, 333 Pine Street, or at the Department of Public Works, 2323 Army street, Fewer noted. Basic considerations in the trees listed include suitability to climate, low maintenance cost, freedom from disease or insect-attack, shallow root systems and the least possible litter problem.

Calendar

July 30 — Tax Section Meeting — 10:30 a.m., Room 200.

July 31 World Trade Association Luncheon Meeting 12 noon, World Trade Club.

HOW DOES ONE *pick a national wine queen from such a lovely bunch? That's the question California wine growers must answer before September 3 when the lucky girl will be crowned at the California State Fair and Exposition. Beginning at the lower left and going clockwise are: Tracy Marston, Kay Gerhard, Vicky Ross, Flora Hoffman, Judy Jo Kinnersley, Carol Bovero, Susan Scott, Bonnie Abbott and Marilyn Lockway.*

Netherlands Look To California Marketing

"The food requirements of The Netherlands will be increasingly in the realm of "sophisticated foods' and California should be in the front ranks of suppliers."

That suggestion was made by Jack Gomperts, president of Calagrex, Inc., of San Francisco, at a recent luncheon of the San Francisco Area World Trade Association in the Ferry Building's World Trade Club. Gomperts only recently had returned from a visit to Holland as a member of a U. S. Department of Commerce trade mission.

A Dutch-born naturalized American citizen, Gomperts, who is a major exporter of agricultural commodities, noted that ". . . canned fruit, fresh fruit and frozen foods have great possibilities. I would like to see a bit more salesmanship and imagination employed in the exploitation of Holland and other European countries as markets for fresh fruit . . .".

Reminding that the United States exports to Holland much more than it imports from that nation, he continued. "The Dutch businessman . . . understands full well that our export drive is by far the best of all alternatives to remedy our balance of payments problem. It is, consequently, as important to them as it is to us."

Radio Programming For This Weekend

SAN FRANCISCO IN THE SIXTIES—Saturday, 8:05 p.m., KNBR: "Some Proposals to Change Redevelopment Programs." Mrs. JoYe Goodwin, housing committee chairman, and/or C. J. Wellington, M.D., co-chairman for redevelopment and urban renewal, National Association for the Advancement of Colored People, San Francisco chapter; Frank Quinn, executive secretary, Council for Civic Unity; John Hirten, executive director, San Francisco Planning and Urban Renewal Association (SPUR).

CONFERENCE CALL — Sunday, 9 p.m., KFRC: "Senior Citizenship in San Francisco." John J. Smith, publisher, Harvest Years magazine; Irving M. Kriegsfeld, executive director, Mission Neighborhood Center; William P. Dumont, civic leader and retired advertising executive.

SAN FRANCISCO PROGRESS REPORT Sunday, 9:45 p.m., KFRC:"Twentieth Anniversary of the Farmer's Market." Frank J. O'Connell, manager of the Farmer's Market, and John G. Brucato, the market's founder . . . , Sunday, Aug. 4, 9:45 p.m., KFRC: "Plans for October French Week Celebration." Jean Tromw, French commercial counsellor in S. F., and Sichel Weill, general chairman for French Week.

HARRY A. LEE, President
C. L. FOX, Executive Vice President
M. A. HOGAN, Secretary
JOSEPH I. HAUGHEY, Editor
CHARLES F. AYRES, Associate Editor

Published semi-monthly and owned by the San Francisco Chamber of Commerce, a non-profit organization, at 333 Pine St. San Francisco, Zone 4, County of San Francisco, California. Telephone EXbrook 2-4511. (Non-member subscription. $3.00 a Year.) Entered as Second Class matter April 26, 1911 at the Post Office at San Francisco, California, under the Act of March 3, 1879.

Circulation: 7,500

BAY REGION  BUSINESS

SAN FRANCISCO CHAMBER OF COMMERCE

VOLUME 20 • NUMBER 15 • AUGUST 9, 1963

Look At It Now---

Look At It Monday!

Petrarch Place and the alleys adjacent to the Chamber Building — now barren — will be tree-and-landscaped . . .

Miller Scores Nevada Effort to 'Pilfer California Industry and Commerce'

"One more link in a long chain of acts of Nevada interests to pilfer California industry" is what Charles C. Miller, manager of the Chamber's transportation department, calls latest attempts to establish furniture storage-in-transit privileges in Reno for final distribution in California.

Miller reported this week that "the California Economic Development Agency joins in the Chamber's concern over Nevada's encroachment on California industry and commerce through the medium of reduced freight rates and charges, and the establishment of tran-it privileges.

"These items, in conjunction with the

Ag Group to Honor S. F. Farmers Mart

The agricultural committee of the Chamber will honor the Farmers Free Market of San Francisco at a luncheon in the French room of the Fairmont Hotel Tuesday (Aug. 13), according to Carl L. Garrison, chairman of the committee.

Nevada State Free Port Law," Miller reminded, "are luring established California business to Nevada."

The Chamber has traditionally opposed (since 1959) this "free port" practice which brings about rates from Reno into California's major distributing areas which are lower than those for service between San Francisco and the same points.

Radio Programming For This Weekend

SAN FRANCISCO IN THE SIXTIES—Saturday, 8:05 p.m., KNBR: "The California League for the Handicapped." Rose Resnick, League director; Mrs. Francis Brydone-Jack, dance instructor for the League's day camp program, and Miss Antonette Willson, professor of English, San Francisco State College.
CONFERENCE CALL—Sunday, 9 p.m., KFRC: "San Francisco as a Tourist Center—Over-rated or Under-sold?" Joe Cannon, co-owner, The Red Balloon; Hal Spitz, executive vice president. Guest Informant magazine, and Thor Smith, S. F. Convention and Visitors Bureau.
PROGRESS REPORT — Sunday, 9:15 p.m., KFRC: "The Sister Cities (San Francisco and Osaka, Japan)." Miss Ellen McGinty ("Miss Sister City") and Mrs. Margaret Smith, personal secretary to Mayor George Christopher. . . . Sunday, Aug. 18, 9:15 p.m., KFRC: "A Summer Work Experience Program for Retarded Children," Isadore Salkind, Morrison Rehabilitation Center.

Water Project Costs Will Be Out of Line

California's annual $3.9 billion agricultural industry "is threatened by evidence that the price of water under the state water project will be prohibitive for most agricultural uses," according to the Chamber.

The assertion was made as the Chamber agricultural committee, comprising a formidable cross-section of the industry throughout the state, announced its policies on developing the state water project. Recommendations of the committee drew the unanimous approval of the Chamber board of directors.

Under the policies proposed, costs of the project would be shared in proportion to the benefits derived. "Yardsticks for measuring the values of these benefits should be agreed on as a basis for cost allocation."

It is also proposed that investigational costs accrued prior to the $13¾ billion water bond proposal to the electorate in November, 1960, "should not be reflected in the price of project water."

Project water which may be available in quantities beyond those under contract should be "offered to agricultural areas as long as possible on a priority basis and at approximately the cost of operation and maintenance." The same is proposed for water "available during interim periods as the project develops."

The board approved the committee's recommendation that "full advantage should be taken of federal funds that may be available . . . for flood control, navigation, recreation and conservation of fish and game.

"Amounts that have been allocated to the State Water Project from the California Water Fund should be interest free. . . ."

The Chamber board also supports enabling legislation permitting loans to agricultural areas "in serious need of special assistance to finance local water distribution systems. . . ."

Maximum repayment time for those who borrow tideland oil funds to develop local water projects is urged, as well as opposition "as a matter of principle" to efforts to divert tideland oil funds away from state water projects.

Amounts collected from large landowners by a contracting agency should be retained by the agency for future availability to reduce the cost of project water, it is recommended.

"The private company inter-tie to bring cheap electric power into the state will be an aid to pumping project water and should be supported."

And finally, it is proposed that "ways to amend the contract (between the state and agencies) to give agriculture every equitable consideration should be defined and pursued. . . ."

Business Book Briefs —

(a new feature . . . see page three)

Section Will Convene

The building code section of the Chamber's technical projects committee will meet at 11 a.m. Wednesday (Aug. 11) in the second floor board of directors room, 333 Pine Street, to hear reports by two subcommittees, according to Wesley T. Hayes, section chairman.

There also will be a discussion of the State Building Standards Commission, Hayes said.

BUSINESS BEACON

By Joe Haughey

BENJAMIN LINSKY, internationally known authority on air pollution who was control officer of the San Francisco Bay Area Air Pollution Control District from 1956 until recently, has joined the faculty of West Virginia University as professor and director of a new air pollution control training program, according to Paul A. Miller, president of the university. . . .

S. F. PLAYERS GUILD has chosen "Puss in Boots" as the children's play to be presented in Bay Area and other California schools for the 1963-64 season, Arthur B. Poole, president, announces. . . .

ROBERT E. HARRIS, advertising and sales promotion manager for KCBS radio, will be one of the featured guest speakers tomorrow (Saturday) at the Valley Writers Council conference in the Hotel St. Claire, San Jose. . . .

STANFORD CAMPUS construction will hit an all-time high this year and another record is in prospect for 1964, the university's news service reports. Total construction outlays during the fiscal year ending Aug. 31 are expected to reach $25 million—triple last year's figure. . . .

MIKE SALERNO, first vice president of the San Francisco Council of District Merchants Associations, has been appointed to the Library Commission by Mayor George Christopher. . . .

TOM MULLAHEY, public affairs director for KRON-TV and a member of the Chamber's regional problems committee, recently attended the National Broadcasters Association editorial conference in Athens, Ga. . . .

Calendar

"THE ADVOCATE," A NEW PLAY, will open this season on Broadway and, simultaneously, viewers in San Francisco and four other cities will see the production on television—marking the first time in the history of the theater and television that such an event has been made possible. KPIX, Channel 5, will be the outlet in San Francisco. The play, starring James Daly and written by a new American playwright, Robert Noah, will open at the Anta Theater in New York on Sunday, Oct. 13, and will be televised. . . .

ALTON M. CRYER, JR., San Francisco district manager, Dodge Division, Chrysler Motors Corporation, was named the outstanding district manager in the entire Dodge western sales area (nine states) at an awards banquet in Detroit Tuesday (Aug. 6). . . .

MAYOR GEORGE CHRISTOPHER *of San Francisco, writer Richard Dunlop and Charles Folker, San Francisco regional sales manager of Chrysler-Plymouth (l. to r.) look over a copy of the* Plymouth Traveler *— its entire August edition is devoted to San Francisco.*

$3.8 Billion Industry

WESCON in Cow Palace Aug. 20-23

When Dr. Lee DeForest put the grid into a glass bulb a half-century ago, he lit the path for what is fast becoming one of the most important industries in the Bay Area—electronics.

In 15 years, the number of electronics firms in the 11 western states increased from 85 employing 11,000 and generating sales of $159 million (in 1949) to 1190 employing 260,000 and selling at approximately $3.8 billion last year.

California, of course, leads the electronics industry, which now tops the aircraft industry as the state's number one employer.

The Institute of Electrical and Electronics Engineers this year became the world's largest professional association. The Western Electronics Show and Convention (WESCON), to be staged August 20-23 at San Francisco's Cow Palace, is expected to be the largest event of its kind ever held in the electronics field. More than 40,000 are expected to attend the convention and view the exhibits in more than 1200 booths.

In what is now an old rooming house, 831 Emerson Street, Palo Alto, Dr. DeForest developed the application of his Audion (as he called the electron tube) which paved the way for almost every form of electronic device, including computers and equipment now used in long distance telephony.

The San Francisco Peninsula also is the birthplace of the rhumbatron, klystron, vacuum tube and television tape recorder. Here is where DeForest, Herbert van Etten, Leonard E. Fuller, Cyril Elwell, Charles V. Logwood, Ralph M. Heintz and Douglas Perham made significant pioneer contributions.

Experts have prophesied that the San Francisco Peninsula, "that superb stretch of American suburbia," is destined to become the foremost electronic center of the world.

Electronics was born in San Francisco, the first city in America and probably the first city in the world to have central district electrical lighting (1879). More than 50 years ago Cyril F. Elwell, who built the first west coast radio-telephone transmitter, began the first important work here on the Poulsen arc—the first practical source of high powered, continuous wave radar frequency energy.

Early San Francisco pioneers in the field included two famous names in the loudspeaker field, Peter Jensen and E. S. Pridham, who later formed the Magnavox Company. In 1927, Philip T. Farnsworth, who worked out of a loft at Green and Sansome streets, announced to the world, at the age of 20, that he had invented all-electronic television.

The klystron, created by Dr. Russell H. Varian while studying at Stanford, is the heart of many radar and microwave relay systems and an important part of the linear accelerator (developed by Dr. William W. Hansen of Stanford) which has opened new horizons in the studies of the fundamental nature of matter.

"TV on tape," the dream of General Sarnoff, head of RCA, was made a reality by Ampex Corporation of Redwood City, pioneer firm in stereophonic sound. Ampex's revolutionary video-tape recorder, which captures sight and sound on magnetic tape, permits immediate life-like rebroadcasting.

Chromoton, a modern development of the color picture tube, was created by Nobel Prize winner Ernest O. Lawrence, director of the University of California Radiation Laboratory in Berkeley.

Reprints available at the Chamber Research Dept., 333 Pine St.

DAWN OF D-DAY
*"Winnie" and "Ike" (top), Normandy ...
Podesta parachutes (center photo; top) ...*

D-Day Not Yet Dimmed

"NUTZ!"
—*that was the cry of the 101st Airborne Division when told to surrender at Bastogne. . . . The division will "surrender" to San Francisco August 15-18 . . .*

LITTLE TOT LISTENS
. . . it's a long way and a long time from Mittel-Europa to Montgomery street ...

JACK PODESTA
. . . he treaded water (c.) and trained in the desert under Patton and saw action in the Ardennes and in the Rhineland. . . . Podesta is president of Podesta Baldocchi Florists and is currently president of the Retail Merchants Assn. . . .

☆   ☆   ☆

Podesta Leads 'Parachute Invasion' of San Francisco

Veterans of the 101st Airborne Division—one of the greatest fighting teams of World War II—will meet in the Sheraton-Palace Hotel August 15-18 for their 18th annual reunion (first to be held in San Francisco), according to Jack Podesta, general chairman.

More than 500 soldiers from all over the nation are expected to attend. Podesta, a Chamber ex-officio director and president of the San Francisco Retail Merchants, said.

The division is the only one in U. S. Army history to have been awarded two Presidential Citation Units. It was the first full division ever to be cited in the name of the President of the United States. The division led the Normandy invasion, fought in Belgium, Holland, the Rhineland and Central Europe. Its defense of Bastogne has become a classic in American combat history.

A special contingent of 50 troopers from the present active 101st Airborne Division at Fort Campbell, Kentucky, the nation's No. 1 combat-ready striking unit, also will attend, as will Alexandre Renaud, wartime mayor of Sainte-Mre-Eglise, a small village in Normandy and the first French community to be liberated on D-Day.

BUSINESSMAN'S BOOKSHELF

Local Newsman Scores With S. F. Guide Book

A GUIDE TO SAN FRANCISCO AND THE BAY REGION, by James Benet, 496 pages, Random House, $5.95.

"Narcissism,"—or inordinate love of self and what one is a part of—is not necessarily synonymous with being a San Franciscan. This James Benet, San Francisco newspaperman whose great-grandmother ran a boarding house in the Gold Rush days in San Francisco, proves. He

is critical, even aloof. But always incisive and scholarly in his "tourist-in-a-hurry" or long-term visitor approach to the City by the Golden Gate. His guide is scholarly, complete—the best thing of its sort since the old WPA grand-daddy of all S. F. guides. Definitely recommended.

A TIME FOR COOKING, by Zada Taylor and Betty Herman, 244 pages, Houghton Mifflin, $4.50.

Excellent; if you have the time for cooking. "California slant" for "harried housewives."

THE DARTNELL INTERNATIONAL TRADE HANDBOOK, Leslie Lewellyn Lewis, editor, 1311 pages, The Dartnell Corporation $17.50.

Revised and expanded version of the Foreign Trade Handbook. Definitive and in depth.

S. F. Quotes

"Happiness, sang Frances Wayne on that great Woody Herman record, is just a thing called Joe.

"It is also a thing called a tree, newly planted and thriving on an otherwise hopeless expanse of concrete."

—HERB CAEN
S. F. Chronicle

AAA Trans'Interpreters New Chamber Members

Among new member organizations of the Chamber is AAA Trans'Interpreters of 391 Sutter St. (Galen Building)—Suite 501. A father-son operation, this new enterprise offers a complete translation service in practically all languages.

One of AAA Trans'Interpreters' principals, Gerald G. Cox, who is blind, works in six foreign languages—German, French, Spanish, Portuguese, Italian and Russian.

His father, Stanley P. Cox, an insurance adjuster and real estate appraiser, is partner in the enterprise.

The organization offers the services of 150 interpreters and translators. Commercial, legal, technical and documentary translations, as well as conference interpreting, are available in African, Middle and Far Eastern, Germanic, Romance, Scandinavian and Slavic tongues.

Conference room facilities also are available at the Sutter St. offices.

These interesting new members were obtained through the efforts of Al Hirsch of the membership department.

CHE VUOL' DIRE LA BELLA BARBARA? — or "What does the beautiful Barbara mean to say to her master?" The master is Gerald G. Cox — also master of six languages besides English. Barbara, an Irish Setter, is being translated into Pekingese.

THE FIRST WOMAN *special representative ever employed by the Chamber membership department — 23-year-old Debra Wittenberg, formerly of Montreal—is presented her Chamber briefcase by Herbert H. Harmon, manager of the Chamber membership department. He explained that her abilities as a good salesman for the San Francisco Chamber first came to his attention when she was employed by his department in a temporary clerical position.*

FCIA at 333 Pine

Donald W. Marken has been appointed Pacific Coast district manager for the Foreign Credit Insurance Association which has recently been granted temporary office space on the first floor of the Chamber building.

Transportation Group To Take a Sharp Look At S.F. Port Problem

O. H. Stieber, general traffic manager, Crown Zellerbach Corp., has been elected chairman of the Chamber transportation subcommittee on the Port of San Francisco.

The group named William R. Donovan, assistant general traffic manager, California and Hawaiian Sugar Refining Corporation, as its vice chairman, and Crown Zellerbach's marine traffic manager, Clyde L. Jacobs, as a consultant.

The minutes of the meeting, prepared by the subcommittee's secretary, Charles C. Miller (head of the Chamber transportation department), indicate concern over "the apparent lack of activity in the improvement and development" of S. F. port facilities under a $50 million state bond issue which was actively supported by the Chamber and approved by the voters in 1958.

Other specific questions discussed at the meeting included: Is San Francisco getting its share of port traffic? Why did Sea-Land Service (containership) move to Encinal Terminal? Why did Weyerhaeuser Line move to Encinal?

Stieber succeeds Russell A. Morin, director of traffic, Fibreboard Paper Products Corporation, as subcommittee chairman.

Not Hard Duty At All

Lester L. Goodman, president of the San Francisco Area World Trade Association, has been named by the Chamber Board of Directors to represent the Chamber at the Japan-America Conference of Mayors and Chamber of Commerce Presidents November 4-8 in Kobe, Japan.

Zellerbach Lauded By Chamber Official

"With the passing this week of James David Zellerbach, chairman of the board of Crown Zellerbach Corporation, San Francisco lost not only a dynamic industrialist but a great hearted gentleman and a true citizen of the world as well.

"Mr. Zellerbach was a positive force in San Francisco for the development and maintenance of the arts.

"He had been president of the San Francisco Symphony Association, a director of the San Francisco Opera Association and of the San Francisco Planning and Urban Renewal Association — to mention just a few of his activities.

"On the international level, Mr. Zellerbach was esteemed as a gentleman and a diplomat who exemplified San Francisco's finest traditions. His services as United States ambassador to Italy from 1956 to 1960 earned him the gratitude of both nations.

"He was noted for his many charitable works and was prominent in many civic organizations dedicated to the betterment of man. He served as a director of the Chamber in 1951, 1952 and 1953.

"San Francisco and the world have lost a highly talented and deeply humane champion for all that's progressive and meaningful in life."

—G. L. Fox
Executive Vice President

BAY REGION BUSINESS
PUBLISHED BY THE
SAN FRANCISCO CHAMBER OF COMMERCE

HARRY A. LEE, President
G. L. FOX, Executive Vice President
M. A. HOGAN, Secretary
JOSEPH I. HAUGHEY, Editor
CHARLES F. AYRES, Associate Editor

Published semi-monthly and owned by the San Francisco Chamber of Commerce, a non-profit organization, at 333 Pine St., San Francisco, Zone 4, County of San Francisco, California. Telephone EXbrook 2-4511. (Non-member subscription), $5.00 a year.) Entered as Second Class matter April 30, 1944, at the Post Office at San Francisco, California, under the Act of March 3, 1879.
Circulation: 7,500

BAY REGION BUSINESS

SAN FRANCISCO CHAMBER OF COMMERCE

VOLUME 20 • NUMBER 16 • AUGUST 23, 1963

June Business Activity Up 5 Pct. in San Francisco

ARCHBISHOP Joseph T. McGucken of San Francisco is shown presenting a citation from he Catholic Broadcasters Association to David M. Sacks, ABC vice president and general manager of KGO-TV here. The award was earned for he Channel Seven documentary on the installation of the Archbishop and its weekly series, 'For Thou Art With Me."

Business activity in San Francisco for the month of June was up 5% from June of last year, according to the Chamber research department.

The June business activity index was 127.8, compared to 121.7 for the month a year ago, based on the 1957-59 average of 100.

Bank debits in San Francisco totalled $7,395,994,000 for the month, a percentage increase of 6.5 over last June's $6,065,363,000. Department store sales rose 1.0%; electric energy sales, by 6.4%; and freight car loadings increased 7.5% over June, 1962.

In Oakland, bank debits were up 13.6% from $797,772,000 to $906,304,000. Department store sales were down 4.2% from last year.

San Jose's bank debits increased to $583,542,000 in June of this year, up 13.8% from $512,961,000 in June, 1962. Department store sales were up 5.2%.

Total estimated employment during June in the 6-county San Francisco-Oakland metropolitan area totalled 1,212,200—an increase of 39,900 over June of last year. Unemployed persons numbered 75,300, or 5.8% of the total civilian labor force.

An estimated 282,400 were employed in the San Jose metropolitan area (Santa Clara County), up 20,000 from last year. There were 19,400 unemployed, 6.4% of the total labor force.

September Important Month for Chamber

Plans are shaping up for two major dedications to take place next month, both of which have had the active interest and participation of your Chamber, according to Randle P. Shields, manager of the public affairs department. These are the New Era Program inaugurating San Francisco International Airport's new South Terminal, and the dedication and establishment of the new San Francisco Produce Terminal at Islais Creek.

Gala events at the airport take place from Tuesday, September 10 and continue (excepting Friday) through Sunday, September 15. The Chamber's big day during this big, six-day celebration will be Wednesday, September 1, when it joins with the Greater San Jose Chamber, the San Mateo County Development Assn. and the Peninsula Division of the League of California Cities for a "New Era Conference" at the airport's Hilton Inn.

Harry A. Lee, S. F. Chamber president, will preside at the conference luncheon. The conference will present business and civic leaders as speakers, individually and on panels. (Final meeting of the public relations advisory committee for the New Era program was held yesterday — Thursday — in Room 200 of the Chamber building.)

The scheduled week in brief: Tuesday, Sept. 10 — Airport Junior Chamber hosts high school student editors and faculty advisors at tour, press conference and dinner; Wednesday, Sept. 11 — New Era Conference at Hilton Inn; Thursday, Sept. 12 — press conference at Hilton Inn, tour of new Terminal Building, press luncheon (this is press day); Saturday, Sept. 14 — Actual inauguration of the "New Era," by Najeeb E. Halaby, administrator of the Federal Aviation Agency (reception from 3 to 6 p.m.); Sunday, Sept. 5 — public review of the new building, with unveiling of a bronze plaque by public utilities commissioner Stuart Greenberg.

Almost on the heels of the big doings at the airport will occur the official dedication of San Francisco's new Produce Terminal at Islais Creek, a three-day public ceremony on September 27-29.

The ultra-modern facility was built to replace the city's century-old produce district, razed to make way for the Golden Gateway Project. The terminal (and the Gateway, for that matter) culminates years of planning and negotiation by the City and by the S. F. Chamber.

According to Milton Ross, spokesman for the San Francisco Wholesale Fruit and Produce Dealers' Assn., the new produce terminal "has been designed to handle the modern transportation, storage and distribution procedures in the fresh fruit, vegetable, poultry and other produce operations more efficiently and economically than ever before."

(Turn to page three)

Look At It Now - - -

NOW SEE THIS...

Yes, it is Petrarch Place, that alley near the Chamber building. Just one edition ago, it was a typically bleak, if useful, San Francisco alley. Today, attractive trees in handsome planter boxes invite passers-by to tarry a moment—and they do. It is all part of the Chamber's landscaping and tree planting program. . . .

THE CHAMBER'S AGRICULTURAL committee honored the Farmers Market and its
founder, John G. Brucato, earlier this month
at a luncheon in the Fairmont Hotel. Occasion was the market's 20th anniversary. It was
a festive event, as the photos above indicate.
In top photo, Mrs. Merl Brock, of Fresno, helps
son, Michael, make a succulent choice. In bot-
tom picture, Brucato gingerly dons the "garlic
wreath" (an honor) as Carl L. Garrison (at
left), committee chairman, and Allan Grant, of
Visalia, first vice president of the California
Farm Bureau Federation, look on.

Leaflet Lists Benefits New Industry Brings

A ready-reference type, illustrated leaflet on
the benefits of new industry to a community
has been issued by the economic research department of the Chamber of Commerce of the
United States.

The leaflet, "What 100 New Factory Workers Mean to Their Community," has been reprinted for the S. F. Chamber's industrial
department and is available to interested
members on request, according to H. C. (Bud)
Marsh, department manager.

It demonstrates that 100 new factory workers can also be interpreted as 359 more people
(on the average), 100 more households, 91
more school children, $710,000 more personal
income per year, $229,000 more in bank de-
posits, 97 more passenger cars registered,
employment for 65 more non-manufacturing
workers, three more retail establishments and
$331,000 more retail sales per year.

The Chamber's new landscape and tree-
planting section, chairmanned by Brian
Fewer, will hold its next meeting on Tues-
day, September 3, at 10:30 a.m. in the
Chamber board room (200) at 333 Pine
Street.

Advisory Committee Named to Coordinate World Trade Fair

An advisory committee of 106 industrial.
commercial and governmental leaders has
been formed to coordinate the seventh U. S.
World Trade Fair, to be held in San Francisco
September 10-12, 1964, it has been announced
by Harry A. Lee, president of the Chamber,
the Fair's coordinating agency.

Headed by Governor Edmund G. Brown of
California, it names as honorary chairman San
Francisco Mayor George Christopher and as
chairman Lester L. Goodman, president of the
San Francisco Area World Trade Association.

The committee includes heads of federal,
state and city agencies and 66 presidents or
board chairmen of California's largest corporations and leaders in the development of
international commerce.

Committee members already are at work on
plans for the many events and activities which
will make up the state's and city's participation in this international event, the first of its
nature ever to be held in the West. Meetings
also are under way with local representatives
of 53 foreign nations stationed in San Francisco.

Lee said the successful efforts of Mayor
Christopher and others to bring the Fair to
San Francisco represent a breakthrough in
San Francisco's program to enhance its posi-
tion as a major hub for world-wide commerce
in the West.

Calendar

August 26—Department Store Management
Study Team—Room 200, 10 a.m.

August 27—Tax Section Subcommittee Meeting—Room 100, 10:30 a.m.

August 28—Contact Club Meeting—Signature
Room, 3rd Floor, John Hancock Building, 255
California, 10:15 a.m.

August 28—World Trade Business Luncheon
Meeting—World Trade Club, 12 noon.

August 28—Building Code Subcommittee
Meeting—Room 200, 6 p.m.

August 29—Press Conference for the 1963
Outstanding Airman of the Year—Oasis
Room, St. Francis Hotel, 10 a.m.

September 3—Landscape and Tree-Planting
Section Meeting—Room 200, 10:30 a.m.

September 5—Civic Luncheon—Sponsored by
the S. F. Chamber and the S. F. Commercial
Club; Speaker: Edwin P. Neilan, president,
U. S. Chamber of Commerce; Commercial Club,
465 California St., 12:15 p.m.

September 11—New Era Conference—Sponsored by the S. F. Chamber, Greater San Jose
Chamber, San Mateo County Development Association, and League of California Cities, Peninsula Division; Hilton Inn, all-day conference
beginning 9:30 a.m.

September 11—Contact Club Meeting—Signature Room, 3rd Floor, John Hancock Building,
255 California St., 10:15 a.m.

September 11—International Air Transportation Luncheon Meeting—World Trade Club,
12 noon.

By Joe Haughey

THE PACIFIC COAST ASSN. OF PORT AU-
THORITIES will hold its 50th annual conven-
tion September 10-13 at the Fairmont Hotel.
PCAPA president Rae F. Watts announced.
More than 300 officials of western U. S. and
Canadian ports are expected to attend. . . .

THE SHERATON-PALACE will host the annual convention of the California Assn. of Independent Insurance Adjusters on Oct. 10-12.
Panels on innovations in forensic loss adjusting
will be headed by N. Newell, president of Fire
Loss Assn.; R. A. Ryan, president of Inland
Marine Loss Assn.; and E. Bart Fisher, president of Casualty & Surety Claims Assn. . . .

MORE THAN 500 WESTERN ADVERTISING
and media executives will gather in San Francisco for the 26th annual meeting of the American Assn. of Advertising Agencies on Sept.
17-19. A heavy schedule of business sessions
covering the many phases of advertising has
been planned, Donald B. Kraft, western region
chairman, announced. . . .

ISHIHARA INTERNATIONAL PRODUC-
TIONS and Nikkatsu Motion Picture Co., Japanese movie producers on location in San Francisco, began filming the dramatic true story of
Kenichi Horie's solo voyage across the Pacific
exactly one year after he sailed into San Francisco Bay, August 12. Actual local participants
in Horie's adventure will re-create their original
roles in "My Enemy, the Sea," to be released in
November. . . .

MRS. WALTER F. KAPLAN has succeeded
Mrs. Eleanor Rossi Reno as president of the
San Francisco Council of Women's Clubs, representing more than 10,000 San Francisco
women. She is the wife of Walter F. Kaplan,
former Chamber director and past president of
the Retail Merchants Assn. . . .

GILBERT DEAN, former publicity director of
Lennen & Newell, Inc., has joined Southland
in Hayward as its public relations director, John
N. Pappas, general manager of the shopping
center, announced. . . .

STANFORD'S FIFTH NOBEL LAUREATE.
William Shockley, co-inventor of the transistor,
has been named first recipient of the Alexander
M. Poniatoff Professor of Engineering Science
chair at Stanford University, effective Sept. 1.
Funds for the endowed chair came from the
Ampex Foundation in honor of Ampex Corp.'s
founder and board chairman. . . .

EICHLER HOMES, INC. reports a 16 per cent
sales increase and a 33½ per cent rise in net
profits for the first six months of this year over
the same period last year. . . .

Members are reminded that the
1963 Directory of Large Manufacturers, covering 13 Bay Region counties,
is obtainable at the Chamber, 333 Pine
Street. Copies sell for $1 each to mem-
bers, $3 to non-members.

EVEN A BOY *with a Brownie finds San Francisco's attractions a source of creative activity.
At Fisherman's Wharf on the Fourth of July,
11-year-old David D. Ayres snapped this unusual shot of Beniamino Bufano's famed "St.
Francis." The shirtless man in the foreground
is the artist, Bufano, himself. On the Fourth,
he was busy with a helper putting last-minute
touches on the work in its new setting in the
Fisherman's Wharf area.*

The Weekend of Sergeant Waite

"A Fabulous Weekend in San Francisco" is ahead for Air Force Senior Master Sergeant Marvin C. Waite and Mrs. Waite, thanks to the efforts of your Chamber in cooperation with the Air Force. Randle P. Shields, manager of the public affairs department, has disclosed.

Sergeant Waite, a senior director technician at Stead Air Force Base, Nevada, is the 1963 "Airman of the Year" choice of the Air Force Association, which sponsors this annual program with the support of the Air Force.

This year's choice has, according to Air Force information, achieved "one of the most remarkable records" in the service since he enlisted in 1950. At the age of 30, he is considered "one of the youngest if not the youngest" senior master sergeants in the Air Force.

Your Chamber's job in this unique "salute" to outstanding military service is no small one and the itinerary arranged for Sergeant Waite during his four-day S. F. visit (Thursday, Aug. 29-Sunday, Sept. 1.) is, indeed, impressive.

It involves residence at the St. Francis Hotel, a press conference, luncheon at the Commercial Club, a bay cruise aboard the *Adventuress*, a Tiburon Champagne Cruise, breakfast (Friday) at Sear's Fine Food Restaurant, the Gray Line's deluxe tour, luncheon aboard the P&O-Orient Line's *Oriana*, visits to the sailing ship *Balclutha* and the Maritime Museum, a shopping tour, dinner at La Bourgogne Restaurant, Ice Follies attendance, breakfast (Saturday) at the Cliff House, a helicopter flight (S.F.-Oakland Helicopter Airlines), luncheon at San Francisco International Airport, visits to the various Golden Gate Park attractions, dinner and floor show at Bimbo's, and brunch (Sunday) on the Sir Francis Drake Hotel Starlite Roof.

The stellar program of entertainment for Sergeant and Mrs. Waite was arranged by the Chamber's Armed Forces Section, Richard C. Ham, chairman.

San Francisco Wins Excellence Prize For Vehicle Safety Drive

San Francisco has been chosen to receive the 1963 state award of excellence for cities in the over 300,000 population category for its vehicle safety check campaign, conducted by the Chamber as part of this year's National Vehicle Safety Check for communities, according to Harry A. Lee, Chamber president.

San Francisco was one of more than 3,500 communities which participated in the national program, sponsored annually by the Auto Industries Highway Safety Committee and *Look* magazine.

The award was conferred by a national board of judges which met in Washington, D.C., late this month.

A total of 101,611 vehicles was checked in San Francisco by city, state and federal agencies, companies with motor fleets, new and used car dealers, schools, garages, car clubs, service stations and the military in cooperation with the Chamber traffic safety and control section, of which Roy E. Matison is chairman, and the Chamber civic development committee, of which Edward C. Sequeira is chairman.

During the campaign, held in May, seven lanes operated for three days and were manned by the U. S. Marines, the U. S. Naval Receiving Station of Treasure Island, the Pacific Telephone and Telegraph Company personnel, the American Society of Safety Engineers, young adults, car club members, Hi Board Council members, workers from businesses, associations, industrial firms, automobile and tire companies, utility companies and others in a city-wide, voluntary effort.

Important Month

(Continued from page one)

On September 26, prior to the three-day celebration, Assistant Secretary of Agriculture George L. Mehren will address a civic luncheon in the Commercial Club, sponsored by the S. F. Chamber and the Commercial Club. Professor Mehren, until his appointment by President Kennedy on August 15, was professor of agricultural economics at the University of California and Director of the Giannini Foundation of Agricultural Economics.

New Chamber Members

Robert Grison   Mack Newman   Roy Stenmark   J. R. Fewry   Frank Groves

MEMBERS NEW TO THE CHAMBER ROSTER include (above, l. to r.) Robert Grison, owner, *Grison Chicken House* and *Grison Steak House*, both on Van Ness Avenue at Pacific; Mack Newman, president, *Mack Newman, Inc.*, 2415 Chestnut Street; Roy Stenmark, president, *Stenmark Construction Co.*, 2190 Folsom Street; John R. Fewry, sales manager, *Smyth Van & Storage Co.*, 3600 Third Street; and Frank Groves, secretary, *Frank Groves Company*, 345 Fourth Street.

WHEEL TO WHEEL BATTLES *between these speedy little single-seater sports cars, called Formula Juniors, are expected at the Jaycee Candlestick Park Road Races on September 14-15. The drivers are Harry Martin, Corte Madera (leading), and Siro Jones, San Anselmo.*

Racing Your Way September 14-15

Sports car road racing returns to San Francisco for the first time in nearly a decade when the Jaycee Candlestick Park Road Races are presented September 14-15. A field of the West's fastest cars and best drivers are expected for the two-day event, sponsored by the San Francisco Junior Chamber of Commerce. The 2.1 mile course to be laid out over Candlestick's sprawling parking lot will feature a special 4000 ft. straightaway on which the bigger modified sports cars should reach speeds of 140-150 miles per hour.

Proceeds from the event will be used for Camp Jaycee, a camp to be developed in the Sierra for youth agencies without facilities; Fishing For Youth, enabling Jaycee members to take youths on Sierra fishing trips; and Operation Shopping, which will give underprivileged children an opportunity to go shopping at Christmas time.

Jaycee project chairman Nick Bowles, committee advisor Bill Dunne, and Terry Rico of the Municipal Railway have announced a unique transportation setup for the event. Special Muni bus service will carry spectators to the course from the Cow Palace parking lot and from regular stops throughout the city.

The Jaycee Road Races are sanctioned by the San Francisco chapter of the Sports Car Club of America.

Research Department Issues Artcraft List

The research department, under Stanley C. Allen, has updated its list of schools of art, craft and design in San Francisco.

Fifteen schools are listed, teaching subjects ranging through fine and commercial art, photography, metalcraft, dress designing, millinery, textiles, ceramics and flower arranging.

Copies are available from the Chamber research department, 333 Pine St., San Francisco 4.

Stewart Cort Named Bethlehem President

Stewart S. Cort, vice president in charge of the Pacific Coast division of Bethlehem Steel Corp. since May, 1961, was named president of Bethlehem Steel on July 31st.

Cort, who succeeds Edmund F. Martin as head of America's No. 2 steel producer (Martin moves up to the newly created post of vice chairman), tendered his resignation from the San Francisco Chamber board by letter. His new post takes him to Bethlehem, Pa.

There's No Denying It: Our City's Attraction Experienced by Many

A total of 4,200 inquiries from individual planning to move to San Francisco were received during the first half of 1963 by the Chamber research department, according to Stanley C. Allen, department manager.

And while visitor requests of all kinds during the period, totalling 8,800, represented a 8 per cent decline from the same period a year earlier, Allen stressed that the inquiries from those planning to move to San Francisco were up by 18.7 per cent from the prior first half's 3,500.

Prospective visitors received the regular "packet," Allen said, consisting of a map and guide to San Francisco, tour brochures, a guide to climate and clothes, lists of hotels, motels and restaurants, and a current calendar of events.

"Newcomer Packets," Allen noted, contain the map and guide along with a booklet on the city's vital statistics (population, climate, housing, taxes, employment, transportation, recreation, etc.) and other items.

Total mail requests for information during the first half of 1963 numbered more than 22,000, and there were more than 24,000 telephone calls and visits to the office. In all Allen said, there were more than 46,000 requests for information, including queries on marketing and economic data, handled by the research department.

During the six months, 28,000 San Francisco maps were distributed.

Chamber Will Choose Year's Livestock Man

California's 1963 Livestock Man of the Year will be chosen by the livestock man award committee of the Chamber during the award group's annual meeting at a luncheon Friday September 13, in the San Francisco Commercial Club.

Chairman of the awards committee is Henry Schacht, director of information, University of California Agricultural Extension Service.

The Livestock Man of the Year has been selected and honored by the Chamber ever year since 1950. The 1962 recipient of the award was D. E. Alexander, of Napa.

The 1963 award will be presented during San Francisco Chamber night at the Cow Palace, Saturday, October 26, as a feature of the Grand National Livestock Exposition.

BAY REGION BUSINESS
PUBLISHED BY THE
SAN FRANCISCO CHAMBER OF COMMERCE

HARRY A. LEE, President
C. L. FOX, Executive Vice President
M. A. HOGAN, Secretary
JOSEPH C. BAUGHEY, Editor
CHARLES F. AYRES, Associate Editor

Published semi-monthly and owned by the San Francisco Chamber of Commerce, a non-profit organization, at 333 Pine St., San Francisco, Zone 4, County of San Francisco, California. Telephone EXbrook 2-4511. (Non-member subscription, $3.00 a year.) Entered as Second Class matter April 25, 1946, at the Post Office at San Francisco, California, under the Act of March 3, 1879.

Circulation: 7,300

BAY REGION BUSINESS

Business Heart of San Francisco

SAN FRANCISCO CHAMBER OF COMMERCE

VOLUME 20 • NUMBER 17 • SEPTEMBER 13, 1963

S.F. Airport's 'New Era' Jets in On $14 Million Wings

"TIN GOOSE" FLYS HIGH AGAIN

Sightseeing flights for the Bay Area press, radio and television newsmen were conducted yesterday by American Airlines at International Airport, marking this weekend's dedication of the new South Terminal. The old Ford Tri-Motor, fully restored to its 1929 condition, will be presented to the Smithsonian Institution when its new air museum is ready for occupancy. It will be on display at the S. F. Airport tomorrow. . . .

Civic Luncheon to Mark Opening of New S. F. Produce Market

Professor George L. Mehren, appointed assistant secretary of agriculture by President Kennedy recently, will be the feature speaker at a civic luncheon in the Commercial Club on Thursday, September 26, celebrating the opening of the new San Francisco Produce Terminal at Islais Creek.

The civic luncheon, sponsored jointly by the Chamber and the Commercial Club, will precede three days — September 27-28-29 — of public festivity at the new produce facility built to replace the 100-year-old produce district in which the Golden Gateway is now rising.

Prof. Mehren

Mehren, professor of agricultural economics at the University of California and director of the Giannini Foundation of Agricultural Economics immediately prior to his federal appointment, has an historical relationship to San Francisco's produce market problems that goes back to 1943. He was co-author with agriculturists W. T. Calhoun and H. E. Erdman at the University of California of the original report on improving San Francisco's wholesale fruit and vegetable market, its potential and its future.

AIRPORT'S MOVING SIDEWALK

Called "Speedwalk," this passenger conveyor— to be 460 feet long and the longest moving sidewalk in the nation — will be operating this winter at the International Airport's concourses B and C (occupied by United Air Lines). . . .

Benefit Performance At Masonic Temple

As a glittering climax to the observance of Cystic Fibrosis Week in San Francisco (Sept. 15-21), the San Francisco chapter of the National Cystic Fibrosis Research Foundation will stage its second annual benefit performance, "An Evening with Joey Bishop," September 21, 8:30 p.m., in the Masonic Memorial Temple Auditorium.

Bishop, serving his third consecutive year as national chairman for the campaign, will be master of ceremonies.

The first major completed element of "The New Era Airport" will be introduced to the public in a day-long preview of the new $14 million South Terminal at San Francisco International Airport on Sunday.

During the preview hours—10 a.m. to 5 p.m. —the public will be invited to inspect the handsome jet-age structure which sweeps in a functional 800-foot arch from the central terminal.

Visitors are also invited to attend the formal dedication of the South Terminal at 10:30 a.m. Mayor George Christopher will unveil a commemorative plaque in the main lobby area on the upper level at Concourse "F." President Stuart N. Greenberg of the S. F. Public Utilities Commission will be master of ceremonies.

PRIME TENANT

Trans World Airlines, the building's prime tenant, is scheduled to commence operations in the South Terminal Monday. Other airline tenants will follow suit as their areas become operational. They include: American Airlines, British Overseas Airways, Japan Air Lines, Lufthansa German Airlines, Pan American World Airways, Philippine Air Line, Qantas Empire Airways, West Coast Airlines and Western Airlines.

Western, second largest South Terminal tenant, will share Concourse "F" with TWA, within six months will acquire additional passenger handling facilities in a new Pier "FF" which will be a twin to TWA's present jet pinwheel, Pier "F."

American and West Coast will continue to use gate positions in Concourse "E," but will shortly transfer all ticketing and baggage handling to the South Terminal.

All airline areas will be staffed for the Sunday public review in order that visitors may be thoroughly informed as to the most modern and functional jet-age terminal building in the world. They will be able to observe the newest methods of baggage handling, ticketing, passenger loading and U. S. Customs controls, as well as to see the ultimate in service refinements built into the terminal's restaurants and cocktail lounges.

KEY ELEMENT

A key element in new era compactness concept is the new $10 million, four-level parking garage now under construction at San Francisco International Airport. This, the first of a three-stage project, will have a capacity for 2,850 cars which will make it the largest garage parking facility in the world. The second and third segments will provide a total of 8,000 stalls. The final effect will be that of four large parking lots stacked one above the other, with entrance and exit ramps *outside* the garage.

S.F. Business Activity for First Half of Year Rises 7.4 Per Cent

Business activity in San Francisco for the first half of this year showed an increase of 7.4 per cent over the same period last year, according to the research department of the Chamber. The Chamber index for the first half of the year was 129.6 compared to 120.7 for the same period last year (based on the 1957-59 average equal to 100). Bank debits, continuing to be the most significant factor, increased 11.2 per cent over the same period last year. The total debits for the first six months of 1963 were $39,780,152,000—up more than four billion dollars from the first half of 1962.

Electric energy sales rose 5.1 per cent. Department store sales slipped 0.3 per cent. Freight car loadings increased 0.6 per cent. (The figures represent comparisons between the first half of this year and the first six months of last year.)

Shares traded on the Pacific Coast Stock Exchange fell from 28 million during the first half of '62 to 25 million this year. However, the value was up $121,868,915 over last year for a six months' total of $702,996,460—a percentage rise of 21 per cent.

The San Francisco Mining Exchange dropped in number of shares traded from 9,111,015 during the first half of last year to 2,313,768 for the similar period this year. Their value also slipped from slightly over a million dollars last year to $108,000 for the first half of 1962.

San Francisco postal receipts amounted to $21,991,509—an increase for the period of 11.4 per cent.

Airline arrivals and departures at San Francisco International Airport numbered nearly 82,000 for the first six months of 1963 —an increase of more than 5,000 from the corresponding period a year ago—up 6.7 per cent. Passengers off-and-on totaled nearly three million, up 365,000 and 14.3 per cent from the previous year. Total air mail poundage increased by nine per cent.

More than 11 million vehicle crossings over the Golden Gate Bridge were registered during the first six months of this year—an increase of nearly 750,000 vehicles and 7.2 per cent over the same period last year. Traffic on the San Francisco-Oakland Bay Bridge numbered nearly 21 million crossings—up more than a million and 5.5 per cent from the first half of 1962.

San Francisco's consumer price index (cost of living) rose to 108.9 based on the 1957-59 average of 100 compared to the June, 1962, figure of 107.5, a rise of 1.3 per cent.

Building permits authorized during the first half of this year reached an alltime high for any six months' period in San Francisco. Permits issued totaled $90 million in valuation— 50 per cent higher than for the same period last year. A total of 7,431 permits were issued —1,731 for new dwelling units. Permits issued for new non-residential buildings had a value of nearly $43 million — 256 per cent higher than last year's $12 million.

In San Francisco there were 10,444 deeds of transfer during the first half of this year, 1,197 or nearly 13 per cent more than last year. Mortgage loans totaled 12,812, an increase of 1,332 or 11.6 per cent over the first half of last year.

Mortgage loans totaled 12,813, an increase of 1,332 or 11.6 per cent over the first half of last year. The value of mortgage loans was more than $52 million over the first half of last year, totaling more than $307 million during the first six months of 1963—a sizeable 20.5 per cent increase.

Building permits issued for the nine-county San Francisco Bay Area (the counties of San Francisco, Alameda, Contra Costa, Marin, San Mateo, Solano, Napa, Santa Clara and Sonoma) were up 16.5 per cent over the first six months of 1962. Total valuation amounted to $627.5 million compared to $538.5 million last year; total valuation of residential building permits was $475.5 million, up 18.3 per cent.

A total of 34,469 dwelling unit permits were authorized in the Bay Area during the first six months this year; of these, 14,347 were for single family units, 1,063 for duplex units, and 19,059 for multi-family units (apartments). Santa Clara County led with 11,352 dwelling units followed by Alameda County with 7,418 and San Mateo County with 4,710.

CONGRATULATIONS are in order for both Dave Rose (l.), composer and arranger, and Herb Caen, San Francisco Chronicle columnist. Both figured in last night's successful POR-TRAIT production of "My Enchanted City" on KRON-TV. Dave composed the musical background for the album which depicts San Francisco's most famous attractions. Larry Russell was KRON-TV's Writer and Producer for the show.

Industrial Trade List is Published

An updated list of more than 150 industrial and trade organizations with offices in San Francisco is available from the San Francisco Chamber of Commerce research department, according to Stanley C. Allen, Chamber research manager.

The list includes such industrial categories as food and beverages; building and construction; forest products; chemicals; power; machinery and metals; and textiles. Also listed are wholesale, retail, service and publishing associations. The presiding officers and headquarters address of each organization are named.

The new industrial and trade organization list may be obtained free of charge at the research desk of the Chamber, 333 Pine street; EXbrook 2-4511, extension 14.

Visiting Frenchmen Presented Packets

The Chamber publicity department and the publicity office of the Wells Fargo Bank recently cooperated in preparing and presenting gift packets to two visiting Frenchmen — Claude Martial Richard, chairman of the board and general manager, and Emile Henri Roussel, vice chairman and assistant general manager, of the Bartissol Company of Banyuls-sur-Mer on the east coast of France.

New Chamber Members

S. C. Marsh   Michael Reuter   Mike Singer   J. L. Reid   W. B. Little

MEMBERS NEW TO THE CHAMBER ROSTER include (above, l. to r.) Standish C. Marsh, manager, Doyle Dane Bernbach, Inc., 255 California Street; Michael Reuter, owner, Samovar Restaurant, 2506 Fillmore Street; Mike Singer, president, International Motor Lodge, Palm Desert, Calif.; Architect John Lyon Reid, FAIA, Reid and Tarics, 1019 Market Street, and W. Buckingham Little, director and partner, Container Laboratories of California, 151 New Montgomery Street.

'Good Politics, Good Government Go Hand-in-Hand'

Edwin P. Neilan, president of the Chamber of Commerce of the United States, discussed the federal government and "pork-barrel spending" at a luncheon in the Commercial Club last week under the sponsorship of the club and the San Francisco Chamber of Commerce. Excerpts from his fiery speech, entitled "They're Throwing It Away Just To Be Big Spenders," follow. Impact of the speech can be measured by the innumerable calls requesting copies of it handled all this week by the Chamber.

—The Editor

"Good political morals and good government go hand-in-hand. . . . We have a right to insist on the highest standards of public morality from the men we elect to office. . . .

* * *

"A number of our national officeholders suport a double standard of morality —one for themselves and another for the taxpayers who foot the bill. . . .

* * *

"Too many of our Senators and Congressmen have become 'bagmen' for their constituents. . . . The voters either tolerate or insist upon the reckless spending of public money for self-serving local projects that do not meet the test of national interest. . . .

* * *

"The party in power has more tax money to spend than at any previous time in history and more ways to spend it. . . . Unless there is a great awakening of public conscience, the 1964 election could well turn into the greatest auction sale of all time. . . .

* * *

"Money the federal spenders have in their give-away bag . . . doesn't fall from Heaven in a once-a-year shower. It represents the hard work and sacrifice of 180 million Americans. . . . Yet the spenders throw it away like rich men's sons on a spree, confident that the supply is inexhaustible. . . .

* * *

"A federal agency that finds itself with unspent funds in the final month of the fiscal year rushes out to find a project that will empty the till by June 30 so that the next year's budget can be increased rather than cut back. And what does this waste cost the taxpayers? I'd be afraid to guess."

* * *

"Of all the federal agencies that spend without justification, the Area Redevelopment Administration, with its program of aid to so-called depressed areas, should top anybody's list. . . . That agency operates on the theory that any kind of federal spending is good spending and it's out to get another $455 million from Congress. . . .

S. F. QUOTES

"New York claims eight million people. Los Angeles claims the Dodgers. Chicago is proud of its industry. But the only civilized city in the United States is San Francisco."

—WILLIAM F. SCHANEN, III

BEFORE KSFO MIKE
. . . U. S. Chamber president Neilan (c), Robert W. Walker, S. F. Chamber director and vice president-executive representative of The Atcheson, Topeka and Santa Fe Railway, and Harvey R. Wright, assistant vice president-traffic of the same company, are interviewed by Carter Smith.

* * *

"We can't consider our American public scandal less shocking than England's just because it involves only the everyday abuse of public trust rather than call girls

and spies and Cabinet Ministers. If anything, we are in worse shape than England if we have come to accept corruption for granted as an unpleasant but necessary part of the democratic process. . . .

* * *

"When we tolerate a pickpocket philosophy in government we impair the value of the dollar, we rob the aged of their pensions, we defraud ourselves. Worst of all, we corrupt the whole moral fiber of the nation. . . .

* * *

"The 50-mile hike has become more popular than touch-football. . . . Everybody has felt a little better for it, especially the foot doctors. . . . But we have far greater need for a moral fitness program that will reawaken the American conscience . . . a new application of morality to the public business. . . .

* * *

"Make no mistake. We get the kind of government we deserve."

San Francisco First in State In Filing of Taxable Returns

San Francisco ranked first in the state during the 1961 income year in the filing of taxable returns, according to the 1962 annual report to the Governor by the California Franchise Tax Board. In San Francisco, 291 taxable returns per 1,000 residents of the city were filed, compared with 205 out of every 1,000 for the entire state.

San Mateo County ranked second with 247 of every 1,000; Alameda County third with 242.

The tax assessed throughout the state on 1961 personal income tax returns aggregated $295,147,000 and exceeded 1960's high of $259,614,000 by 13.7 per cent, the board reported.

Again indicating San Francisco's leadership in the personal income column, the board noted that this county had the highest aver-

age tax assessed in 1961—$119.11 per taxable return. Santa Barbara County's second place —$116.90—was a nose ahead of Marin County's third, $116.49. The average for the state as a whole was $85.20, an increase of 9.3 per cent over 1960's mean value of $77.92. (The figure is exclusive of fiduciary and non-resident returns.)

CORPORATION TAXES

The board "collected $290,869,922 in bank and corporation franchise and corporation income taxes in the 1961-62 fiscal year, compared with $272,717,949 in the 1960-61 fiscal year" for a gain of 6.7 per cent.

Corporate taxes "accounted for 17.8 per cent of the State's General Fund revenues in 1961-62."

And the board pointed out, "Calendar year collections scored an even more impressive gain than fiscal year collections. For the 1962 calendar year they totaled $305,936,391, compared with collections of $270,024,786 in the 1961 calendar year and $274,145,569 in 1960 calendar year."

PROFITS HIT PARADE

The board reported, "Corporate net profits (net income less net losses) subject to the bank and corporation franchise tax reached a new peak of $3,716,550,000 in the 1961 income year. This figure is $199.3 million or 5.7 per cent greater than 1960's total . . . and exceeds the record high of $3,633,711,000 established for the 1959 income year."

In 1961, firms engaged in finance, insurance and real estate ventures "showed a remarkable increase of over $100 million, or 13.6 per cent, rising from $763,351,000 in 1960 to $866,877,000 in 1961."

By Joe Haughey

A RECORD ATTENDANCE of more than 500 leading advertising and media executives from throughout the United States will gather here for the 26th annual Western Region Convention, American Association of Advertising Agencies, next Wednesday through Friday (Sept. 17-19) at the Mark Hopkins Hotel. . . .

PAN AMERICAN AIRWAYS has been designated as a New York World's Fair official ticket and information center for San Francisco and the Bay Area. . . .

BENJAMIN F. BIAGGINI, a former Chamber director, has been elected executive vice president and a director of the Southern Pacific Co., according to president D. J. Russell. . . .

THE COW PALACE now has exclusive right to its name, according to California Attorney General Stanley Mosk. An oval design in which the words "Cow Palace" appear has been submitted to the U. S. Patent Office. Action was taken after it was learned that several eastern livestock emporiums were also using the name. . . .

MATSON NAVIGATION CO. has established an electronic computer center at its headquarters, 215 Market street, under management of Wilbur Frye, formerly research department information systems manager. . . .

THE SAN FRANCISCO ACTOR'S WORKSHOP pre-subscription season opens in the Encore Theater, Mason near Geary, tonight (Friday) with Garcia Lorca's *The House of Bernarda Alba*. This is a violent tragedy stemming from a mother's domination of her five daughters. Lorca was Spain's foremost poet-dramatist prior to his assassination in 1936 during the Spanish Revolution. . . .

CHARLES A. ROGERS, San Francisco registrar of voters, states the voter registration drive is in full swing. Forty deputy registrars are stationed throughout the city. Many of the stations are open evenings and Saturdays, he said. . . .

A COURSE for trainee registered representatives preparing to take the New York or Pacific Coast Stock Exchange examinations will begin September 23 at the University of California Extension Center, 55 Laguna Street. . . .

"FORTY-NINER HIGHLIGHTS" will be sponsored on KTVU Channel 2 again this year by Delco Battery, starting Tuesday (Sept. 17), 8:30 to 9 p.m., with highlights of this Sunday's game with the Minnesota Vikings. Delco is sponsoring the highlight telecasts of all 14 regular season 49er games. . . .

United We Stand—Divided We Surely Would Have Fallen Low

Efforts to sever the San Francisco-Oakland Standard Metropolitan Statistical Area have been stymied, for the time being, according to reports from Washington.

Chamber Executive Vice President G. L. Fox assembled data and documents necessary to head off the proposal—which would affect statistics from vital sources on population and its trends, employment volume and structure, traffic, newspaper circulation, telephone usage, charge accounts, banks, corporations and other key indices of the general Bay Area economy.

The theme, in essence, is: "united we stand, divided we fall."

In reviewing the history of efforts during the last 15 years to define both standard metropolitan areas and a consolidated area, Fox noted that, concurrent with the move to split off the East Bay from San Francisco, "representatives of Sacramento, San Joaquin, Santa Cruz and Yolo Counties requested the San Francisco Chamber of Commerce to recognize them as parts of the Bay Region in its publications and otherwise.

"Consequently," he reminded, "the Chamber published five-county, six-county (S.M.S.A.), nine-county and twelve-and then 13-county (when Santa Cruz was added) sub-totals in statistical tables.

"While data for the six-county Metropolitan Area are of dominating importance," he continued, "the term 'Bay Area' generally refers to nine counties and the term 'Bay Region' to 13 counties."

LOSS IN RANK

Fox stressed that the San Francisco-Oakland Metropolitan Area (comprised of the six counties of Alameda, Contra Costa, San Francisco, San Mateo, Marin and Solano) ranks sixth nationally in economic wealth. Opposed is a proposal to create a new San Francisco Area which would rank 14th in the nation and a new East Bay alignment of counties ranking 16th.

The proposal was predicated also on a parallel plan combining Solano and Napa counties as a new economic entity.

"In all reality and logic, San Francisco and Oakland are economically interdependent," Fox stated, "and any

FRANCIS V. CLIFFORD, 41, graduate of the University of San Francisco (1944), succeeds the late Harold Berliner as president of the 63-year-old San Francisco manufacturing firm, The Hockwald Company. Hockwald makes and distributes maintenance supplies. . . .

hierachical ambitions on the part of either would eventually destroy the economic health of both."

The office of statistical standards of the Bureau of the Budget recognizes this fact, Fox added, in its definition:

"The general concept of a standard metropolitan statistical area is that of an integrated economic unit having as its nucleus a city (or two contiguous cities) above 50,000 in population with a large volume of daily travel and communication between the central city and other parts of the area. . . ."

DEFINITION FITS

The existing metropolitan area fits the Bureau definition exactly — with San Francisco (the central city in this instance) having the preponderance of employment for the area and the impetus for a heavy flow of traffic both ways.

The circulations of three San Francisco metropolitan newspapers throughout the proposed 13-county San Francisco Consolidated Area are part of the Chamber concept of the realistic range of the actual economic interdependence of a natural geographic unity.

Telephone calls between San Francisco and downtown Oakland and Piedmont average about 1.5 million a month in each direction, according to the Pacific Telephone and Telegraph Company.

The economic unity and homogeneity of the Bay Region is attested also by credit account information.

PROOF UNNECESSARY

Commented the *San Francisco Examiner* in a recent editorial: "The economic oneness of the Bay Area is so evident that we would never had thought proof necessary." Arthur Caylor, *News Call Bulletin* columnist, asserted, "the move to spilt the area would merely damage everybody concerned."

Philip G. Lasky, vice president, Westinghouse Broadcasting Company, added:

"Dismemberment of the unified economic force of the San Francisco-Oakland Standard Metropolitan Area would reduce the impact of this area upon the business world."

BAY REGION BUSINESS

SAN FRANCISCO CHAMBER OF COMMERCE

VOLUME 20 • NUMBER 18 • SEPTEMBER 27, 1963

BECOMING BEAUTY—*The Marina's historic Palace of Fine Arts, relic of the 1915 Panama-Pacific Exposition, awaits in its current condition of stately ruin the magic of a modern renovation depicted above. The artist's sketch shows the concept under an estimated base bid of $4¾ million plus additional ornamentation. Architects for the job are William Gladstone Merchant & Associates and Welton Becket and Associates (architects and engineers), with Hans U. Gerson coordinating architect. The Palace of Fine Arts was advertised for bids September 18. Bids will be received November 13.*

Salute to France Fete, Chamber Event Oct. 21 At Commercial Club

A civic luncheon will be held Monday noon, October 21, at the Commercial Club as a highlight of the Festival of France, to be celebrated October 18-27.

Sponsors include the Chamber, the Commercial Club and the San Francisco Area World Trade Association.

Georges Desbrière, president of the Paris Chamber of Commerce, will discuss "The French Economy in 1963." Harry A. Lee, Chamber president, will preside.

The 10-day Festival, of which Michel Weill is general chairman, will include a military ceremony at the Palace of the Legion of Honor, bicycle races and folk dancing in Golden Gate Park, a Bal Populaire in honor of visiting French sailors, a Bal de l'Elegance, a poodle show, exhibits of French art and scores of other events.

S. F. Quotes

"Your town (San Francisco) has more volunteer salesmen around the country than any other city in the world."

—EDWIN P. NEILAN,
1963 President,
Chamber of Commerce
of the United States

Safety Check Award Luncheon Wednesday

Frank Lowrey, of Washington, D. C., assistant manager, National Vehicle Safety Check traffic safety and control section of the Chamber at a luncheon Wednesday in the Commercial Club.

The plaque commemorates San Francisco for winning the State award of excellence for cities of more than 300,000 population in the 1963 voluntary community vehicle safety check.

Business Community Hosts 4000 Teachers On B-E Day, Oct. 11

A cordial invitation has been extended to San Francisco business and industrial firms to participate in the coming 13th annual Business-Education Day, Friday, October 11, sponsored by the Chamber and the Board of Education.

Randle P. Shields, manager of the Chamber public affairs department and business coordinator for the annual event, expecting to arrange for more than 4,000 teachers to visit business and industrial concerns, noted:

"This is a terrific event and complements our annual Education-Business Day, held in the spring of the year, when members of the business community visit our schools.

"These exchanges have proved invaluable in the knowledge obtained by businessmen of school work in progress, and in the development of school cur-

(Turn to page three)

BUSINESS BEACON

By Joe Haughey

EVENING COURSES for the fall term of the School of Advertising, Golden Gate College, get under way at the turn of this month, with three courses scheduled—radio and television, advertising production, and general advertising. Instructor in each case will be David Meblin, Pacific Coast manager, television division, Avery-Knodel, Inc.; N. B. Cole, general manager and treasurer, Johnson Printing Plates, and Arthur M. Arlett, account executive, Hoefer, Dieterich & Brown, and director of G. G. College's advertising program....

BALLET "63" with leading dancers of the San Francisco Ballet is currently on a 54-city tour which will take it east to Illinois and south of the border into Mexico. The tour is under the direction of Columbia Artists Management....

CONGRESSMAN William S. Mailliard, of San Francisco, is one of five U. S. delegates to the United Nations General Assembly. On taking his seat at the recently opened 18th UNGA, Mailliard said, "San Franciscans have always had a proprietary interest in the United Nations since 1945 when its charter was drafted and signed in our city."...

S. F. LIFE UNDERWRITERS Association has hired Helen Vasil as its new executive secretary, succeeding Mrs. Caye McKibbin, who held the post for almost 12 years. Mrs. McKibbin accepted a new position within the industry. Miss Vasil has had extensive public relations and editorial experience....

AMERICAN SOCIETY of Chartered Life Underwriters, San Francisco chapter, will present diplomas to underwriters who have successfully completed the CLU course at a conferment dinner Tuesday (Oct. 1) at 8 p.m. in the San Francisco Bar Association Lounge, Mills Tower, according to Leo H. Evart, CLU, president of the local chapter....

KRON-TV announces the appointments of Roy A. Meredith and Allan W. Kohlwes to future documentary programs. Meredith has had extensive experience as a film writer and director for the National Broadcasting Company, the Westinghouse Broadcasting Company and the Columbia Broadcasting System....

DELTA NU ALPHA, San Francisco chapter No. 48, transportation fraternity, hosts Pacific south coast regional meeting and workshop at the Marines Memorial Club Saturday (Sept. 28). Fifteen chapters from California and Arizona have been invited....

"A NEW EMPHASIS on Urban Renewal" will be discussed Wednesday (Oct. 2) by Ferd Kramer, a Chicago mortgage banker, at a luncheon of the San Francisco Planning and Urban Renewal Association (SPUR) in the St. Francis Hotel....

COW PALACE directors have engaged Stanford Research Institute to develop a master capital improvement plan, according to Fred P. Cox, president of the Cow Palace board of directors. Estimated cost of the study to determine land need and uses, and a traffic flow plan, is $28,000 to $32,000....

ANTHONY J. CELEBREZZE, Secretary of Health, Education and Welfare, will be the main speaker at a coronation ball and banquet on October 12 at the Fairmont Hotel as part of the city's Columbus Day celebration, according to William J. Marsico, president of the event. The holiday will be capped off Sunday, October 13, by a parade, traditional re-enactment of the landing of Columbus and other festive events....

JOSEF KRIPS, new conductor and musical director of the San Francisco Symphony Orchestra, will have a solid rehearsal schedule with the orchestra before the gala non-subscription concert opening the 52nd Symphony Season on November 29. The internationally famed musician said he will fly to San Francisco on November 24, adding, "I am looking forward to San Francisco and the opportunity to help make the orchestra one of the 'few' in the world."...

THE 1963 BIENNIAL meeting of the Family Service Association of America, the professional organization for more than 300 agencies in the United States and Canada, will be held in the Sheraton-Palace Hotel here November 13-16. The theme: "Strength to Families Under Stress." The local arrangements committee is headed by Mrs. S. Marshall Kempner and Mrs. Philip S. Boone....

ARMY STREET TERMINAL project received a major boost this month with the awarding by the San Francisco Port Authority of a $15,084,000 contract—largest in the port's history for substructure work—to Manson Construction and Engineering Company and General Construction Company, both of Seattle, first big phase of the ship-truck-rail terminal (a $25 million project) at Islais Creek....

TWO SCHOLARSHIPS have been established by the California Cotton Industry ($1000 and $200, respectively) for the young ladies chosen to serve as 1964 California Maid of Cotton and her first alternate. The judging will take place during the weekend of November 15-16 at Fresno....

NEW PAINTINGS by artist William Morehouse are currently on exhibit at Bolles Gallery, 729 Sansome street. The show, also including serigraphs by Joseph Fay, will continue through October 11....

SAN FRANCISCO MAIL CARRIERS have completed a field-test of a new harmless repellant designed to "Halt" attacking canines. Out of 10 mailmen bitten in San Francisco, the one man in the program could not get his "Halt" aerosol capsule out of his pocket. In 24 instances, "Halt" was effective. If the Post Office decides the repellant is effective enough for nation-wide use it could save the Government $1 million annually....

SAN FRANCISCO COUNCIL, Navy League of the United States, in cooperation with the city and the 12th Naval District, is sponsoring the art exhibit, "Old Navy—1776-1860," at the S. F. Maritime Museum, October 10 through November 3. This is a collection of 88 prints and watercolors from the Franklin Delano Roosevelt collection....

SEA CADET Review, the second annual for San Francisco, will be conducted aboard the USS Midway on Saturday, October 5, berthed at the Alameda Naval Air Station. The review will be conducted by the Navy League and Naval Sea Cadet divisions sponsored by the League's San Francisco Council....

BACCHIC BELLE—*National wine queen Marilyn Lockway, the prettiest wine seller of all, inspires that book of verse, that jug of wine (and hose!) and things fermenting for October 19-26—the National Wine Week celebration. San Francisco's Wine Fair will be staged on the Fulton Street Mall, between Hyde and Larkin Streets, October 19 and 20.*

USF MANAGEMENT Development Center is presenting a total of five workshop discussions on new products on Thursday evenings through October 10....

PHILIP S. BOONE, San Francisco advertising executive, has been elected president of the San Francisco Symphony Association, succeeding the late J. D. Zellerbach....

THIS WEEK, ending today (Friday) is "Project Concern Week," proclaimed by Mayor George Christopher. Proceeds from the varied activities centering around Chinatown are to go to Project Concern medical facilities in Hong Kong....

THE SCOTCH GARDENER, Jim Kerr—a member of the Chamber Landscape and Tree Planting Section—has begun his third year on KCBS Radio at a new time, 8:35 a.m. every Saturday. The program is sponsored by Leslie-Agriform Corp....

TWENTY UNEMPLOYED workers will be trained in San Francisco as office machine servicemen under a 52-week program beginning Monday (Sept. 30), financed by a $18,580 grant provided through the Manpower Development and Training Act of 1962 by the Department of Health, Education and Welfare. The program will be conducted at John Adams Adult School, 1860 Hayes Street....

NEW DIRECTOR of alumni relations at the University of San Francisco is the Reverend Thomas J. Sullivan, S.J., a 1931 graduate of USF and a pre-war teacher there. He succeeds the Reverend Francis J. Callahan, S.J., the university's vice president for development....

BERNIE RAUSCH, KTVU staff photographer who covers the San Francisco news beat for Channel 2, was recently named honorary mayor of the city in a proclamation issued by Mayor George Christopher. Rausch, a native of Germany, became a U. S. citizen on August 6....

OCEAN TRANSPORTATION will be fully explored in the repeat of a popular, 12-week seminar presented by the Management Development Center, University of San Francisco, held each Wednesday from 4 to 6 p.m. in the seventh floor conference room at 550 Montgomery Street, beginning next Wednesday (Oct. 2). Steamship and terminal executives, and legal advisors will be discussion leaders. Moderator will be Leo C. Monahan, the Center's staff seminar leader....

"COFFEE, TEA OR LETTUCE?" *queries Western Airlines stewardess Joanne Bears of her strange passenger—Benny the Bug—to the dismay of his traveling companion, Ted Huggins (enroute to the California Chemical Company ortho sales meeting at Minneapolis).*

France Still Leading Market for the U. S.

France continues to be a leading market for American products despite tariff difficulties foreseeable within the European Common Market.

That's the opinion of F. Paul Farish, recently retired general manager of the American Chamber of Commerce in France who addressed the San Francisco Area World Trade Association last week at the World Trade Club.

Farish pointed out that more than 2,000 American firms still are selling their products to France—a business volume running at the rate of almost $1 billion annually.

"American traders and businessmen, concerned over the rising tariff on some agricultural products are perhaps overlooking a parallel trend to lower tariffs in other marketing areas," he said.

Proposed Height Limit on Downtown Buildings is Opposed by Chamber Directors

Efforts to limit heights of commercial buildings in San Francisco's central business district have been decried by G. L. Fox, executive vice president of the Chamber.

Following a reaffirmation of a long-standing policy on the part of the Chamber by the board of directors, Fox stated that "the Chamber is primarily interested in the economics of the situation and also the reputation of the community and its attractiveness to major builders and investors.

"Tinkering with the floor area ratio in the C-3 district is hazarding the welfare of the city and adversely affecting the business climate," he warned.

Chamber action was in challenge of efforts to reduce the present ratio of 20 feet of floor space to one square foot of site which presently applies to inside lots. (A 25:1 ratio is allowed for corner lots.)

"The Chamber," Fox continued, "is seeking to enhance San Francisco as a major management and executive headquarters center for the western United States and is continuing its policy to make our community as attractive as possible to accomplish this goal.

"San Francisco has geographical characteristics which are more limiting than those which prevail in most other communities. It is a city which cannot spread and, to fulfill its destiny, must grow upward."

A currently proposed amendment to reduce the limit in the planning code would, Fox pointed out, make a building now under construction—and deemed highly desirable by the business community—not permissible to build.

"Likewise, construction of an announced structure would not be permissible under the proposed amendment inasmuch as it would have a floor area ratio of 23.8 to 1.

"Certainly, such magnificent improvements are desirable for San Francisco and every effort to attract them, rather than reject them, should be made."

Fox warned, ". . . If the city invokes a law which would prohibit such investors as are engaged (in major construction projects currently under way or planned) from determining what is economically feasible in the improvement of San Francisco property, such a law would adversely affect other property values. . . ."

Amended Maritime Mediation Bill is Backed by Directors

Directors of the Chamber have voted support of the Bonner Bill (HR 1897), as amended, providing for extended mediation in maritime disputes, according to G. L. Fox, executive vice president of the Chamber.

Action of the board followed the recommendation of the Chamber transportation committee of which Russell A. Morin, director of traffic, Fibreboard Paper Products Corporation, is acting chairman.

"This bill is intended to provide better machinery than now exists for the prevention of work stoppage in major maritime disputes affecting public interest," Morin said. "It is designed to protect the legitimate interests of both management and labor.

"The bill would provide a logical step-by-step procedure of bargaining mediation with work continuing throughout procedures.

"Specifically, it would authorize the President to appoint a national emergency board to seek settlement by mediation within 60 days in any major dispute involving the American merchant marine. Parties involved would be required to continue work for another 90 days should a solution not be found within the original mediation period."

West Germany Honors Wilson

James P. Wilson, Chamber world trade department manager, was presented the Officers' Cross of the Order of Merit of the Federal Republic of Germany at a champagne reception Wednesday last week.

Siegfried von Nostitz, newly appointed German Consul General to San Francisco, made the presentation.

B-E Day—

(Continued from page one)

ricula preparing youngsters for business life in their adult years," Shields said.

"We need the participation of many more firms in the B-E Day program," he stressed, "and it is still not too late to sign up to host a group of teachers."

In a letter to Chamber members, Chamber president Harry A. Lee stated: "The knowledge of business gained by teachers on B-E Day will be reflected in the basic attitudes of many future citizens. . . ."

The San Francisco Board of Education cooperates fully in the annual program. Schools will be closed October 11 to permit the teachers a full day for participation. School coordinator for the program is Ray Del Portillo, language teacher at the Francisco Junior High School.

SUPERSONIC AIRCRAFT—*At the recent dedication of San Francisco International Airport's $14 million south wing, a model of the British-French version of the supersonic aircraft Concorde was put on display by British Overseas Airways. Shown viewing the model above (l. to r.) are: John Dodd, BOAC manager, San Francisco; Najeeb A. Halaby, Federal Aviation Agency administrator; Tom Orpin, BOAC manager, USA; Mayor George Christopher; Ross Stainton, general manager, western routes, BOAC; and Ron Cockman, BOAC station manager at S. F. Airport.*

Car Demurrage
osals Opposed
amber Board

arrage rules and changes advocated rican Association of Railroads have ed in their entirety by the Chamber irectors, according to G. L. Fox, ecutive vice president.

f the board followed the recom- of the Chamber transportation com- which Russell A. Morin of Fibre- r Products Corporation is acting

sought by the railroad group and the Chamber:

me for loading and for unloading m 48 hours to 24 hours, except

on (coal excepted) of Saturdays, d holidays as penalty days after f free time be eliminated;

nation of Rule Nine (average entirely, coal excepted;

murrage charges (set forth in sec- le seven) which now provide a 4 for each of the first four days ation of free time, if any, and $8 bsequent day, be amended to pro- charge per day for the first and s, an $8 charge per day for the ourth days, and a $16 charge for quent day.

CALENDAR

EMBERSHIP MEETING, John Hancock loor, Signature Room, 255 California.

ANDSCAPE & TREE PLANTING SEC. 200, 10:30 a.m.

RAFFIC SAFETY & CONTROL SEC. ercial Club, 12 noon.

ORLD TRADE ASSOCIATION LUNCH. NG: Danish Trade Mission; World Trade

DARD OF DIRECTORS MEETING, Com. Room 1, 12 noon.

AY REGION COUNCIL, Jr. Chamber of oom 200, 2 p.m.

ONTACT CLUB, John Hancock Bldg., ecutive Suite, 255 California, 10:15 a.m.

EW ZEALAND TRADE GROUP MEET. 00, 10 a.m.

XECUTIVE COMMITTEE MEETING, n.m.

INTER-CITY SECTION TRIP to San reat Golden Fleet, 8:30 a.m.

BUSINESS-EDUCATION DAY.

HARRY A. LEE, President
L. FOX, Executive Vice President
M. A. HOGAN, Secretary
JOSEPH I. HAUGHEY, Editor
RLES F. AYRES, Associate Editor

ni-monthly and owned by the San Francisco Commerce, a non-profit organization, at 333 Francisco, Zone 4, County of San Francisco, elephone EXbrook 2-4511. (Non-member sub- 00 a year.) Entered as Second Class matter a, at the Post Office at San Francisco, Cali- the Act of March 3, 1879.

Circulation: 7,500

New Chamber Members

Irene Snook   C A. Barbanell   Toshio Yamada   James K. Speck   Jan Johnston

New Chamber members (l. to r.) are: Irene Snook, owner, *Irene Agency* (professional personnel consultant), 343 Sansome Street; Clifford A. Bar- banell, president, *Barbanell-Liever, Inc.,* 405 Montgomery Street; Toshio Yamada, general manager, S. F. branch, *Kasho Co., Ltd.,* 25 California Street; James K. Speck, manager, S. F. office, *Carl Byoir and Associates, Inc.,* and Jan Johnston, owner-operator, *Chez Antoinette* (massage parlor).

Businessman's Book Shelf—

THE SIERRA, by W. Storrs Lee, G. P. Putnam's Sons, New York—price $5.95.

"This is the morning of creation, the whole thing is beginning now. The mountains are singing together."

Thus rhapsodized the great poet-naturalist John Muir on first viewing Vernal and Nevada Falls in Yosemite. Multitudes have had similar feelings, more or less articulated, since. And they may be experienced any day, anywhere throughout the whole range of the mighty California mountain barrier known as the Sierra.

W. Storrs Lee, educator and a man who knows his mountains *(The Green Mountains of Vermont)* intimately as Muir learned to know them, has written a colorful historical account which will do much to enrich today's seeker of the wonders of the out-of-doors. This is both a history of great events and of human frailties and strengths, written for popular appeal but based on solid scholarship.

—C. F. Ayres

Air-Surface Tariff Law Change Sought

Amendment of federal law to allow com- mon carriers to file joint air - surface tariffs between all areas, including air terminal areas, has been voted support of the board of directors of the Chamber.

Action of the board, announced by G. L. Fox, Chamber executive vice president, fol- lowed a recommendation of the Chamber transportation committee.

'Money' Show Looks At Charities, Sports

"Are Charities Worthwhile?" and "Eco- nomics of Athletics" are the topics for the next two "Money in Motion" panels on KRON-TV.

"Are Charities Worthwhile?" will be tele- vised Sunday, 2 p.m. Participants: John R. Beckett, chairman, 1963 United Crusade Campaign (president Transamerica Corp.); Allan E. Charles, trustee of Presbyterian Medical Center and of Stanford University; and Kenneth R. Ford, donations and contribu- tions counsellor, Standard Oil Company of California.

"Economics of College Athletics" will be televised Sunday, October 6, at 2 p.m. Panel- ists: Pete Newell, director of athletics, Uni- versity of California; Dr. Paul Stagg, who holds the same position at University of the Pacific; and Chuck Taylor, their counterpart at Stanford.

PLANNING ACTION

The city planning commission, which yester- day presented its report on the proposed Downtown Plan, has scheduled three more reports during October, to be followed by pub- lic hearings.

Height limits, northeastern waterfront: report—Fri- day, October 4, 3 p.m., Board of Supervisors Cham- bers; hearing—Thursday, October 23, 3 p.m., room 282,.City Hall.

R-3 Zone (permitting frame apartment buildings with 40-foot height limit): report—Thursday, October 10, 3 p.m., room 282, City Hall; hearing—Thursday, October 31, 3 p.m., room 282, City Hall.

Sign regulations: report—Thursday, October 17. 3 p.m., room 282, City Hall; hearing—November 4-8, time and place to be announced.

CARL L. GARRISON
...honors on a 'silver platter.'

Panel Discussion On Supreme Court

"Money in Motion," the panel show on KRON-TV (Channel 4), will consider the uestion, "What Does the Supreme Court lean to the Average Citizen?" Sunday, Oc- ber 20, 2 p.m.

Participants will be: William P. Gray, pres- ent of the State Bar of California and part- er, Gray, Binkley & Pfaelzer; Dr. Frank C. ewman, dean of the University of California Law School; and U. S. Supreme Court Justice eter Stewart.

The program, moderated by Lloyd D. Luck- ann, coordinator, division of instruction, City College of San Francisco, is sponsored by the orthern California Council of Intere in America in cooperation with the Federal eserve Bank of San Francisco.

1,000 Teachers Visiting Busine

More than 200 companies, representing v. ments of the business, industrial and c he community of San Francisco, today e are hosting in excess of 1,000 tea en the city's schools in observance is annual Business Education day. Public schools will be closed for the gram, which is sponsored by the Bo ucation and the Chamber. Groups of from as few as four to as m a 150 are being briefed on the activit ads of the commercial-industrial enter

BAY REGION BUSINESS

AN FRANCISCO CHAMBER OF COMMERCE

VOLUME 20 • NUMBER 19 • OCTOBER 11, 1963

CARL L. GARRISON
. . . honors on a 'silver platter.'

Carl L. Garrison of Woodside Named Livestock Man of Year

Carl L. Garrison of Woodside (San Mateo County) has been named California's 1963 "Livestock Man of the Year" by the statewide livestock man award committee of the Chamber. Award committee chairman Henry Schacht, who announced the selection commented: "On any list of the factors that have brought the state livestock industry to the No. 1 position in California's economy, Carl Garrison's leadership deserves to be underscored."

Garrison, who was born in 1911 in Lassen County, has been manager of the Porter Estate Company—which has extensive livestock and ranching interests in California and Nevada—since 1951. He is an active partner in the Atherton Cattle Company. From 1945 until 1951 he was manager of the Cow Palace.

The award—a beautiful silver tray—will be presented officially to Garrison by President Harry A. Lee of the San Francisco Chamber during the October 26 evening performance of the Grand National Livestock Exposition, Horse Show and Rodeo at the Cow Palace.

Garrison was the first chairman of the California Beef Council in 1954 and was re-elected to that office for the year 1959-60. He presently is a director and member of its executive committee. He also served four years as vice president and director of the National Beef Council.

He has been a director of the California Cattlemen's Association since 1953, chairman of the Grand National Junior Livestock Exposition advisory committee since 1962 and a member of the livestock advisory committee for the Grand National Livestock Exposition.

His activities in behalf of agriculture and animal husbandry have been numerous: he was president of the California Aggie Alumni Association for two years (University of California, Davis), a member of the first University of California advisory committee to the College of Agriculture created by president Robert Gordon Sproul, and chairman of the subcommittee on Agricultural Extension Service policy for the University.

Garrison also has been effective in the agricultural programs and activities of the San

Navy Day Luncheon To Feature Address By Paul B. Fay, Jr.

"Your Navy and the Defense Department" will be discussed by Paul B. Fay, Jr., Undersecretary of the Navy, at a San Francisco Navy Day luncheon Thursday, October 24, in the Commercial Club.

The event is jointly sponsored by the San Francisco Council of the Navy League of the United States, the Chamber and the Commercial Club.

Harry A. Lee, Chamber president, will preside. Chairman of the day will be Robert D. Cherrigan, president of the S. F. Council of the Navy League.

The speaker, Undersecretary Fay, is a native of San Francisco and a graduate of Stanford University. His responsibilities in the Navy Department cover personnel, industrial relations, the bureau of medicine and surgery, the Judge Advocate General's office, and personnel, Marine Corps.

Reservations for this important civic luncheon may be made with the Chamber. Check of $3.75 a person should accompany your reservations. The price includes tip and tax.

Francisco Chamber of Commerce — serving, for several years, as vice chairman of the Chamber agricultural committee before becoming chairman in 1962.

During his leadership, the Chamber agricultural committee spearheaded numerous campaigns of mutual farm-city

(Turn to page 2)

'anel Discussion)n Supreme Court

"Money in Motion," the panel show on RON-TV (Channel 4), will consider the 1estion, "What Does the Supreme Court lean to the Average Citizen?" Sunday, Octo er 20, 2 p.m.

Participants will be: William P. Gray, pres ent of the State Bar of California and part r, Gray, Binkley & Pfaelzer; Dr. Frank C. ewman, dean of the University of California aw School; and U. S. Supreme Court Justice otter Stewart.

The program, moderated by Lloyd D. Luck an, coordinator, division of instruction, City ollege of San Francisco, is sponsored by the orthern California Council of Invest in merica in cooperation with the Federal eserve Bank of San Francisco.

,000 Teachers Visiting Business and Industry Today

More than 200 companies, representing all gments of the business, industrial and serv e community of San Francisco, today (Fri ay) are hosting in excess of 4,000 teachers om the city's schools in observance of the 3th annual Business Education day.

Public schools will be closed for the day's rogram, which is sponsored by the Board of ducation and the Chamber.

Groups of from as few as four to as many 450 are being briefed on the activities and als of the commercial-industrial enterprises

of the city, visiting offices and plants and facilities on conducted tours. Luncheons are planned in all cases.

The largest group—450 teachers—will hear redevelopment and planning leaders — public and private—at a special program in the Marines Memorial Theater. This concerns the city's "Big Build" — the major construction under way or planned at present.

The San Francisco Area World Trade Association is hosting a group; the Chamber itself will play host to about 20. A large group will

be the guests of the Western Insurance Information Service. Pacific Telephone will entertain and educate about 170.

Oil companies, steamship firms, airlines, railroads, newspapers, the California Dental Association, the Heart Association, hospitals, dairies and the Salvation Army (hosting 75), are among those participating in the event.

The teachers choose their programs from a general list under broad categories: communications, distribution, finance and service, manufacturing and transportation.

July-August Business Activity Shows Healthy Upswing in S.F.

San Francisco business activity for July and August rose 15.2 per cent and 11.4 per cent, respectively, over the same months last year, according to the Chamber research department.

The Chamber index—based on the 1957-59 average equal to 100—stood at 138.4 for July and 136.8 for August compared to 120.1 and 122.8 for the corresponding months of a year ago.

Department store sales in August reached their highest peak of the year and surpassed any month of 1962 excepting the Christmas shopping months of November and December. Sales climbed 3.3 per cent over August of last year after having slipped 3.5 per cent in July under the previous July.

Bank debits in San Francisco totaled $7,-395,994,000 for July, up 24.6 per cent from the same month last year, and $7,139,488,000 for August, up 20.3 per cent.

Electric energy sales were up 4.5 per cent in July and down 0.6 per cent in August. Freight car loadings increased 11.3 per cent in July and slipped 6.1 per cent in August.

Oakland bank debits for July totaled $1,-029,210,000, up 18.0 per cent from $871,646,-000 for July of last year, and $956,217,000 in August of this year compared to $946,132,000 —a gain of 1.0 per cent.

San Jose bank debits increased to $651,-277,000 in July, up 17.9 per cent from the same month last year, and amounted to $572,-721,000 in August compared to $588,035,000 for August of 1962.

July employment in the six-county San Francisco-Oakland Metropolitan Area (San Francisco, Alameda, Contra Costa, Marin, San Mateo and Solano) totaled an estimated 1,214,000, up 31,000 over July, 1962. August employment numbered 1,224,000 persons, an increase of 28,900 over August of last year. Unemployment numbered 70,000 persons, or 5.4 per cent of the total civilian labor force, in July, and 66,400 in August, or 5.1 per cent of the labor force.

An estimated 299,100 persons were employed in the San Jose Metropolitan Area (Santa Clara County) during July, up 21,500

'LIVESTOCK' MAN—

(Continued from page one)

concern, including a drive to assure farm users of adequate water at reasonable rates under the California water project.

Elected by his peers as California's 1963 state "Livestock Man of the Year," Garrison became an honorary State Future Farmer (1948), a director of the International Rodeo Association (1946-51), a director and secretary of the California Reined Cow Horse Association and an honorary director of the California Rodeo at Salinas.

Garrison also:

• Graduated from the College of Agriculture with a B.S. degree in animal husbandry, 1933;

• Became farm advisor in San Joaquin County in July, 1935; remained until February, 1941, when called to active duty with the U. S. Army Air Force during World War II. Served with the Air Force until January, 1946 when released as a Colonel in the Air Force Reserve;

• Served as president, Californians for Fairs.

He will be honored at a noon luncheon of the Chamber's agricultural committee on October 15 at the St. Francis Hotel.

Garrison's portrait will be permanently displayed at the Cow Palace with those of others who have received the award since its inception in 1950.

from last year. During August 308,700 workers were employed, up 18,400 from the month a year ago.

PACIFIC TELEPHONE recently dedicated six trees to the memory of famous stage stars who performed at the old California Theater, now the site of PT&T's downtown business office (444 Bush Street). Affixing brass name plate to one of the aggregate planters are Sydney G. Worthington, PT&T, San Francisco division manager; Brian Fewer, Supervisor of street tree planting, Dept. of Public Works, and chairman of the Chamber landscape and street planting section; A. Ralston Page, grandson of W. C. Ralston, founder of the California Theater in 1869; and Peter Tamaras, President of the San Francisco Board of Supervisors. The six trees were named for Edwin Booth, Lotta Crabtree, Laurence Barrett, John McCullough, Barton Hill and Adelaide Neilson.

'Eiffel Tower' Takes Over Union Square

Sections of the 110-foot replica of the Eiffel Tower—constructed for the Festival of France, October 18-27—will be fitted into place today.

The replica of the Eiffel Tower will remain as the dominating feature of Union Square throughout the ten days of the Festival, with flags and bunting in the surrounding streets adding to the gaiety and daily musical programs.

At the corner of Maiden Lane and Grant avenue, the Cafe de France—"a typical Parisian sidewalk cafe"—will be operated by Saks Fifth Avenue, serving soft drinks, beer, wine or coffee.

Georges Desbrière, president, Paris Chamber of Commerce, will speak on "The French Economy in 1963" at the Festival of France luncheon Monday noon, October 21, at the San Francisco Commercial Club. Sponsors are the Chamber, the San Francisco Area World Trade Association, and the Commercial Club.

The Festival opens officially Friday, October 18, 11 a.m. at Union Square, with Jean Auburtin, Mayor of Paris, participating.

New Chamber Members

Hugh Grogan   *Juan M. Dulay*   *Harry Ho*   *Jennie S. Woolley*   *Charles E. Smith*

MEMBERS NEW TO THE CHAMBER ROSTER INCLUDE (above, l. to r.) Hugh Grogan, president, *Sentinel Life Insurance Company*, 47 Kearny street; Juan M. Dulay, managing owner, *Dulay Realty*, 1122 Market street; Harry Ho, owner, *Ho's Cuisine Restaurant*, 45 Turk street; Mrs. Jennie S. Woolley, controller, *Retailers Credit Association of San Francisco, Inc.*, 15 Stockton street; and Charles E. Smith, *fire prevention engineer-consultant*, San Rafael.

By Joe Haughey

Some of Old S. F. Has Returned ..

The San Francisco Historical Monument, a newly dedicated state park within the city, has become a stellar new tourist attraction.

The monument consists of a block square park, the restored Hyde street pier and four historic California vessels, and the Haslett Warehouse, soon to be filled with a display of early Western rolling stock.

The monument was built with $2 million of tidelands oil royalty money, conceived by the San Francisco Maritime Museum in 1948 and engineered by the State Division of Beaches and Parks. The square was designed by internationally known landscape architect Thomas Church.

The vessels on display include the last of the San Francisco Bay ferries, the *Eureka* (the only extant "walking beam" ferryboat on the North American continent); the three-masted lumber schooner, *C. A. Thayer;* a double-ended steam schooner, *Wapama;* and a hay scow built in 1891 at Hunters Point, the *Alma.*

The vessels are open to the public daily

OLD FERRYBOAT IS BACK
... Eureka 'rediscovered' ...

from 10 a.m. to 10 p.m., with an admission charge of $1 per adult, 50 cents per youngster to 18, but no charge for children under 6.

The Great Golden Fleet of the San Francisco Chamber was on hand bright and early to greet the old vessels as they were towed to their moorings at the Maritime Museum.

THEME OF THIS YEAR'S San Francisco International Film Festival (the seventh annual) is a worldwide view of contemporary life, according to Irving M. Levin, founder and director of the event. More countries have entered the festival, Levin says, than ever before, including: U.S.A., Japan, France, Italy, Great Britain, Brazil, Czechoslovakia, Holland, Korea, Yugoslavia, India, Poland, Argentina, Denmark, Russia, Mexico, Greece, the Philippines, and China....
AMERICAN AIRWAYS announces order of three new all-cargo jet aircraft, Boeing 707, model 321C. This will bring the line's all-cargo jet fleet to 11, largest in the industry, according to Axel Mikkelsen, district sales manager. . . .

QUEENLY BOUQUET — *Every wine expert knows the bouquet is the harbinger of good things to come. Here Alessandro Baccari, chairman of the Baccari Wine Festival (this month) is favored with a lovely boquet indeed. From left to right are: Queen of the Grapes (Gigi Annaloro), Queen of the Festival (Susan Franz) and Queen of the Wines (Pamela Crow).*

WELLS FARGO Bank reports a 20 per cent gain in net earnings during the first nine months of 1963, as well as all-time highs in total assets and deposits. The bank's president, Ransom M. Cook, listed total assets of $3,489,957,296 (a gain of $347 million over September 30, 1962) and total deposits of $3,041,995,683. . . .
MURIEL TSVETKOFF, executive director of the San Francisco Advertising Club, was presented the "Woman of Achievement Award" Tuesday night (Oct. 8) by the Pacific and San Francisco groups of the Business & Professional Women's Clubs. The presentation was made by Mrs. Ruth Church Gupta at a dinner in the Women's City Club. . . .
CONTRACT TO DESIGN the largest shopping center in the history of Gilroy has been awarded to the San Francisco architectural firm of Weber & Fairfax. . . .
A SERIES of financial management courses will be offered by San Francisco State College November 5 through December, on five consecutive Tuesday evenings (7:00-9:30). Cost of the series will be $30. Direct inquiries to Dale L. McKeen, School of Business, San Francisco State College, San Francisco 27 (JU 4-2300, ext. 740 or 381). . . .
MORTIMER FLEISHHACKER, JR., San Francisco business executive and civic leader, has been named to the board of regents of the University of San Francisco. . . .

THE NETHERLANDS National Tourist Office has opened western area offices here in the International Building, 601 California street, under the direction of Mrs. Julie Goss Lynch. The offices have jurisdiction over 13 western states....
NETHERLANDS CONSUL Johannes Tjaardstra, who has held his San Francisco post for more than six years, has been transferred to the post of economic secretary at the embassy in London....
COMPLETE CLEARANCE by the government of U.S. exports by air at 22 airports, including San Francisco International, began this month, according to the Air Transport Association of America....

THE "GREAT GOLDEN FLEET" will observe Columbus Day by landing at Coyote Point Yacht Harbor today at 11:30 a.m. A luncheon, sponsored by the San Mateo County Italian-American Federation and the San Mateo Chamber of Commerce, will be held at noon in the College of Marin Cafeteria on the Coyote Point campus...,
JACK BATES has joined KRON-TV's news staff. He's had 13 years news-gathering experience on radio and television in Nebraska and has handled publicity and public relations for the Lincoln (Neb.) and Duluth (Minn.) Chambers of Commerce....

(Continued on page four)

Truck Accident Rate Cut Drastically

Accidents involving the Scavengers Protective Association have been cut 83.8 per cent in five years, according to John P. Moscone, president of the Association.

Under a program—originally inspired by the annual Chamber vehicular safety check and headed by George Kasnoff, safety consultant for the organization—the Association has found that time taken for educational discipline within the organization has paid off in thousands of dollars.

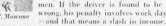

"Truck accident frequency numbered about one a day five years ago," Moscone said.

Under the present effort to curb accidents, a safety committee has been set up by Kasnoff. Hearings are held and the drivers, who share positions on the committee along with directors, judge their fellow men. If the driver is found to be in the wrong, his penalty involves work day losses —and that means a slash in income.

John P. Moscone　　　　　　　　*George Kasnoff*

Firm personnel also is involved in checking vehicles, blocks under wheels, and numerous mechanical safety factors.

Cooperating with the safety program is F. Bussi, Local 315, Sanitary Truck Drivers, and Manuel C. Conti, executive secretary of the Scavengers Protective Association.

"This is the closest thing to a self-insured program we can conceive of," Moscone said. "With more than 108 trucks traveling at all hours, we felt such a program was imperative. It's not only imperative, it is also invaluable."

: the Fulton Street Mall. The "comprimario" ith the California champagne bottle is Otto feyer, wine fair executive committee chairman. he Fair will benefit the Opera Association.

Radio Programs This Weekend

Radio shows scheduled this weekend by the Chamber publicity department:
TOMORROW, 8:05 p.m., KNBR, "San Francisco in the ities." Participants: Douglas Anderson, director, Adult raining Center; Stan A. Ousman, director of safety, Western reyhound Corporation. Subject: "Helping the Retarded Help hemselves and Industry."
SUNDAY, 9 p.m., KRFC, "Conference Call." Participants: imes McCarthy, San Francisco Planning Director; Attorney asper W. Weinberger; and Attorney Harold Nachtrieb. Sub-ct: "Height Limits on the Bay Front."
SUNDAY, 9:45 p.m., KFRC, "Progress Report." Partici-ant: Harry Bacigalupi, president, California Grape Products oro . and secretary of the Wine Institute. Subject: San Fran-aro Wine Festival."
Moderator (all three programs): G. L. Fox, Chamber execu-ve -ice president.

BUSINESS BEACON—

(Continued from page three)

, 20-PAGE supplement to the *Riverside (Calif.) 'ress-Enterprise*, devoted to the grand opening f the Palm Springs aerial tramway, is available a the Chamber's research department. The tram-/ay, rising 8,516 feet over the sheer slopes of pectacular Mt. San Jacinto, provides an un-aralleled vista of mountain and desert stretch-ng beyond the Salton Sea. Its cars are patterned fter those of Swiss trams, but are one-third arger. . . .

:AN FRANCISCO is one of seven cities in the ation chosen as key centers for the observance f National Hat Week (Oct. 14-21) by the Hat :ouncil, Inc. Monday, October 14, will be Hat)ay. During the week-long promotional period o heighten consumer interest in fall 1963 head .eur, the Council proposes special events for his city, Atlanta, Boston, Chicago, Minneapolis-t. Paul, Seattle and Washington, D. C. . . .

members. . . .

* * *

"Great accomplishments in a city come to those who insist that the future shall be not a little better, but far better than the present.

"There are far more failures which are the lot of those who advocated nothing, who were simply opposed, or who risked too little too late than those who want so much so soon for their beloved San Francisco.

* * *

"Through population growth and radical shift of functions, the most changing urban region in the United States will probably be the Bay Area with the possibility, but not the assurance, of San Francisco as its hub.

* * *

"San Francisco can become a shoddy, faceless city or a great headquarters center. Courageous planning coupled with equally courageous action increases our chances for the greater San Francisco.

* * *

"The next great step for the City of San Francisco is to prepare to accommodate and complement its new (produce) facility with the rapid transit corridor study. . . . This study will look ahead at least a decade to putting the city in a position where it can set the stage for business development, for the expansion of the tourism industry, for cultural and recrea-tional facilities, and for housing for all citizens to match the transit system.

* * *

"Daniel Burnham may be 'old hat' to San Franciscans, but his advice to 'make no small plans' never had more valid application than today when you have proof in the San Fran-cisco Produce Terminal of what great plans can finally mean to you and to your city."

 analyst in the industrial economics division at Stanford Research Insti-tute.

Tom Borek

Borek succeeds Stanley C. Allen, now with Marshall Banking and Marketing Consultants, Hayward, California.

CALENDAR

October 15—Membership Orientation Meeting — Executive Suite, 2nd Floor, John Hancock Building, 255 California Street, 10:45 a.m.

October 15—Capital Improvement & Land Use Section Meeting—Room 200, 10:30 a.m.

October 15 — Transportation Conference — Room 200, 12:30 p.m.

October 16 — Retail Merchants Association Board of Directors Meeting—Bohemian Club, 8 a.m.

October 16—World Trade Association Lunch-eon—World Trade Club, 12 noon.

October 17—Board of Directors—Room 1, S. F. Commercial Club, 12 noon.

October 21—Festival of France Luncheon—Speaker: Hon. Georges Desbriere, President, Paris Chamber of Commerce—S. F. Commercial Club, 465 California Street, 12 noon.

October 21 — S. F. Council of District Mer-chants' Associations Meeting — Room 200, 8 p.m.

October 23—Contact Club Meeting—Executive Suite, 2nd Floor, John Hancock Building, 255 California Street, 10:15 a.m.

October 23—World Trade Association Lunch-eon—World Trade Club, 12 noon.

October 24 — Navy Day Luncheon — Speaker: Paul B. Fay, Jr., Undersecretary of Navy — S. F. Commercial Club, 465 California St., 12 noon.

October 26 — Inter-City Section Trip to Cor-ning, California.

REGION BUSINESS
PUBLISHED BY THE
RANCISCO CHAMBER OF COMMERCE

HARRY A. LEE, President
G. L. FOX, Executive Vice President
M. A. HOGAN, Secretary
JOSEPH I. HAUCHEY, Editor
CHARLES F. AYRES, Associate Editor

Published semi-monthly and owned by the San Francisco Chamber of Commerce, a non-profit organization, at 333 Pine St., San Francisco, Zone 4, County of San Francisco, California Telephone EXbrook 2.4511. (Non-member sub-scription, $1.00 a year.) Entered as Second Class matter April 26, 1941, at the Post Office at San Francisco, Cali-fornia, under the Act of March 3, 1879.

Circulation: 7,500

BAY REGION BUSINESS

SAN FRANCISCO CHAMBER OF COMMERCE

VOLUME 20 • NUMBER 20 • OCTOBER 25, 1963

City Propositions G and J Voted Support of Chamber

Directors of the Chamber have gone on record in support of Propositions G and J in the city elections next November, according to G. L. Fox, executive vice president. Both of these measures would extend to certain city employees benefits which the majority of the city's civil servants now enjoy. "Their passage would be in the interest of equity," Fox noted.

MORE THAN 50 schoolteachers were hosted by the Chamber in the recent Business-Education Day, during which more than 4,000 were guests of the community's business firms and the Chamber. Gallantly opening a Yellow Cab taxi door enroute to luncheon at the Fairmont is Michael R. Martin of James Lick Junior High School.

Chamber Radio Shows on Tap for Next Two Weeks

Saturday — San Francisco in the Sixties. "The Bay Area Sports Scene—Its Strengths and Its Weaknesses." Panel: Prescott Sullivan, S. F. Examiner sports columnist; archery expert Doug Morgan; Thomas R. Rooney, producer. San Francisco Sports and Boat Show. KNBR. 8:05 p.m.

SUNDAY— Conference Call. "Merchandise Delivery and the Parking Problem in the Bay Area." Panel: Captain I. Thomas Zaragoza, San Francisco Police Traffic Director; Russell Be an, secretary-manager, Draymen's Association of San Francisco; Thomas Burke, secretary, local 85, Teamsters' Union. KFRC, 6 p.m.

SUNDAY San Francisco Progress Report. "An Industry Participates in Education." W. K. Evans, Jr. S. F. district sales manager, Shell Oil Company. KFRG, 9:45 p.m.

SATURDAY, November 2 - San Francisco in the Sixties. "The Economic Contribution of the Brewing Industry to San Francisco and the State." Panelists: John Burer, assistant to the president, General Brewing Corp. (Lucky Lager); George Osoke, executive secretary, California Brewers Assn. KNBR. 8:05 p.m.

SUNDAY, November 3 Conference Call. "The Public Relations Man and San Francisco's Image." Panel: Clay Bernard, assistant to the vice president—sales, public relations, Western Airlines; George B. Pottorff, regional representative, The Sperry & Hutchinson Co. (S&H Green Stamps); Arthur I. Blum, principal, Art Blum Public Relations. KFRC, 6 p.m. (All programs moderated by G. L. Fox.)

S. F. Quotes

"San Francisco is a mad city, inhabited for the most party by perfectly insane people whose women are of a remarkable beauty."
—Rudyard Kipling

The Chamber board's action resulted from a recommendation of the San Francisco Municipal Conference.

Proposition G would provide health service coverage for the employees of the Parking Authority who do not now enjoy this benefit although they've been granted retirement benefits available to all city employees.

Proposition J would raise death benefits for retired policemen and firemen to a maximum of $750 per beneficiary, consistent with what other city employees now have. The estimated annual cost of this increase would be $50,950.

Other measures on the November ballot, dealing with civil service and retirement benefits, were opposed by the Chamber board as, in some instances, "piecemeal tinkering" that eventually would harm rather than strengthen the city's civil service structure.

The propositions which the Chamber board opposes are: A, C, D, E, F, and I. Fox stressed that omission of other propositions in the board's last action does not imply approval of them. Some are still under study.

Proposition A would allow city employees to retire before age 60 and earn thereafter unlimited salaries without repaying the city. Currently, employees who leave city service after 55 and before 60 must repay the city for excess earnings.

Proposition C would grant employees full

(Turn to page three)

THE BANK OF AMERICA, enhancing its property at Pine and Montgomery streets, had 17 Indian laurel fig trees planted recently. Assisting Myron Tatarian, manager of the San Francisco Department of Public Works, are Emily Carnahan (l.) and Carol Boedeker.

Jim Wilson to Attend Nat'l Foreign Trade Council's Convention

James P. Wilson, manager of the Chamber's world trade department, will attend the 50th National Foreign Trade Convention in the Waldorf-Astoria Hotel, New York City, on November 18-20.

Wilson also will preside as outgoing president of the National Association of World Trade Secretaries at an election session to be held in conjunction with the NFT Council convention on the afternoon of November 20.

The Chamber's world trade manager noted he has been promoting San Francisco as the 1965 convention site for the National Foreign Trade Council and will continue his efforts during the New York convention.

Seattle to See S. F. Collection

Jules Charbneau, the Microcosmic Man who has the largest collection of the smallest objects in the world, is publicizing San Francisco in no small way at Seattle.

Charbneau—one of the most youthful of octogenarians—is exhibiting more than 30,000 of his priceless collection of miniature objects at the Seattle world fair grounds.

Almost everybody who attended the San Francisco world's fair in 1939 remembers his collection of amazing miniatures.

His world travels have netted him an enviable collection of art works and miniatures from every part of the globe. He has been a collector since he was eight years old.

Charbneau also has a business office at 55 New Montgomery street devoted to appraisals for insurance, for sales or tax purposes.

JULES CHARBNEAU
...the 'Microcosmic Man'

By Joe Haughey

:ALIFORNIA MUSIC Foundation's season se-ies opens Sunday afternoon, November 10, at p.m. with a performance of the General Platoff !on Cossack Chorus and Dancers at the Curran 'heater....

7ARNER BROTHERS Company of Bridge-ort, Conn., apparel manufacturers, has complet-d negotiations with Crocker Land Company or construction of new West Coast headquarters nd distributing facilities in Crocker Industrial 'ark....

'ROJECT CONCERN'S recent dinner-show and drive was a gratifying success, according to tennis Wong, San Francisco chapter chairman. 'roject Concern is a non-profit medical relief rganization providing medical care, food and lothing to refugees living in Hong Kong and :owloon....

'WO MEMBERS of the KPIX art department, Iichael F. Dattel and Peter Girolami, have een honored for outstanding achievement in ne field of commercial art. Dattel has been auded for the third consecutive year by the irt Directors and Artists Club of San Francisco. *. A.,* a national bi-monthly magazine of com-nercial art, has selected a Girolami design for lisplay in its annual competition....

CANCER FACTS for Men" and "Cancer Facts or Women," two well-known pamphlets of the imerican Cancer Society, have been completely eworked and are now available in new editions rom the Society's San Francisco branch (OR -7979)....

IEMBERS of Macy's Hi Board have signed up 0,000 teen-age volunteers to assure Christmas mployment for a group of mentally retarded tudents. Macy's Hi Board is composed of girls vho are interested in fashion, writing and art. Saturday, November 16, will be a Fashion Fund Drive for Goodwill Industries....

'ORT OF SAN FRANCISCO handled 3,964,000 ons of cargo in the first nine months of the ear for a gain of 212,000 tons over the same eriod last year, according to Rae F. Watts, port lirector....

'RESIDENT KENNEDY this month signed the Alcatraz Commission bill which provides for he appointment of a five-man body to study and recommend possible uses of Alcatraz Island. The bill was introduced by San Francisco Con-tressman John F. Shelley....

SUNSET MAGAZINE and Sunset Books an-iounced this week two major expansion moves: i new edition of the magazine and a new office uilding for the book company. The new "des-ert edition," to be circulated in Arizona and parts of southern California and Nevada, brings .o four the number of regional editions. A new, $600,000 building, similar in style to the present Menlo Park structure, will be built across the street from the existing plant....

KPIX, THE GROUP W (Westinghouse) tele-vision station in San Francisco, has been hon-ored for its recent telecast of the Chinese opera, "The Golden Coin Leopard." Yin-Shou Che, consul general of the Republic of China; Dr. T. Kong Lee, president of the Chinese Chamber of Commerce, Albert Lim and H. K. Wong, Chinatown civic leaders, presented a scroll to KPIX general manager Louis S. Simon....

THE ROYAL PHILHARMONIC Orchestra will be heard under the direction of Sir Malcolm Sargent in the Opera House Saturday evening, November 23, a special off-subscription event of the California Music Foundation....

RICHARD A. BUSCHMAN has been named resident manager of the Sheraton-Palace Hotel. He joined the Sheraton Corporation of America in 1954 and came to the Sheraton-Palace in 1959 as administrative services manager....

GOLDEN GATE COLLEGE total enrollment for the fall semester is nearly 15 per cent higher than it was a year ago, according to president Russell T. Sharpe. Enrollment as of October 17 totaled 2,007....

PUBLIC HEARINGS will be held in San Fran-cisco on October 30 by the Bay Area Air Pollu-tion Control District to decide whether a million Bay area used motor vehicles must install air pollution control devices and whether a network of inspection and installation stations will be established. Time and place: 10 a.m., room 1194, 455 Golden Gate avenue....

SF's INTERNATIONAL FILM Festival will, for the first time in its seven-year history, have entry applications, posters and other relevant data distributed abroad by the U. S. State Department, according to Cyril Magnin, member of the festival's board of directors and its legis-lative committee....

S. R. NEWMAN, western regional sales man-ager here for United Air Lines since 1944, has been named to the new post of assistant to the vice president-general sales manager. H. E. Mor-ley, district sales manager here for seven years, succeeds Newman, and James J. Hartigan, for-merly assistant to the sales manager, Great Lakes Region, succeeds Morley....

THE PORT AUTHORITY'S $2 million mod-ernization of Piers 29, 31 and 33, occupied last April by Pacific Far East Line, brought an immediate 26 per cent jump in the amount of cargo handled at the steamship line's San Fran-cisco facilities, a letter from PFEL's vice presi-dent for operations, George J. Gmelch, to port director Rae F. Watts discloses....

RUDOLPH A. PETERSON has been named president and chief executive officer of Bank of America, succeeding S. Clark Beise, president since March, 1954. Beise will retire as an active officer of the bank at the end of this month, but continue as a director and as chairman of the executive committee....

PACIFIC COAST port and shipping executives have agreed to join in pressing for lower rail-road freight rates on midwestern corn exported through the west coast. Action followed declara-tion by federal officials that a rate cut is essen-tial if the U. S. is to obtain a larger share of the booming Japanese corn market....

"PERFORMER'S CHOICE 4," the first of this season's public concerts presented by KPFA, will be given Wednesday, October 30, at the listener-sponsored FM station's San Francisco studio, 321 Divisadero street, by pianists Joan Goodwin and Dwight Peltzer, and percussionists Roland Kohloff and Peggy Cunningham Luc-chesi....

A THESIS titled "The Use of Mortgage Loan Brokers by Savings and Loan Associations in the San Francisco Bay Area," written by Richard S. Fazackerly, vice president and assistant loan manager of San Francisco Federal Savings, has been selected for inclusion in the "Thesis Mono-graph" being published by the American Savings and Loan Institute's Graduate School at Indiana University....

KPIX NEWS recently filed its 20,000 news film, making its library one of the largest in northern California, according to Deacon Anderson, KPIX news director....

THIRD ANNUAL Women Executives All-Day Seminar (for those aspiring to be executives as well) will be held Saturday, October 26, begin-ning at 8:30 a.m. at the Management Development Center of the University of San Francisco....

WHY CARL SMILES—*You would, too, if sur-rounded by such a bevy of beauties, all waiting on you hand and foot. Carl L. Garrison, the San Francisco Chamber's "Livestock Man of the Year," looks happy indeed as he is assisted at the plate by, left to right: Livestock Queen Ju-dith MacMillan, Rodeo Queen Virginia Arm-strong, Horse Show Queen Susan Farnow and Miss Grand National (Sheila Shaul). That's why Carl smiles!*

SEVENTH ANNUAL California Industrial De-velopment Conference will be held Friday, November 8, at the Sheraton-Palace Hotel, ac-cording to conference chairman George M. Dean, vice president, Pacific Telephone....

S & N ENTERPRISES, newly organized mail order merchandisers, search for new and mar-ketable products and welcome correspondence from manufacturers of items suitable for selling by mail. The firm is located at 26 Hamilton street....

PHILLIP R. SLEDGE, of San Carlos, has been advanced to director of sales for the San Mateo office of Carl Hanauer Company. Sledge has instituted a comprehensive sales training pro-gram for the development of specialists in the field of municipal bonds....

JOSEF KRIPS, conductor and musical director of the San Francisco Symphony Orchestra, is conducting 16 concerts of the New York Phil-harmonic prior to his debut here on November 29. Season tickets for the 52nd season of the San Francisco Symphony are still available. For information or reservations, call UNderhill 1-4008....

TOM FRANKLIN, long-time Bay Area televi-sion news reporter, has been appointed manager of public relations and advertising for Century City, Los Angeles, according to Frederick J. Gebers, executive director of the huge Alcoa development....

A RARE COLLECTION of oil paintings and etchings, titled "Masters of the American Scene" will be presented at Maxwell Galleries, 551 Sut-ter street, beginning Monday (Oct. 28) through November 16....

TAR GARD COMPANY is one of the fast grow-ing small businesses in San Francisco. It manu-factures and markets a new cigaret filter invent-ed by a Millbrae aeronautics engineer, Herbert A. Lebert. Already distributed in San Francisco, Los Angeles, Portland, Seattle, San Diego and Phoenix, Tar Gard will be introduced in Hawaii and Ohio in November and throughout the na-tion early next year, according to Robert W. Dailey, the firm's president....

COMMERCIAL AVIATION'S next seven to nine years should be the most stable the indus-try has ever known, according to L. B. Maytag, president of National Airlines. This will result from a combination of factors, Maytag said, including the ideal qualities of present types of jet aircraft, their long service before threatened by the advent of supersonic aircraft and "the strong actions of the CAB this year in facing the economic realities" in regulating the indus-try....

(Turn to page four)

New Chamber Members

Milena Vesic   *Leola Bragg*   *Georg H. Lenk*   *T. R. Upton*   *Mrs. V. M. Upton*

NEW CHAMBER MEMBERS—Top panel, left to right: Milena Vesic, director, *School of Paris*, 35 Grove street; Leola Bragg, owner, *Civic Manor Motel*, 825 Polk street; Capt. Georg H. Lenk, owner, *Captain's Galley*, 2241 Chestnut street; T. Russell Upton and Mrs. Veryne M. Upton, co-owners, *Upton's Restaurant and Catering Service*, 2419 Lombard street.

Adrian E. Scharlach   *E. W. Nicholson*   *Mark H. Lazarus*   *John A. Vietor*   *Dean Erickson*

Left to right (above): Adrian E. Scharlach, owner, *Claremont Residence Club*, 1500 Sutter street; E. William Nicholson, manager, *Laurel Motor Inn*, California street and Presidio avenue; Mark H. Lazarus, general agent, *Massachusetts Mutual Life Insurance Company*, 601 California street; John A. Vietor, publisher and editor, *San Francisco Magazine*, 319 Pacific avenue; Dean Erickson, director, *Western Business College (Speedwriting Secretarial School)*, 785 Market street.

BUSINESSMAN'S BOOKSHELF

Sutro in Tribute—a Forest and Now a Book

ADOLPH SUTRO, A BIOGRAPHY, by Robert E. Stewart, Jr., and Mary Frances Stewart, Howell-North (Berkeley, California). Price $6.

Sutro Forest—that part of it which hasn't fallen before bulldozers—is a silent and continuing tribute to Adolph Sutro who himself had had the trees planted — and who also made the University of California Hospital at the base of the mountain possible by his generosity.

With little formal education, a brilliantly practical mind and a stubborn will, Sutro arrived in San Francisco in 1850. After having constructed the world-famed four-mile Sutro Tunnel in Comstock country—which involved a long but victorious battle with the Virginia City mine owners and the San Francisco "Bank Ring" — he invested heavily in San Francisco sandlots, built Sutro Baths, provided the city with many parks, railways and roadways. His greatest idea was to establish a library for scholars from all over the world on the heights overlooking the present Cliff House and Seals Rocks. (His enormous collection of books only recently has found a home on the campus of the University of San Francisco.)

A practical engineer, he also appreciated the aesthetic, even if at times it took the form of a craze for outlandish 19th century bric-a-brac.

Among the saddest days in the life of this doggedly honest Prussian-born engineer were during his term as mayor of the city he so loved; wily politicians broke his spirit. But he spent his last days on his beloved Sutro Heights "with the plaintive barking of the seals his funeral dirge."

HIGHLY RECOMMENDED.

—*Joe Haughey*

MARK TWAIN'S SAN FRANCISCO, edited by Bernard Taper. McGraw Hill Book Company, Inc., New York, Toronto, London. Price $6.95.

This is a series of rare and specially San Franciscan pieces written by Mark Twain during his stay here in the saucy sixties of the last century—written before he attained fame as one of world literature's greatest humorists. Although Twain keeps company with such satanic scoffers as Voltaire, Dean Swift and Juvenal, much of the material here is on a lesser level. He excoriates children in the manner of a W. C. Fields and he often writes in the hoopskirt and high-button shoe style of his times. A "must," however, for collectors of San Franciscana. Pump's caricatures of the time—including splendid drawings of Emperor Norton—add a rollicking touch to Twain's sometimes bitter and somber humor.—*J. H.*

Propositions G, J Voted Approval by Chamber Directors

(Continued from page one)

pension allowances from the city in addition to social security benefits. As it now stands, social security and the city pension plan are integrated, a formula which was approved by the voters in 1958.

Estimated increased annual cost to the city, should Proposition C be approved, has been set at $3,372,814.

Proposition D would extend city-supported health benefits to teachers who resign from the San Francisco District to retire under the State Teachers' Retirement Plan.

The city health service currently is costing the public almost $2 million a year in subsidized benefits, it was reminded. Proposition D, it was claimed, would add an estimated $54,376 to the annual cost of the health benefits.

It means, it was further noted, that taxpayers would "have to pick up $18 a month in excess costs for each teacher involved in this proposal."

Proposition E would provide $25 a month increase in the retirement allowance for a group of employees retired before July, 1947, at an annual cost of $86,240.

It was pointed out that "this group has had three grants of this kind in the past 15 years" and that "these pensioners have already received a greater pension increase than the increase in cost of living since 1947."

Proposition F would provide pay parity for police and firemen. It would also place the Fire Prevention and Investigation Bureau, now under jurisdiction of the Fire Commission, under the fire chief, and would integrate the salvage corps personnel into the fire department.

Policemen currently receive maximum pay $16 above that of firemen ($693 as compared with $677). It was noted that "policemen are difficult to recruit while the supply of firemen is ample." In recent times there have occurred numerous incidents in which policemen have taken the examination to switch to the fire department.

It was reminded that San Francisco firemen "now receive a salary as high as any in the state."

The other items in the proposition are, in the Chamber's view, "riders" which should not appear on the same proposal with parity pay. They are not of the same nature. The Chamber at this time reserves opinion on their merit.

The annual public cost of carrying out the terms of Proposition F (pay parity) has been estimated at $392,000.

Proposition I would fix the pay level of police sergeants midway between that of patrolman and lieutenant, a 2½ per cent increase at an annual cost of $59,947.

Sergeants' salaries are presently closer to the lower grade. It was noted, however, "this is the third police increase presented in the past two years and represents piecemeal tinkering with pay schedules."

In addition, it was reminded, "this increase makes the sergeant's salary identical to that of inspector ($806 a month) and may lead to future requests for pay adjustments."

CALENDAR

October 29 — Capital Improvement & Land Use Section Meeting, Room 200, 10:30 a.m.

October 29—Jr. Chamber Board of Directors Meeting, Room 200, 12:15 p.m.

October 30 — World Trade Association Luncheon, World Trade Club, 12 noon.

November 5 — Landscape & Tree-Planting Section Meeting, Room 200, 10:30 a.m.

November 5—Jr. Chamber Board of Directors Meeting, Room 200, 12:15 p.m.

November 6 — Contact Club, John Hancock Building, 3rd Floor, Signature Room, 255 California street, 10:45 a.m.

November 6 — World Trade Association Luncheon, World Trade Club, 12 noon.

November 7 — Regional Problems Section Meeting, Room 200, 10 a.m.

November 7—Board of Directors Luncheon Meeting, Commercial Club, Room 1, 12 noon.

Maxwell Opens PR Firm Office

Walter J. Maxwell, formerly with the Chamber's membership relations department, and Mrs. Zoila Maxwell announce the opening of the firm of Maxwell & Maxwell, public relations consultants.

Offices are at 315 Montgomery street, suite 302 (DO 2-5755).

The new agency presently handles accounts in the fields of catering, architecture and building, and electronics.

Business Beacon—

(Continued from page two)
HYATT HOUSE HOTELS and Motels have issued "Traveler's Expense Book" to customers to clear up confusion on new expense account policies of federal government. . . .

Pacific Gas and Electric Co.; Louis G. Milone, area director the American Economic Foundation.

Sunday, Nov. 3 — "Modern Health Insurance Program for Senior Citizens." Panelists: H. Harold Leavey, vice president and general counsel, California-Western States Life Insurance Co.; A. B. Halvorsan, vice president of Occidental Life Insurance Co. and chairman of the executive committee of Western 65 Health Insurance Assn.; F. Britton McConnell, former California insurance commissioner.

Moderator of all "Money in Motion" programs is Dr. Lloyd D. Luckmann, coordinator division of instruction, City College of San Francisco.

"Money in Motion" is sponsored by the Invest-in-America Northern California Council.

Agriculture a $12 Billion Annual Industry

California agriculture creates $12 billion annually in new wealth, according to the agriculture department of the San Francisco Chamber of Commerce.

California leads all other states in the value of farm products.

California farmers produced $3.34 billion worth in 1962—a new record, an amount greater than the value of all of the gold mined in this state since the Gold Rush in 1849.

This $3.34 billion swells into more than $12 billion as it flows through the channels of trade, commerce, and industry.

Directly or indirectly, farming in California is responsible for three out of every four jobs in the state.

Farming, alone, absorbs the services of 323,000 workers, on the average— 428,000 at peak harvest. Hired year 'round workers account for 94,300; farmers and family members, 93,800; hired temporary domestic workers, 102,500; foreign contract workers, 33,300 ('62 figures).

For every 100 employed in agriculture, another 263 are employed in such closely related industries as canning, preserving, packaging, transporting, storing, and selling.

California's fruit and vegetable canning and preserving industries pay out more than $225 million in wages to 45,000 employes annually.

Other food and kindred product processors pay approximately $675 million to over 110,000 employes each year.

BAY REGION BUSINESS
PUBLISHED BY THE
SAN FRANCISCO CHAMBER OF COMMERCE

STATEMENT OF OWNERSHIP, Management and Circulation, required by Act of October 23, 1962; Section 4369, Title 39, United States Code, of BAY REGION BUSINESS, published semi-monthly at 333 Pine Street, San Francisco, California 94104, for October 21, 1963:
1. The name of the publisher is San Francisco Chamber of Commerce, 333 Pine Street, San Francisco, California; the editor, Joseph I. Haughey, 333 Pine St., San Francisco, California; the Managing Editor, Joseph I. Haughey, 333 Pine St., San Francisco, California.
2. The owner is San Francisco Chamber of Commerce, 333 Pine Street, San Francisco, California 94104.
3. There are no known bondholders, mortgagees or other security holders owning or holding 1 per cent or more of total amount of bonds, mortgages, or other securities.
4. Circulation: (This information is required by Sections 4355a, 4355b and 4356 of Title 39, United States Code) 7,500.

BAY REGION BUSINESS

SAN FRANCISCO CHAMBER OF COMMERCE

VOLUME 20 • NUMBER 21 • NOVEMBER 15, 1963

K. C. Chamber Executive Named Successor to G. L. Fox

William E. Dauer, 38-year-old executive vice president of the Kansas City Chamber of Commerce, has been named to assume the chief executive post of the San Francisco Chamber of Commerce on January 1, it was announced by Harry A. Lee, Chamber president.

He will succeed G. L. Fox, who is retiring as executive vice president of the Chamber after more than 20 years of service with the Chamber. Fox will continue to serve as a consultant until July 1, 1964.

Dauer, a native of Lincoln, Nebraska, has been a Chamber of Commerce executive since 1950 and has headed the Kansas City Chamber since 1959. Nationally known for his achievements in Chamber administration and for an aggressive approach in community development, he was elected this year to the presidency of the American Chamber of Commerce Executives Association.

Small Business Administrator to Speak Here Monday

"Is Small Business on the Way Out?"

That's the title of an address on federal government policy relating to independent business to be given by Eugene P. Foley, Administrator, Small Business Administration, at a Chamber luncheon Monday noon (November 18) at the St. Francis Hotel.

Cooperating with the Chamber in sponsoring the event are the National Federation of Independent Business, the San Francisco regional office of the Small Business Administration, the Western Association of Small Business Companies, and the San Mateo County Development Association.

Chairman of the day will be Donald Hietter, chairman of the Chamber Small Business Section.

The speaker took office as Administrator of the Small Business Administration on August 7, 1963. His prior experiences included two years as legal counsel to the Senate Small Business Committee and the post of Deputy to the Secretary of Commerce. A Minnesotan, he took his A.B. from St. Thomas College in St. Paul and also studied at the University of Vienna. He received his LL.B. from the University of Minnesota and later was an instructor in philosophy of law at St. Mary's College, Winona, Minnesota.

Tickets, $3.75 each, can be obtained at the Chamber, 333 Pine street, EXbrook 2-4511.

Public Relations Discussion Set

A panel of experts will be asked, "Does Public Relations Pay Dividends" Sunday at 2 p.m. on the popular television public service show, "Money in Motion," over KRON-TV.

The program is arranged by the Invest-in-America Northern California Council in cooperation with the Federal Reserve Bank of San Francisco and KRON-TV (channel 4).

Moderator is Dr. Lloyd D. Luckmann, coordinator, division of instruction, City College of San Francisco.

Under Dauer's direction, membership income of the Kansas City Chamber increased by 30 per cent in four years and advertising income from the *Kansas Citian,* one of the nation's leading Chamber publications, was more than doubled.

A believer in automation for higher efficiency, Dauer installed the most modern equipment and procedures in the Chamber offices.

ACCOMPLISHMENTS

Among other accomplishments in his Kansas City post, Dauer organized a non-profit industrial foundation and in 19 days raised $1,200,-000 to finance it. He also lured the champion American Football league team from Dallas, Texas, to Kansas City.

Last year, the Chamber of Commerce of the United States awarded his organization the top Program Work award for cities of more than 500,000 population. For two consecutive years, his Chamber has been nationally recognized for the excellence of its legislative work.

Dauer's Chamber of Commerce career began when he was graduated from Nebraska Wesleyan University in 1950 and joined the Grand Island, Nebraska, Chamber of Commerce as assistant manager. In 1951, he accepted the *(Continued on page four)*

WILLIAM E. DAUER

. . . a Marine has landed

Transportation Man Of The Year Named By Delta Nu Alpha

P. Steele Labagh, a key man on the Chamber's transportation committee during the last decade, is this year's Delta Nu Alpha "Man of the Year."

Labagh, who is traffic director here for the California Packing Corp., received the honor during the recent transportation fraternity's annual convention at Denver.

He is chairman of the export-import traffic committee and a member of the executive committee of the National Industrial Traffic League, chairman of the traffic committee of the Grocery Manufacturers Association of America, and chairman of the traffic committee of the Canners League of California.

In addition, he is a founder-member of the American Society of Traffic and Transportation, a sustaining member of the Associated Traffic Clubs of America.

Record For Construction Permits

Total value of construction permits issued in San Francisco during the first 10 months of 1963 reached $169,072,964, a figure already surpassing last year's record total for 12 months, according to Thomas W. Borek, manager of the research department of the Chamber.

The 1962 12-month total value for construction permits was $156,-184,401. The 1963 10-month figure exceeds it by $12,888,563.

When compared with the 1962 10-month figure, Borek noted, the upsurge in building permit valuation is dramatically emphasized—an increase of $41,363,407, or 32.4 per cent.

The bulk of the $169,072,964 thus far this year is accounted for mainly by office buildings, Borek said. The valuation in that category is $44,945,786, while multi-unit dwellings accounted for $40,287,161.

Major boost to the upsurge in construction permit values was the Dillingham Corporation's permit for the new Wells Fargo building at Montgomery and Sutter streets—approximately $20 million.

BUSINESS BEACON

By Joe Haughey

AMERICAN BUSINESS WOMEN'S Assn. recently held its convention in Cleveland. San Francisco delegates included: Lois Gallagher (Charter chapter delegate), Mrs. Jennie Wooley (Golden Gate chapter "Woman of the Year") and Mrs. Laila Gasho (past president—Charter chapter)....

Lois Gallagher

S. F. PRESS CLUB has re-elected Rene Cazenave, president; Ed Reynolds, first vice president; J. Rufus Klawans, second vice president; Bob Nicholas, secretary, and Virgil Elliott, treasurer. A change in the club name from Press and Union League Club to the San Francisco Press Club was authorized at the annual membership meeting....

TRANS WORLD AIRLINES has commenced non-stop jet flights between San Francisco and St. Louis with 600 mph Convair 880 equipment, according to Charles C. Tillinghast, Jr., TWA president....

PURITY STORES, Inc., has returned to San Francisco after an absence of seven years, with the acquisition of four Siri's Markets accounting or total annual sales of approximately $8 million....

THREE INTIMATE CONCERTS will be presented in the Little Theatre of the San Francisco Jewish Community Center, 3200 California street, commencing with a performance by the Repertory Musicians Sunday, November 24, at 1:30 p.m. On Sunday, January 12, it will be the Aeolian Ensemble, and on Sunday, March 22, the Bach-to-Mozart Group. Among the talented musicians are such well-known artists as cellist Boris Blinder, flautist Paul Renzi and oboist Raymond Duste, to mention only a few....

THREE FULBRIGHT-HAYS lectureships in journalism for American instructors in El Salvador, Nicaragua and Spain will be awarded early in 1964, according to the committee on international exchange of persons of the Conference Board of Associated Research Councils. The teaching posts will be at the University of El Salvador, the National University of Nicaragua and the Catholic University of Navarra, Pamplona, Spain....

KITTY HAWK dinner and dance, an annual event, will be held Friday evening, December 13, at Alameda Naval Air Station, according to R. P. Bartlett, vice president of the National Aeronautics Assn., sponsor. Tickets are available from Bartlett at $6 each, Standard Oil Co. of Calif., SUtter 1-7700 (Ext. 2926)....

A NEW METHOD for participating in world fairs is now offered by Exhibit Design Associates, 1185 Bayshore boulevard—a plan which can out to determine the advantages offered by a particular show, a budget proportionate to the anticipated business and a design for an exhibit consistent with the market and the budget....

SANDY GLASER—Mission High School senior—will captain 10,000 teenage volunteers tomorrow in a drive to collect materials needed by Goodwill Industries to train and employ handicapped students during the Christmas holidays. The one-day drive, sponsored by Macy's Hi Set, involves students from both parochial and public schools. Wooden furniture is especially needed—and pickups can be arranged by calling DOuglas 2-8781....

"HOLLYWOOD PARTICIPATION and cooperation will be a permanent part of the San Francisco International Film Festival. It deserves ALL Hollywood support," Arthur Freed, MGM producers and president of the Academy of Motion Picture Arts and Sciences, has promised.

PHILIPPINE COCONUT Oil and California meat by-products are being blended into a foreign trade package that promises to bring the Port of San Francisco some 75,000 tons a year in new cargo business. Port officials disclosed the import-export arrangement in connection with a lease on a 2½-acre site in the Islais Creek terminal area granted to Baker Commodities, Inc., of Los Angeles, tallow producers and exporters.

LEO P. McDERMOTT, recently of the United States Air Force, has joined the staff of Douglas G. Hertz, Business and Financial Consultant, Monadnock Building, and will be active in public relations for the Bolema Club, Inc., and the Atherton Country Club now building in Novato.

"NOT TAKING UP SMOKING is the best way to prevent lung cancer," according to a leaflet for teenagers distributed by the American Cancer Society, San Francisco branch....

EXPLORERAMA, a series of feature-length films presented and narrated in person by world famous explorer-photographers, currently is being shown in Morrison Auditorium in Golden Gate Park on Sundays—two complete shows each day, beginning at 1:30 p.m. and 3:15 p.m.

BANK OF CALIFORNIA has purchased additional property in Portland (Ore.) just one block from the bank's present Portland office, according to Charles de Bretteville. The bank president said plans call for a multi-story banking structure....

S. F. CONSERVATORY OF MUSIC announces a series of seven concerts by Bay Area pianist Dwight Peltzer. The first of the series will take place tonight (Friday) at 8:30 at the Conservatory Auditorium, 1201 Ortega street....

NATIONAL SPORTS AND BOAT Show will be held in the Cow Palace from January 31 through February 9, 1964. Floor plans and space rates may be obtained from the show's office here, 325 Pacific avenue (DO 2-2442)....

DUNGENESS CRAB, nearly 40 tons of it (cooked), from Metlakatla, Alaska, was flown by Pan American Airways to markets in the Pacific Northwest and Hawaii during a four-month period, according to Harold Graham, Pan Am's vice president for cargo sales....

HILLER AIRCRAFT Company has received a $953,000 contract from the U. S. Army Transportation Research Command to design a giant rotor system powered by turbojet engines, it was announced by Col. N. A. Gage, Jr., commanding officer of TRECOM....

THE INSTITUTE OF INDUSTRIAL Relations of the University of California announces the appointment of Professor Lloyd Ulman as director, succeeding Professor Arthur M. Ross....

ROGER W. GRAY of the Food Research Institute, Stanford University, has been elected president of the Western Farm Economics Association....

PAINT-UP TIME *for the world's largest Burgermeister bottle recently slowed down noon-day traffic as autoists watched three workmen swing-ing high above the street at the San Francisco location of the Jos. Schlitz Brewing Co. The huge container, 18 feet tall, would hold 166,400 ounces of beer—enough to fill 13,867 regular bottles.*

FACTS ON FARMING in the state are contained in a folder just published by the California State Chamber of Commerce, titled "What California Agriculture Means to You." Single copies are available free at the State Chamber main office, 350 Bush street....

A SIX-ACRE, $1 MILLION shopping center in Livermore will be designed by the San Francisco architectural firm of Weber & Fairfax. The site is being developed by the Granada Investment Co. of San Francisco, owner of the property, to service the new community of Granada Village.

ED HART, formerly news editor of KPTV, Portland (Ore.), has been added to the news staff of KRON-TV as a newscaster....

FINANCIAL TITLE CO. directors have elected Fred Quontamatteo, executive vice president, to the board. Financial Title, headquartered in Walnut Creek, is a subsidiary of California Financial Corporation, San Francisco....

SIX DOCUMENTARIES, each an hour long, will be seen on KRON-TV. They are produced by David Wolper & Associates and co-sponsored by Citizen's Federal S&L Association (through Botsford, Constantine & Gardner, Inc., San Francisco)....

ASSIGNMENT FOUR, KRON-TV's award-winning documentary series, is the winner of the only first-place award given a West Coast station by the New York International Film Festival. The honor was for "the best local series produced by a local station" ("Skid Row")....

"THE CARETAKER," by Harold Pinter, combining farce, tragedy and menace, opens tonight (Friday) in the Marines Theater as the San Francisco Actor's Workshop's second major production of the 1963-64 season. It is scheduled for a four-week run....

THE SAN FRANCISCO PUBLIC LIBRARY distributes an average of 13,311 books a day, it was announced by Marjorie Ford, librarian in charge. A total of 3,776,867 books circulated during the last fiscal year, an increase of more than 225,000 over the previous year. Officials see a growing interest in non-fiction—history, travel and biography.....

MEL PINSLER, northern California broadcasting and newswriting specialist, has joined the news staff of KTVU, news director Al Helmso announced....

S. F. Quotes—

"Serene, indifferent of Fate,
Thou sittest at the Western Gate;
Upon thy heights so lately won
Still slant the banners of the sun."
—Bret Harte

TREES DESTROYED by vandals on Polk street have been replaced by the district's merchants as part of the Chamber's continuing program to mantle the city in greenery. With Brian Fewer of the Department of Public Works supervising the enterprise, some 37 trees were planted. Above—serving on a "Vigilance Committee" to prevent vandalism, are (l. to r., standing) Brian Fewer, Jr., Gary Gordon, Dick Peterson, John Tindell and Harry Doherty. Kneeling are Fred Arndt and Harry Eisler.

S. F. September Business Shows
An Accelerated Rate of Growth

September business activity in San Francisco topped last year's same month by 16.8 per cent — highest increase for any month this year — according to the Chamber research department.

The Chamber business index was 135.4 compared to 15.9 for the same month last year. (The index is based on 1957-59 equaling 100.)

September bank debits, rocketing to 30.4 per cent over September of last year, totalled $7,123,945,000 — compared to $5,462,761,000 for the same month last year.

Electric energy sales rose 4.7 per cent over the corresponding months. Department store sales slipped 4.7 per cent.

San Jose bank debits increased 15.5 per cent, up $55,357,000 from $485,130,000. Department store sales rose 2.1 per cent.

Employment during September in the six-county San Francisco-Oakland Metropolitan Area totalled an estimated 1,234,000, an increase of 26,000 over September of last year. Unemployed workers numbered 60,000, or 4.6 per cent of the total civilian labor force.

An estimated 310,000 persons were employed in the San Jose Metropolitan Area (Santa Clara County), up 14,300 from the same month last year. Unemployed numbered 12,800, or 4.0 per cent of the total labor force.

GILT-PLATED jackhammers roared into action to mark the official ground-breaking of the new 18-story 111 Pine Building. On hand at the site of the $7.5 million project were (l. to r.) Walter H. Shorenstein, owner-developer; David Sherwin, Metropolitan Life Insurance Co.; Edward T. Haas, owner-developer and board chairman of Haas & Haynie, general contractors; and Harry A. Lee, Chamber president. Architect is Mario Gaidano.

Business Man's Bookshelf

THE GREAT EARTHQUAKE AND FIRE, SAN FRANCISCO, 1906, by John Castillo Kennedy, William Morrow and Company, New York. Price $5.00.

For three days—from Wednesday, April 18, through Friday, April 20, 1906—the people of San Francisco were involved in a battle for survival that might be said to rival the fall of Troy or the sack of Rome. The enemy was fire—a holocaust brought on by the cataclysm of a great, if brief, earthquake.

When the last fires smoldered on Saturday, April 21, 400 people had died, four square

.OWELL S. DILLINGHAM (r.), president of he Dillingham Corporation, was welcomed to a ecent Chamber luncheon in the Sheraton-Palace lotel, where a model of the new 43-story Wells 'argo Building was unveiled. Wells Fargo president Ransom Cook (left) and Harry Lee, president of the Chamber, joined in the appraisal of he building to be the tallest in San Francisco. 'rojected completion date for the project is 966. The luncheon was attended by more than 50 business and civic leaders.

miles (520 blocks) had burned and 28,188 buildings had been destroyed. The homeless were legion—hundreds of thousands left the city, camped out in Golden Gate Park, stood in interminable bread lines, worked (sometimes under the duress of bayonet) to clean up the ruins. The loss was estimated at $500 million.

But during the epic three days, as the fire swept along a multitude of fronts, water supplies failed and the fire fighters despaired but fought on, mean and petty men often became great—and great men greater.

Mr. Kennedy's work, with its focus on the three-day agony, is certain to be THE definitive work that must stand for a long time.

THE CROOKEDEST RAILROAD IN THE WORLD, by T. G. Wurm and A. C. Graves, Howell-North Books, Berkeley, Calif. Price $3.75.

For a period of 34 years, ending in early July, 1930, Mt. Tamalpais and the Muir

Woods area were served by a little railway that twisted over 8½ miles of trackage to the mountain's summit.

With fine inns in the woods and at the summit, and gravity cars in which visitors could coast serenely from the top into Mill Valley through the splendor of redwood forest by day or on a magically moonlit night, the Mt. Tamalpais and Muir Woods Railway must have been one of the sheer delights of the world.

BUILDINGS OF THE BAY AREA, compiled by John Marshall Woodbridge and Sally Byrne Woodbridge, Grove Press, New York. Price (paperbound) $1.95.

This is an excellent guide which need not be confined to those with a special interest in architecture.

—C. F. Ayres

Water Policy Committee Takes to the Air

Members of the Chamber water policy subcommittee will fly to Los Angeles to confer with officials of the Metropolitan Water District of southern California Tuesday, November 26, in response to an MWD invitation to discuss state water problems in general.

Chamber subcommittee members will include Harry A. Lee, President of the S. F. Chamber; Carl L. Garrison, Chairman of the Chamber Agricultural Committee and 1963 State "Livestock Man of the Year"; committee Vice Chairman Wm. Hunt Conrad, public relations, Kern County Land Co.; Earl Coke,

Vice President, Bank of America; Robert T. Durbrow, Irrigation Districts Association; G. L. Fox, Chamber Executive Vice President; Oral L. Moore, Manager, Hetch Hetchy Project and Eng. Bureau; Jack T. Pickett, Editor, California Farmer; Randle P. Shields, Manager, Chamber Agricultural Department; Bert L. Smith, Vice President, Farm Credit Banks of Berkeley; and Joe Haughey, Chamber Publicity Manager.

A Convair plane will leave San Francisco at 8 a.m. for the meeting with MWD officials at 10:45 a.m.

New Chamber Chief—

(Continued from page one)

post of manager of the Lexington. Nebraska. Chamber and within one year had more than doubled membership income.

Returning to the Grand Island Chamber as manager in 1952. he spent the next four years there and. during that period. increased membership income from \$24.000 to \$42.000. established a program of meetings in which 65 per cent of the membership participated, set up a non-profit industrial organization and brought three new industries to the city.

Moving on to management of the Springfield, Missouri. Chamber in 1956. he increased membership income by five times in three years and Springfield led all cities in Missouri for those three years in acquisition of new industry. Dauer left Springfield in 1959 to head the Kansas City Chamber.

CIVIC LEADER

Dauer has been active in civic affairs. including Boy Scouts. state prison work. Boys Club. Y.M.C.A.. United Fund. and church activities.

He is a past member of the Small Business Administration's loan committee and currently serves on the U. S. Commerce Department's seven-state Export Expansion Council.

Dauer received the Junior Chamber of Commerce distinguished service award in 1956 and the Rotary International award in 1959.

He served as president of the Nebraska Chamber of Commerce Managers in 1954, was a director of the Missouri Chamber of Commerce Executives from 1957 through 1959 and was a director of the Southern Chamber of Commerce Executives during the same period. He has been a director and officer of the American Chamber of Commerce Executives for the past five years. He has also served as an instructor at the Rocky Mountain Institute and the Southwestern Institute.

During World War II, Dauer saw action in the South Pacific as a Marine with the 6th Division and was wounded in the Guam and Okinawa campaigns.

He is married and has two school age children.

Radio Programs on Tap This Weekend

SATURDAY, 8:05 p.m., KNBR, San Francisco in the Sixties, "Food Brokerage and the Bay Area Economy." Panelists: Don Auterbury, president, Associated Grocery Brokers of San Franrisco; Earl Rains, secretary, AGBSF; Clarence E. Brown, industry relations and publicity chairman, AGBSF.
SUNDAY, 9:45 p.m., KFRC, San Francisco Progress Report, 'The Santa Fe Plan to Redevelop the East Bay Mud fl ts." Panelist: Robert W. Walker, vice president, Santa Fe Railway.

New Chamber Members

C. F. Montgomery   W. M. Wyman   G. G. Cox   S. P. Cox   Prof. Kolitsch

MEMBERS NEW TO THE CHAMBER ROSTER are (l. to r. above): Claude F. Montgomery, owner-manager, *Hardware Products Co.,* 2700 18th street; W. M. Wyman. owner, *Trend Lighting, Inc.,* 712 Montgomery street; Gerald G. Cox and Stanley P. Cox, partners, *AAA Trans'Interpreters,* 391 Sutter street, and Prof. Vlado Kolitsch, *violin teacher,* 1332 25th avenue.

Salvatore DiGrande   Ray Prince   George D. Gavin Robert R. Weber Geoffrey W. Fairfax

Left to right (above) are: Salvatore DiGrande, owner and cook, *Naples Pizzeria and Italian Restaurant,* 1224 Grant avenue; Ray Prince, assistant vice president, *Consolidated Mutual Insurance Co.,* 601 California street; George D. Gavin, manager, *California Masonic Memorial Temple,* 1111 California street; Robert R. Weber, A.I.A., and Geoffrey W. Fairfax, A.I.A., partners, architectural firm of *Weber & Fairfax,* 254 Sutter street.

Chamber Calendar of Events

November 18 — **Small Business Luncheon;** *Speaker: Eugene P. Foley, Small Business Administration; St. Francis Hotel, 12 noon.*

November 18—S. F. Council of District Merchants Association, *Room 200, 8 p.m.*

November 19—**Traffic Safety & Control Sub**mittee Meeting, *Room 200, 10 a.m.*

November 19—**Jr. Chamber Board of Direc**tors, *Room 200, 12:15 p.m.*

November 19 — **Transportation Conference,** *Room 200, 12:30 p.m.*

November 20—**Retail Merchants Board of Di**rectors Meeting, *Bohemian Club, 8 a.m.*

November 20 — **Contact Club,** *John Hancock Bldg., 3rd Floor, Signature Room, 255 California St., 10:15 a.m.*

November 20—**World Trade Assn. Luncheon,** *World Trade Club, 12 noon.*

November 21 — **Board of Directors Meeting,** *Room 1, Commercial Club, 12 noon.*

November 26—**Jr. Chamber Board of Direc**tors, *Room 200, 12:15 p.m.*

November 26 — **Water Policy Subcommittee Meeting;** *Host: Los Angeles Metropolitan Water District; Los Angeles Flight, 8 a.m.*

November 27 — **World Trade Association Luncheon,** *World Trade Club, 12 noon.*

November 29—**A.I.D. Food Preservation and Canning Study Team,** *Room 200, 2 p.m.*

S. F. Quotes

"... In any part of the city, a totally unexpected and unexplored San Francisco can be discovered—just around the corner in the very next moment."

—*Herb Caen*
SF CHRONICLE

BAY REGION BUSINESS

SAN FRANCISCO CHAMBER OF COMMERCE

VOLUME 20 • NUMBER 22 • NOVEMBER 29, 1963

100 Amendments to Building Code Recommended by Chamber Board

Chamber directors have approved 100 proposed amendments to the San Francisco building code. according to G. L. Fox. executive vice president.

The board acted on recommendation of the Chamber's building code section. of which Wesley T. Hayes. of Graham & Hayes. structural engineers. is chairman.

Many of the changes have become necessary. Fox noted. because of the development of new structural materials in recent years. Such changes. in general. would be an updating of the code to bring it into closer agreement with national codes.

Sections dealing with structural timber. structural steel and reinforced concrete would be modified to coincide with latest specifications of the American Institute of Steel Construction. provisions of the American Concrete Institute's building code. the Steel Joist Institute's specifications. and the light gage steel specifications of the American Iron and Steel Institute.

The board also took cognizance of the rise of new materials in studying sections relating to fire resistive standards of finishes and the increasing use of plastics in construction.

Code changes would be revised "to regulate the life hazard from smoke emission as well as that of flame spread and to regulate the use of plastics as building material."

JOSEF KRIPS, *world-renowned Vienna-born maestro, and new permanent conductor of the San Francisco Symphony Orchestra, will make his debut here as the S. F. Symphony begins its 52nd season at 9 o'clock tonight in the War Memorial Opera House.* (See San Franciscana, page three.)

Jack Gomperts Elected President Of S. F. Area World Trade Assn.

Jack Gomperts, president of Nordisk Andelsforbund California. has been elected 1963-64 president of the San Francisco Area World Trade Association. affiliate of the Chamber, according to G. L. Fox. executive vice president of the Chamber. Gompert succeeds Lester Goodman. chairman of Getz Bros. & Co.. Inc.

"The San Francisco World Trade Association is the oldest, largest and most active international trade organization on the West Coast. boasting the second largest international world trader membership in the country," according to Fox.

Gomperts has had 44 years experience in the food processing and packaging industry. In 1935 he founded the San Francisco firm of Jack Gomperts & Company. which became one of the largest independent export distributors of dried fruits. canned fruits. canned vegetables and tree nuts in the country.

Gomperts served on the board of directors of the California Dried Fruit Export Association for 30 years.

He now serves on the board of directors of the Netherlands Chamber of Commerce in the U. S., and the Swedish Chamber of Commerce of the U. S. and is a member of the Regional Export Expansion Council in San Francisco. Earlier this year Gomperts served as a member of the U. S. Trade Mission to the Netherlands.

He was decorated in 1960 by Her Majesty Queen Juliana as an officer in the Royal Order of Oranje Nassau. and by the King of Sweden as an officer in the Royal Order of VASA. Gomperts lives in San Mateo.

SAFETY AWARD—*Three men deeply involved in the annual traffic safety check sponsored by the Chamber display the 1963 State Award for Excellence in the communities of more than 300,000 population category. Left to right above are: Clifford Luster, personnel supervisor for Pacific Telephone, who headed the annual traffic safety check which won this year's honor; G. L. Fox, executive vice president of the Chamber; and Walter Lunsford, representative of the Auto Industries Highway Safety Committee.*

Bird to Appear On TV Program

"What Can American Youth Learn from European Business."

That provocative question will be probed on the KRON-TV program. "Money in Motion." Sunday (Dec. 1) at 2 p.m.

Panelists on the show. arranged by the Invest-in-America Northern California Council in cooperation with the Federal Reserve Bank of San Francisco and Channel 4. are:

William J. Bird. western vice president. John Hancock Mutual Life Insurance Co.; Dr. John W. Cowee. dean. Graduate School of Business Administration. University of California at Berkeley. and Dr. Robert E. Dockson. dean. Graduate School of Business Administration. University of Southern California.

Moderator of the show is Dr. Lloyd D. Luckman. coordinator. division of instruction. City College of San Francisco.

Jr. World Trade Officials Named

Ronald P. Hostetter. of Mark Ross & Co.. has been elected president of the Junior World Trade Association for 1963-64.

Hostetter succeeds Peter M. Horn. of John Stanley Horn Co.

Other new officers elected by the association board are: Jan M. Berghout. General Steamship Corp.. Ltd.. vice president; David A. Cassinelli. Crocker-Citizens National Bank. secretary. and J. T. Kettlewell. Pacific Vegetable Oil Corp.. treasurer.

By Joe Haughey

OHN M. KINARD has been elected president
f the California Manufacturers Association.
:inard is president of the Riverside Cement Co.
)ther new officers: Horace M. Blinn, vice presi-
ent, Continental Can Co., vice president-North-
rn California; William H. Fellows, president,
)ld Colony Paint & Chemical Co., vice presi-
ent-Southern California; Warner W. Henry,
resident, the W. W. Henry Co., treasurer, and
.rne-t F. Blackwelder, president, Blackwelder
lanufacturing Co., secretary. Among new direc-
)rs are: Charles W. Griffin, vice president,
:&D, California Packing Corp., San Francisco;
:. R. Grunsky, vice president, personnel and
idustrial relations, Ampex Corp., Redwood
:ity; William R. Knapp, plant general manager,
'alstaff Brewing Corp., San Jose, and R. L. Mc-
:innis, plant manager, International Harvester
:o., Emeryville. . . .

:ALIFORNIA'S gross farm income figure of
pproximately $3.3 billion annually is expanded
o about $13 billion by totaling the value of
ndustries dependent on agriculture, Milton
'eague, president of the California State Chamer, told a Farm-City Week audience at Santa
!osa. . . .

VILLIAM E. WADSWORTH has been appoint-
d vice president-education of the San Francisco
leadquartered Automation Institute of America,
t was announced by Vernon D. Patterson, presi-
lent. Wadsworth joined the AIA faculty in 1956.

FORECAST '64" twelfth annual UCLA Busi-
iess Forecast Conference, will be held Decem-
ier 12 at the Statler Hilton Hotel in Los An-
eles. . . .

IcGRAW-HILL announces publication of new
ook by Joseph W. McGuire, "Business and
ociety." Book deals with interrelationships of
abor, government and business, and "explores
he history of business philosophy and econom-
cs and its effect on contemporary business and
ociety," says publisher. . . .

}ANTAS Airways announces purchase of two
nore Boeing 707 V-Jets at cost of approximately
10.5 millions. . . .

TRANS WORLD *Airlines will become the first
iir carrier to inaugurate Boeing pure jet service
vithin the country with first schedules operating
ionstop from the Bay Area to New York begin-
ting Tuesday. In front of the above TWA all-
urgo jet is a Cochran Equipment hydraulic lift
vhich can load up to 13 pallets of freight into
the cabin within an hour. The cabin holds 90,000
pounds of freight.*

"BUILDING DESIGN DATA," a quick reference handbook to help architects and engineers
take greater advantage of latest technological
advances in building design and construction,
has been published by United States Steel Corp.

SOUTHERN PACIFIC will spend $90 million
on new rail equipment in 1964, including 133
new locomotives at a cost of about $34 million,
according to Donald J. Russell, president of the
company. . . .

ARTHUR A. DAILEY, general advertising manager for Santa Fe Railway at Chicago, retires
tomorrow (Nov. 30) after more than 25 years
with the road. Under Dailey's tutelage, the popular little Indian boy, Chico, rose to a prominent
point in Santa Fe's advertising campaign and
has become a well-known corporate image. . . .

SPECIAL SHORT SERIES are being offered by
the San Francisco Symphony Association to Bay
Area music patrons who are unable to purchase
tickets for the complete season. Each of the
four 5-concert series provides a representative
cross-section of the 18 regular programs to
be presented by the San Francisco Symphony
Orchestra. . . .

DAVID AND IGOR Oistrakh, famous Russian
father and son violinists, will appear in joint
concert with symphony orchestra at the War
Memorial Opera House Thursday evening, January 9. Mail orders are available from Sherman
and Clay, 141 Kearny street. . . .

MOSCOW CHAMBER Orchestra will be heard
as the next attraction in the California Music
Foundation's season series at Masonic Auditorium on Saturday evening, December 7. Tickets
available at Sherman and Clay. . . .

BALLET CELESTE will present five 2:30 matinees on Dec. 8-14-15-21-22, and two special evening performances Dec. 14 and 21 at the Harding
Theatre, Divisadero at Hayes. The ballet will be
"the authentic and complete version" of Tchai-
kovsky's "Nutcracker."

JACK R. WAGNER, program manager for
KNBR-NBC, has been appointed to serve on the
Governor's Advisory Committee on Emergency
Communications by Governor Edmund G.
Brown. . . .

FRED DREXLER, senior vice president of Industrial Indemnity Insurance Co. of San Francisco, is one of seven prominent Californians
named by Governor Brown to the Workmen's
Compensation Study Commission established by
the Legislature in its last session. Also appointed
were Charles P. Scully, attorney, and Wendell J.
Phillips, union official. . . .

OAKLAND-BORN Nathan Oliveira is currently
exhibiting 66 oils, drawings, prints, gouaches
and watercolors at the San Francisco Museum of
Art, McAllister at Van Ness. The exhibition will
continue through December 8. . . .

SALES AND EARNINGS of Lucky Stores, Inc.,
during the nine-month period ended September
29, improved over the comparable period in
1962. Sales — $188,221,054 — represented a 10.9
per cent increase. Earnings, after taxes—$2,015,-
066 (90 cents a share)—were up by 18.8 per cent.

HERBERT G. DRAKE, business development
manager of N. W. Ayer & Son, Inc., has been
elected to the board of directors of the San Francisco Advertising Club, filling the vacancy created by transfer of Joseph Cross to Compton Advertising in New York. . . .

"STREETS IN UNIFORM" will trace the history of those streets in San Francisco named for
the military on "Bay Area '63" Sunday (Dec. 1)
1:30 to 2 p.m. On KPIX, Channel 5. . . .

NBC-TV's *(Channel 4)* Perry Como *Kraft Music
Hall, which originated live from the War Memo-
rial Opera House Nov. 21, was lauded by the
Chamber for bringing a new honor to the city.
Chamber president Harry A. Lee personally con-
ferred on the show's star, singer Perry Como, an
Ambassador Extraordinary card.*

"1963 OFFICE SALARIES: 17th Survey Sum-
mary Guide to Salary Rates"—compiled by the
National Salary Survey Committee of the National Office Management Association—has been
published and is being distributed by the Mc-
Graw-Hill Book Company. The publisher announces this is the first time an edition of the
surveys is being made widely available to the
general public. . . .

NATIONAL AIRLINES reports it has boosted
its advertising budget to $4½ million, a $1 million increase over last year's budget for advertising and promotion. . . .

'THE COMMITTEE'—a group of young political and social satirists—will headline the San
Francisco Advertising Club's annual Christmas
party Wednesday (Dec. 4) in the Grand Ballroom of the Sheraton-Palace Hotel. . . .

FAVORITE CHILDREN'S CLASSICS compose
a special series of 90-minute films on KRON-TV.
The next in the series, sponsored by Macy's of
California, will be the Laurel and Hardy opus,
"Chumps at Oxford," tomorrow (Saturday) at
3:30 p.m. on Channel 4. On December 7, it will
be the cartoon, "Hoppity Goes to Town" and on
December 14 Robert Louis Stevenson's "Kid-
napped." . . .

A WEEK OF NEW AMERICAN CINEMA i-
being offered at the Richelieu Theatre, 1075
Geary boulevard, December 2-7 inclusive. The
exhibition of short, 16mm works, a joint venture
of Canyon Cinema and the American Frontier
Theatre, represents the first programming of
films by the new generation of independent
American film artists. . . .

WILLIAM W. SULLIVAN, a native of San
Francisco and a graduate of the University of
Santa Clara, has been named manager of the
new San Bruno office of the Bank of California.

AMERICAN CANCER SOCIETY'S S. F. Branch
raised a total of $237,067.50 during the 1963
Cancer Crusade, according to the branch president, J. W. Mailliard III, who noted this was a
9 per cent increase over last year. O. Cort Majors
headed the drive. . . .

Early San Francisco's Crime of Passion Adds Up to Fascinating Book

WHO KILLED MR. CRITTENDEN? by Kenneth Lamott, David McKay Co., Inc., New York, N. Y. Price $4.95.

One of the most remarkable trials ever held in San Francisco unfolds in this book—the first time the trial of Laura D. Fair has ever been fully reported. The scandalous carryings-on between Laura Fair and the respectable lawyer-politician, A. P. Crittenden, provided gossip for years to come in and around San Francisco, because the affair involved many of the most prominent personages of the period. Although dealing essentially with a crime of passion, the book contains many interesting historical facts about the days of the Comstock Lode and the roaring West of the 1860s and '70s.

Kenneth Lamott is the author of several books, also has written for the *Yale Review*, the *New Yorker*, *Show*, *Harper's*, *Contact*, and *Newsweek.—Yvonne Heatley*

OUR NATIONAL PARKS: YOSEMITE, SEQUOIA, KINGS CANYON, HAWAII, by Frances Wood, Follett Publishing Company, Chicago. Price $1.95.

A simply written yet comprehensive guide to California's and Hawaii's unusual National Parks, generously supplemented by full-color illustrations. An excellent armchair tour, reference or guide book, and souvenir of the Parks' unique natural assets—sequoias, desert life, volcanoes, and rugged Sierra scenery. Mentions accommodations, trails and off the beat attractions sometimes neglected by the peregrinating Californian—*Laura Laird*

Calendar

December 3—Landscape & Treeplanting Section, *Room 200, 10:30 a.m.*

December 3—Jr. Chamber Board of Directors, *Room 200, 12:15 p.m.*

December 4—Contact Club, *Signature Room, 3rd floor, John Hancock Bldg., 255 California st., 10:15 a.m.*

December 4—Street, Highway & Bridge Section, *Room 200, 10:30 a.m.*

December 4—World Trade Assn. Luncheon, *World Trade Club, 12 noon.*

December 5 — Board of Directors, *Room 1, Commercial Club, 12 noon.*

December 9—Action Course in Practical Politics, *Room 200, 3:30 p.m.*

December 10—Membership Orientation Meeting, *3rd floor, John Hancock Bldg., 255 California st., 10:45 a.m.*

December 10—Agricultural Committee, *Garden Room, Fairmont Hotel, 12 noon.*

December 10—Jr. Chamber Board of Directors, *Room 200, 12:15 p.m.*

December 11—World Trade Assn. Luncheon, *World Trade Club, 12 noon.*

December 12—Executive Committee, *Room 200, 11 a.m.*

December 12—Aviation Section, *Torino's, 12 noon.*

The San Francisco Symphony

FRENCH BAROQUE . . . S.F.'s home of opera and symphony . . .

The San Francisco Symphony Orchestra has a tradition which closely parallels the colorful history of the city.

And with the advent of Josef Krips, great Viennese interpreter of Mozart and Beethoven, in the Symphony's 52nd season (1963-64), the orchestra enters upon a new era of growth and musical maturity. The excitement of a new concert season has always been a part of San Francisco's dynamic uniqueness.

Indeed, music in San Francisco has come a long way since a woman violinist in the Gold Rush days "taxed strength and muscle by alternating musical offerings with gymnastic skills" in the city's El Dorado gambling saloon on the Barbary Coast.

The first concert performed in San Francisco, in 1850, was described as "an exquisite execution of the classics on a trombone by Signor Lobero." A Hungarian violinist, Miska Hauser, led the city's first chamber music group, described by him as "a mental quadrologue of equally attuned souls." (The viola player later succumbed to an attack of indigestion.)

The orchestra today comprises more than 100 musicians. Its members form the core of musicians for the ballet, the opera, and various other orchestral groups—cultural legatees of a musical tradition as proud as the city itself.

Although the present musical organization was founded in 1911, the orchestra's roots antedate this by more than half a century. San Francisco's world of symphonic music was spawned in the opulent, turbulent period of the Gold Rush.

After gold was discovered at Coloma, Rudolph Herold organized the city's first known "symphonic group" in 1854, which continued to give concerts for more than 25 years. Herold, a pianist and conductor, led an orchestra of 60 pieces in the first of his concerts in 1865. He was followed by such distinguished conductors as Louis Homeier, Gustav Hinrichs and Fritz Scheel. (The latter, highly esteemed by Brahms, Tschaikovsky, and Von Bulow, founded the Philadelphia Symphony Orchestra.)

The first major orchestra to allow women to perform, the San Francisco Symphony Orchestra also has fostered such prodigies as Yehudi Menuhin, Ruth Slenzynska, Ruggiero Ricci, Patricia Benkman and Grisha Goluboff.

In the '50's and '60's singers Eliza Bisccianti, Catherine Hayes and Madam Anna Bishop gave San Francisco its first reputation as an opera-loving community. .The famed Tivoli Opera House, beginning in 1879, had operatic performances every day in the year without a break for 26 straight years (a record in the history of the American theatre). The great Luisa Tetrazzini was discovered by the colorful manager of the Tivoli, William H. (Doc) Leahy.

Reprints available at the Chamber Research Dept., 333 Pine Street

World Traders to Hold Christmas Party

"Christmas . . . San Francisco Style" will be observed by the San Francisco Area World Trade Association Wednesday, December 11, in the Champagne Room of the Mark Hopkins Hotel.

There will be a variety of events during the luncheon, including a parade of international styles, music, songs and dance—"and a sleighful of surprise packages."

Reservations may be made by telephoning EX 2-4511 (Ext. 42). Tickets are $5.75 per person, or $55 per table of 10.

New Chamber Members

A. H. Dunham   W. P. Fuller III   Angelo Sangiacomo   S. A. Mannis

NEW TO THE CHAMBER ROSTER are (l. to r. above): William
t, *Olsten's of San Francisco, Inc. (temporary personnel)*, 703 Market
I. Dunham, district manager, *Dale Carnegie Courses*, Suite 907, Sheraton-
V. Parmer Fuller III, director-western glass sales, *Pittsburgh Plate Glass*
mery Street; Angelo Sangiacomo, *Builder*, 320 Sixth Avenue, and Samuel
by Mannis, 185 Post Streete.

Helped
s of
. Exhibit

n of Chamber officers and
and National Livestock Ex-
/ Palace added up to a sig-
on to the show's overall

ı was presented the "Cali-
fan of the Year" award by
t Harry A. Lee — both
boy regalia — during the
nance.
champion steer was pur-
ır director B. M. Eubanks,
grand champion hog was
Ellis Brooks.
epresented on the Chamber
ght or donated toward the
National animals.

Weekend
ograms

radio shows this weekend
stography and international
oadcasts follow:
. 30), 8:05 p.m., "San Francisco in
anning and Planting for the Future."
ahry, manager, publicity department,
ewer, chairman, Chamber landscape
(also supervisor of street tree plant-
of Public Works), and Bill Graves,
events, Chamber landscape and tree

1), 9 p.m., "Conference Call" panel
ı promotion of the city. Panelists:
Harleen Studios, S. F.). president of
aphers of California, Inc.; Edwin
nrison office of United Press Interna-
ird Russell, assistant sales manager,
ı Suppliers, San Francisco.
), 9:45 p.m., "San Francisco Progress
iert F. Ernicke, economic counsel to
Washington, discussing international

e shows is Chamber executive vice

DISTINGUISHED VISITOR — *Braj Kumar
Nehru, India's Ambassador to the United States,
was featured speaker this month at a luncheon
sponsored by the Chamber and the San Francisco Area World Trade Association. He discussed
"American Enterprise in India's Future." Shown
during a post-luncheon chat are (l. to r.): William A. Muriale, vice president-international
division, Bank of America; Nehru, and James P.
Wilson, secretary of the WT Assn.*

Foley Report: Growth Of Small Business's Healthy, Promising

The growth of small business ivestment
corporations providing venture «pital for
burgeoning industry — and, often, he management know-how — has been cotinuously
encouraging, according to Eugene ʾ. Foley,
federal administrator of the SmallBusiness
Administration.

And California, with its develoment of
many new enterprises involving nw mate.
rials, techniques and products, haseen the
licensing of more SBIC's than any ther state
in the Union, Foley noted.

Foley addressed a meeting co-spoisored by
the San Francisco Chamber of Commrce, the
National Federation of Independent 3usiness,
the SBA San Francisco Regional Ofce, the
Western Association of Small Busins Com.
panies, the San Mateo DevelopmentAssocia-
tion and the President's Executive Advisory
Board.

Since passage of the SBA bill in)58 and
licensing of the first SBIC in 1959, he program has seen the growth of 678 SB'ʾs providing $475 million in venture captal for
8,500 small business enterprises, Fley reported.

And even during the "past 18 moths—a
period of market depression, economi uncer-
tainties and abundant adverse critism of
(the program), 122 new licensees cate into
the program, bringing more than $43million
in private capital with them," Foley id.

Foley was introduced by Emmett t Solomon, president and chief executive ocer of
Crocker-Citizens National Bank, whoserved
as chairman of the day.

$21 Billion in Assets Aggregatea By Banks Headquartered Here

The 10 banks headquartered in San Francisco had aggregate total assets of $21,216,-
557,013 as of September 30, according to statistics available at the research department of
the San Francisco Chamber of Commerce, 333
Pine street.

Bank of America, largest banking institution in the world, had assets on June 30 of
$13,687,402,920, it was noted by Thomas W.
Borek, manager of the Chamber's research
department.

Here's the September 30 breakdown on the

other nine: Wells Fargo ($3,489,95296),
Crocker Anglo (now Crocker Citizis —
$2,467,325,235), Bank of California $960,-
147,436), Hibernia ($251,721,477), acific
National ($229,536,625), San Francis‹ Na-
tional ($50,814,409), Golden Gate Nional
($39,107,440), Bank of Canton ($31,59895)
and Bank of Trade ($8,949,280).

The 10 banks maintained 114 offices ; San
Francisco, 1,190 in all counties of thestate
(Bank of California total—32—also in udes
branches in Oregon and Washington).

BAY REGION  BUSINESS

SAN FRANCISCO CHAMBER OF COMMERCE

VOLUME 20 • NUMBER 23 • DECEMBER 13, 1963

The Changing of The Guard - - - 1964 Officials Elected

HARRY A. LEE   WILLIAM J. BIRD   WILLIAM A. DAUER   G. L. FOX

(See stories on page three of this edition)

PRESIDENTIAL MESSAGE

Cit's Problems 'Fewest, But Greatest"

by William J. Bird
Western Vice President
John Hancock Mutual Life Insurance Company

Action of 1e San Francisco Chamber of Commerce in 1964 will be to concentrate spcial emphasis upon major economic problems obstructing the city's growth wile at the same time continuing its interest and committee activity in the)roader areas of community development.

Never befre have a few problems so shaped a city's destiny as those now facing the grwth of San Francisco. Nor have such problems presented a citizenry more hallenging opportunities.

The tange:d freeways of the Bay Area and snarled traffic conditions in downtown an Francisco are challenges that must bring about a network of freeways an public transportation which should become the envy of cities throughout th nation.

The exchnge of blighted areas for new residential and business construction)uld not only increase tax revenues but would create better housing and wrking conditions for our citizens. Leadership in this effort to improve our tandard of living would stand as a goal for civic leaders everywhet.

The righ of humans as expressed in better working relationships between the nny races that make up the citizenry of San Francisco and more leadership on he part of business in creating equal rights between these races is a challenge or justice and equality.

Turning iese impossible tasks into genuine accomplishments will be the aim of the Sa Francisco Chamber in 1964. It will call upon the cooperation of public offials—whose interests are the same; upon businessmen large and small—whose uture hinges upon the results; and upon the greater numbers of employed itizens—whose very existence depends upon our success.

To accelrate our efforts, the Chamber must look within and be sure that it is up) date in its financial support, its program; and its manpower ·1ganization.

Our abity to achieve results will be determined by the degree of cooperation nd support given by the entire business community, the political leadrs of the city, and labor interests.

... Bill Bird (left) and Bill Dauer

Freeway Safety Record Lends Strong Support To New Construction

A strong point supporting the construction of more freeways is their safety record, according to J. P. sinclair, assistant state highway engineer.

sinclair provided an example in San Francisco to bear out his statement—a comparison between the 1962 traffic experience on the Embarcadero Freeway and on Park-Presidio Boulevard.

During that year, the freeway carried 31,500 vehicles per day on the average, Sinclair said, yet its accident total for the year was only 11—nine property damage and two injury—and there were no fatalities.

In contrast, Park-Presidio carried 34,000 vehicles per day on the average and there were 110 accidents (10 times those of the freeway), 62 property damage mishaps (seven times those of the freeway) and 48 injury accidents (24 times the freeway) accounting for 74 persons injured (37 times). There were no fatalities.

CALENDAR

December 18—CONTACT CLUB, Signature Room, 3rd floor, John Hancock Bldg., 255 California. 10:15 a.m.
December 18—WORLD TRADE ASSOCIATION LUNCHEON, World Trade Club, 12 noon.
December 18—TRANSPORTATION CONFERENCE, Room 200, Chamber building, 12:30 p.m.

Chamber Helped In Success of Livestock Exhibit

The participation of Chamber officers and
directors in the Grand National Livestock Exposition at the Cow Palace added up to a significant contribution to the show's overall
success.

Carl L. Garrison was presented the "California Livestock Man of the Year" award by
Chamber president Harry A. Lee — both
decked out in cowboy regalia — during the
October 26 performance.

The 1963 grand champion steer was purchased by Chamber director B. M. Eubanks,
and the reserve grand champion hog was
bought by director Ellis Brooks.

Ten companies represented on the Chamber
Board either bought or donated toward the
purchase of Grand National animals.

Chamber Weekend Radio Programs

S. F. Chamber radio shows this weekend
feature flowers, photography and international
trade. Times of broadcasts follow:

KNBR, Saturday (Nov. 30), 8:05 p.m., "San Francisco in
the Sixties" panel on "Planning and Planting for the Future."
Panelists: Joseph I. Baughey, manager, publicity department,
S. F. Chamber; Brian Fewer, chairman, Chamber landscape
and tree planting section (also supervisor of street tree planting division, S. F. Dep't of Public Works), and Bill Graves,
chairman-promotion and events, Chamber landscape and tree
planting section.
KFRC, Sunday (Dec. 1), 9 p.m., "Conference Call" panel
on photography's role in promotion of the city. Panelists:
Carl Harleen (Dickey & Harlern Studios, S. F.), president of
the Professional Photographers of California, Inc.; Edwin
Hoffman, of the San Francisco office of United Press International Photos, and Richard Russell, assistant sales manager,
Brooks Camera and Photo Supplies, San Francisco.
KPRC, Sunday (Dec. 1), 9:45 p.m., "San Francisco Progress
Report" presents Dr. Albert F. Eenicke, economic counsel to
the German Embassy at Washington, discussing international
trade opportunities.
Moderator of all three shows is Chamber executive vice-
president G. L. Fox.

DISTINGUISHED VISITOR — *Braj Kumar
Nehru, India's Ambassador to the United States,
was featured speaker this month at a luncheon
sponsored by the Chamber and the San Francisco Area World Trade Association. He discussed
"American Enterprise in India's Future." Shown
during a post-luncheon chat are (l. to r.): William A. Muriale, vice president-international
division, Bank of America; Nehru, and James P.
Wilson, secretary of the WT Assn.*

$21 Billion in Ass By Banks Headqu

The 10 banks headquartered in San Francisco had aggregate total assets of $21,216,-
557,013 as of September 30, according to statistics available at the research department of
the San Francisco Chamber of Commerce, 333
Pine street.

Bank of America, largest banking institution in the world, had assets on June 30 of
$13,687,402,920, it was noted by Thomas W.
Borek, manager of the Chamber's research
department.

Here's the September 30 breakdown on the

BAY REGION

SAN FRANCISCO CHAMBER OF COMMERCE

BUSINESS

VOLUME 20 • NUMBER 23 • DECEMBER 13, 1963

The Changing of The Guard - - - 1964 Officials Elected

HARRY A. LEE   WILLIAM J. BIRD   WILLIAM A. DAUER   G. L. FOX

(See stories on page three of this edition)

PRESIDENTIAL MESSAGE
City's Problems 'Fewest, But Greatest'

by William J. Bird
Western Vice President
John Hancock Mutual Life Insurance Company

Action of the San Francisco Chamber of Commerce in 1964 will be to concentrate special emphasis upon major economic problems obstructing the city's growth while at the same time continuing its interest and committee activity in the broader areas of community development.

Never before have a few problems so shaped a city's destiny as those now facing the growth of San Francisco. Nor have such problems presented a citizenry more challenging opportunities.

The tangled freeways of the Bay Area and snarled traffic conditions in downtown San Francisco are challenges that must bring about a network of freeways and public transportation which should become the envy of cities throughout the nation.

The exchange of blighted areas for new residential and business construction would not only increase tax revenues but would create better using and working conditions for our citizens. Leadership in this effort to improve our standard of living would stand as a goal for civic leaders everywhere.

The rights of humans as expressed in better working relationships between the many races that make up the citizenry of San Francisco and more leadership on the part of business in creating equal rights between these races challenge for justice and equality.

Turning these impossible tasks into genuine accomplishments will be the job of the San Francisco Chamber in 1964. It will call upon the cooperation of public officials—whose interests are the same; upon businessmen large and small—whose future hinges upon the results; and upon the greater numbers of employed citizens—whose very existence depends upon our success.

To accelerate our efforts, the Chamber must look within and be sure it is up to date in its financial support, its program; and its manpower utilization.

Our ability to achieve results will be determined by the degree of cooperation and support given by the entire business community, the several leaders of the city, and labor interests.

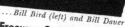

. . . Bill Bird (left) and Bill Dauer

Freeway Safety Record Lends Strong Support To New Construction

A strong point supporting the construction of more freeways is their safety record, according to J. P. Sinclair, assistant state highway engineer.

Sinclair provided an example in San Francisco to bear out his statement—a comparison between the 1962 traffic experience on the Embarcadero Freeway and on Park-Presidio Boulevard.

During that year, the freeway carried 31,500 vehicles per day on the average, Sinclair said, yet its accident total for the year was only 11—nine property damage and two injury—and there were no fatalities.

In contrast, Park-Presidio carried 31,000 vehicles per day on the average and there were 110 accidents (10 times those of the freeway), 62 property damage mishaps (seven times those of the freeway) and 48 injury accidents (24 times the freeway) accounting for 71 persons injured (37 times). There were no fatalities.

CALENDAR

December 18—CONTACT CLUB, Signature Room, 3rd floor, John Hancock Bldg., 255 California, 10:15 a.m.

December 18—WORLD TRADE ASSOCIATION LUNCHEON, World Trade Club, 12 noon.

December 18—TRANSPORTATION CONFERENCE, Room 200, Chamber building, 12:30 p.m.

By Joe Haughey

BAY AREA FOOD BROKER *leaders gathered at KNBR-NBC radio, 420 Taylor street, to participate in the taping of a recent Chamber discussion show, "San Francisco in the Sixties." Left to right are: Earl Rains, secretary of the Associated Grocery Brokers of San Francisco; Clarence E. Brown, industry relations and publicity chairman of the association; Delwin Ensminger, merchandising manager of KNBR-NBC sending; G. L. Fox, executive vice president of the Chamber and moderator of "San Francisco in the Sixties," and Don Atterbury, president of the grocery brokers group.*

Here's Your Line-up of Luminaries for New Year

Dwyer   Sutherland   Eskildsen   Bird   Loberg   Weir   Ellis   Wilkinson

13 New Directors Elected
To Fill Out 31-Man Board

Thirteen new directors have been named to fill the board of the Chamber Elected in November to run the Chamber next year.

The nominees for directors are:

Eskildsen

Dwyer

Sutherland

Bird Jr.

Ellis

Loberg   Pindorf   Lawrence

BUSINESS BEACON

By Joe Haughey

OHN W. MAILLIARD III, president of Mailliard and Schmiedell, San Francisco, has been elected national chairman of the National Food Brokers Association.

Mailliard served as president of the s. F. Chamber in 1953. Mailliard has served in San Francisco as chairman of the March of Dimes, commissioner of the Redevelopment Agency, and director of Bay Area Educational Television. For many years, he has served as director of the California Academy of Sciences, American Cancer society (s. F. chapter), Wells Fargo Bank, and Pacific Mutual Life Insurance company. . . .

HIGH SCHOOL JOURNALISM awards in a contest sponsored by the San Francisco International Airport Junior Chamber of Commerce went to Linda johnson, editor of the sequoia (Redwood City) High school Times (first), and Bill Galstan, editor of the Oceana (Pacifica) High School Breakers (second). . . .

DON SHERWOOD, "the world's greatest disc jockey," is back with his cronies—Herb Kennedy and Wally King—at KSFO. Between them, the three account for 73 years of broadcasting—Kennedy 30, King 22, and sherwood 21. . . .

CALIFORNIA COUNCIL Table, KSFO discussion show moderated by stuart R. Ward, asks the question, "should Our Immigration Laws be Changed?" sunday (Dec. 15) at 8:05 p.m. Panelists include: J. C. Russell, long-time student of immigration; s. M. saroyan, engaged in refugee resettlement activities since 1946, and Eugene L. Rendler, attorney and student of immigration matters. . . .

JOSEPH M. ANELLI has been named the San Francisco Recreation and Park Department "Gardener of the Month" for November. Anelli, who joined the department in june, 1959, received a $25 U.S. savings Bond from the Levi Strauss Trust Fund and a certificate for a pair of Levi jeans. For 21 years prior to joining the department, Anelli operated his own nursery. He is in charge of the Strybing Arboretum Rock Garden. . . .

ERNEST BORN, former professor of architecture at U.C. has been retained to develop conceptual designs for the new rapid transit subway stations to be built in San Francisco, Oakland and Berkeley. Born was designer of the 1959 Embarcadero development plan for the S. F. Port Authority. . . .

SKYWAY EXPRESS—*New American Airlines Astrojet freighters took to the skies this month to provide new speed, greater capacity for the nation's airfreight shippers in time for the upcoming holiday rush. San Francisco is among the cities served. The cargo jets carry 45 tons.*

A 10-POINT PROGRAM for California business has been outlined by Milton M. Teague, president of the California state Chamber. The objectives: "an economical and equitable tax structure; reasonable industrial insurance programs; equitable labor-management relations; practicable, low-cost water development and distribution; maintenance of profitable agricultural production; transportation, recreation and national resources development; exploitation of California's excellence in research and development; inducement of industrial expansion and new industries in the state; expansion of markets locally and abroad, and mobilization of all California business to get together, plan together and act together." . . .

BERTOLT BRECHT's "The Caucasian Chalk Circle" is the next (third) major production of the Actor's Workshop, opening tonight (Friday) in Marines' Theater, staged by Carl Weber, a former director in Brecht's renowned Berliner Ensemble, the epic adaption of an oriental fable will be performed on a revolving stage, complete with masks, music and some 100 roles. . . .

MANAGEMENT CONsULTANTS Cresap, McCormick and Paget have moved to enlarged offices in the American International Building, 206 Sansome street (SUtter 1-8421). . . .

NEW OFFICERs of Mission street Merchants are: Frank J. Goni, branch manager of Bay View Federal savings and Loan Association, president; Richard Bon Omi, of Bon Omi stores, Jack Fanburg, owner of Ann Lee Apparel and Fanburg's, and John Cockerham, manager of Grayson's Mission store, vice presidents; Philip Hunter, controller, Redlick's, treasurer, and Anthony Mannina, CPA, secretary. . . .

FIVE HUNDRED California leaders in industry, science, government and education will meet in sacramento January 27-28 to launch a sweeping attack on problems confronting the state in the next two decades, according to University of California Extension. The meeting will take place at sacramento's Hotel El Rancho. . . .

PROF. VLADO KOLITSCH, director of Professional Violin studios here, is booked for a series of concerts in the western states and will next be heard in San Francisco in early spring. . . .

GRACE BUMBRY, mezzo soprano and the famed "Black Venus" of Beyreuth a couple of seasons ago, will dedicate an aria to the late President John F. Kennedy at her 3 p.m. concert in the Curran Theater sunday (Dec. 15)—"O tion fatale" from Verdi's Don Carlo, a favorite of the President. . . .

AMONG MEMBERs of Governor Edmund G. Brown's new Coordinating Council on Urban Policy are Roy sorenson, general secretary of the San Francisco YMCA, and Edward P. Eichler, president of Eichler Homes, Inc. . . .

TWO MEMBERs of the advisory board of San Francisco state College have been announced by president Paul Dodd. They are: joseph F. Edelstein, of York & Co., members of the Pacific Coast stock Exchange, and Norman N. Fromm, administrative executive of Fromm & sichel, Inc. . . .

CABOT, CABOT & Forbes, nationally-known real estate developers, have announced the appointment of Bradley W. stark as assistant to Paul P. shepherd, manager of the San Francisco office. CC&F recently disclosed plans for a 600-acre San Francisco Bay Industrial Park on land in South San Francisco. . . .

JOHN W. PETTIT, an ambassador extraordinary of the Chamber and vice president emeritus of the Yellow Cab Co., recently was officially complimented and commended by the S. F. Board of Supervisors "for the excellence of your representation of our city during your recent travels throughout Latin America. Supervisor (Peter) Tamaras recalled to his colleagues the tremendous scope of your itinerary and the fact that wherever you stayed you brought the name of San Francisco to friendly notice." . . .

BAY AREA FOOD BROKER *leaders gathered at KNBR-NBC radio, 420 Taylor street, to participate in the taping of a recent Chamber discussion show, "San Francisco in the Sixties." Left to right are: Earl Rains, secretary of the Associated Grocery Brokers of San Francisco; Clarence E. Brown, industry relations and publicity chairman of the association; Delwin Enzminger, merchandising manager of KNBR-NBC (standing); G. L. Fox, executive vice president of the Chamber and moderator of "San Francisco in the Sixties," and Don Atterbury, president of the grocery brokers group.*

SAN FRANCISCO'S GLAMOR came in for a good share of nationwide publicity in a recent edition of Holiday Inn magazine. The national publication, claiming a circulation of more than 300,000, features San Francisco and offers the motor hotel chain's new $3 million Holiday Inn in South San Francisco as the ideal resting-place or meeting location for tourists or businessmen visiting the city. The story of "San Francisco—Colorful Crossroads of the World" (and of the south city Holiday Inn) is spotlighted with a full-color cover picture of the Golden Gate. . . .

TRANSPORTATION accounts for one-sixth of our gross national product, yet remains one of the least researched fields in all American industry, according to Under Secretary of Commerce Clarence D. Martin. He predicted a completely computerized system will be developed for handling freight billing, during a recent talk at Stanford University. . . .

H. LIEBES, LEADER in women's fashions in the West for 99 years, announces it will finish its 100th year in business with a new store in Marin County. The firm signed a lease for a 15,000-square-foot branch in the Northgate Regional Shopping Center (San Rafael), a project of the Draper Companies. . . .

STATE CHAMBER General Manager Clark Galloway reported its opposition to creation of civilian police review boards which, he said, "would undermine police morale and hamper effective police work by placing an outside authority in judgment over police actions". . . .

WILLIAM E. ROBERTS, president and chief executive officer of Ampex Corporation, has been elected to the board of directors of Wells Fargo Bank. . . .

POLAND'S "HOW TO BE LOVED" won this year's San Francisco International Film Festival Golden Gate Award as best out of 22 entries from 17 countries. . . .

Here's Your Line-up of Luminaries for New Year

| *Dauer* | *Sutherland* | *Eubanks* | *Bird* | *Hazelrig* | *Desky* | *Hull* | *Miss Hogan* |

13 New Directors Elected To Fill Out 31-Man Board

Thirteen new directors have been elected to the 1964 board of the Chamber. Eighteen incumbents fill out the 31-man board.

The thirteen new directors are:

Joseph K. Allen, vice president, Utah Construction & Mining Company; Charles A. Anderson, financial vice president, Kern County Land Company; Robert M. Desky, deputy city attorney; F. Marion Donahoe, president, Citizens Federal Savings and Loan Association.

Dwight H. Hart, Jr., general manager, Clift Hotel; Wesley J. Huss, partner, Lybrand, Ross Bros. & Montgomery; F. E. Kriebel, assistant to vice president-systems freight traffic, Southern Pacific Company; Philip G. Lasky, West Coast area vice president, KPIX-TV.

James P. Mitchell, vice president-public relations, Crown Zellerbach Corporation; Thomas K. Procter, vice president, Coldwell Banker & Company; Kenneth R. Rearwin, vice president, Merrill Lynch, Pierce, Fenner & Smith, Inc.; Sherner L. Sibley, vice president and general manager, Pacific Gas & Electric Company; and Teller Weinman, general merchandise manager, The Emporium.

Re-elected directors:

Ross Barrett, president, Foster and Kleiser; William J. Bird, western vice president, John Hancock Mutual Life Insurance Company; G. C. Briggs, general sales manager-retail, Standard Oil Company of California, Western Operations, Inc.; Ellis Brooks, president, Ellis Brooks Chevrolet; G. E. Coon, regional vice president, San Francisco, American Airlines, Inc.; J. R. Dant, president, States Steamship Company.

Preston G. Drew, manager, San Francisco division, Shell Oil Company; B. M.

Allen

Anderson

Donahoe

Huss

Desky

Hart, Jr.

Kriebel

William J. Bird Succeeds Harry Lee As Chamber President

William J. Bird, western vice president, John Hancock Mutual Life Insurance Company and 1963 vice president of the Chamber, has been elected president of the 113-year-old organization — oldest chamber of commerce in the West — according to G. L. Fox, executive vice president.

G. L. Fox

Bird's election by the 31-man Chamber board of directors, was announced at a breakfast meeting of the Chamber's 1963 and 1964 boards in the Garden Room of the Fairmont Hotel.

Bird, former executive vice president of the Greater Boston Chamber of Commerce and former manager of external affairs of the Chamber of Commerce of the United States, succeeds Harry A. Lee, vice president of J. Walter Thompson Company, 1962-63 president of the Chamber.

Succeeding Fox as executive vice president is William E. Dauer, 38-year old executive vice president of the Kansas City Chamber of Commerce who will assume his new post January 1. Fox, who has served the Chamber for more than 20 years, will act as a consultant until July 1, 1964, date of his retirement.

Three Chamber vice presidents were elected: D. Clair Sutherland, senior vice president, loan administration, Bank of America N.T. & S.A.; B. M. Eubanks,

Lasky

Mitchell

Procter

Rearwin

Sibley

Weinman

Directors—

(Continued from page 3)

..ubanks, partner, Stewart, Eubanks, Meyerson & Company ﹍. P. Garling, Jr., ice president, Macy's California; H. P. ;ough, regional vice president, General Meyerson & Company; J. P. Garling, Jr., ublisher, *San Francisco Examiner* and *an Francisco News-Call Bulletin;* Richard C. Ham, attorney; Paul E. Hazelrig, president, Kilpatrick's Bakeries, Inc.

I. W. Hellman, chairman of the board, Wells Fargo Bank; Jerome W. Hull, vice president, The Pacific Telephone and Telegraph Company; Ray B. Mattson, president, Wilbur-Ellis Company; D. Clair Sutherland, senior vice president, Bank of America N.T.&S.A.; and Robert V. Walker, vice president-executive representative, The Atchison, Topeka & Santa Fe Railway System.

College Education Financing Discussed

KRON-TV's "Money in Motion" will seek answers to the question, "How Can a Student Finance a College Education?" at 2 p.m. Sunday (Dec. 15).

The show, moderated by Dr. Lloyd D. Luckmann, coordinator, division of instruction, City College of San Francisco, is arranged by the Invest-in-America Northern California Council in cooperation with the Federal Reserve Bank of San Francisco and KRON-TV.

Panelists Sunday will be: Leonard H. Hildebrandt, educational director, United Student Aid Fund; Miss Gayle Lombardi, chairman, College Planning Conference, San Francisco Youth Association (and a senior at Lowell High School), and Benjamin McKendell, assistant director, College Entrance Examination Board.

Businessman's Bookshelf

PICTORIAL HISTORY OF THE WILD WEST by James D. Horan and Paul Sann. Crown Publishers, Inc., 419 Park Avenue South, New York City.

Billed as "the whole story truly told with pictures of the West from lawlessness to order," this is a *must* for collectors of Western lore. It does belittle the legend of Joaquin Murieta, the 'Robin Hood of the Golden West" and ignores the last and greatest of the train robbers, Roy Gardner, who made Southern Pacific as miserable in the late twenties as Black Bart did Wells Fargo in earlier days.

THE SARDONIC HUMOR OF AM-BROSE BIERCE, Edited by George Barkin. Dover Publications, Inc., New York City. $1.00 paperback.

Bierce, of course, is part of San Francisco's literary tradition which involves such names as Mark Twain, Jack London, Bret Harte, Frank Norris, William Saroyan, Robert Louis Stevenson and Rudyard Kipling. The Juvenal of San Francisco's Gaslight Era, Bierce vanished mysteriously one day in Mexico in 1913 after a long career in journalism here— including the writing of a column for the *Hearst Sunday Examiner.* Bierce, like Dean Swift, attacked corrupt and hypocritical social institutions of his times.

SAN FRANCISCO, AN INFORMAL GUIDE. By Ben Adams. $1.95 paperback. Hill and Wang, New York City (Revised).

Most San Francisco guides take a stereotyped and hackneyed approach to the city. This one, however, sets out boldly in search of the strange and least known aspects of the city—its delightful small restaurants, the lively arts, night life, shopping tours. A quest for other than the mundane. (Chamber credited for an assist in book flyleaf).

EIGHT IMMORTAL FLAVORS. B Johnny Kan and Charles L. Leon; Howell-North Books, Berkeley, Cali fornia. $5.95.

The only cookbook to emanate from San Francisco's Chinatown and th ONLY cookbook dealing strictly wit Cantonese cookery to be published i this country. Three-quarters of th recipes are simple to prepare. And th remaining ones are for ceremonial o banquet type dishes. Definitely recom mended.

Officers—

(Continued from page 3)

general partner, Stewart, Eubanks, Meyerson & Company; and Jerome W. Hull, vice president (operations), The Pacific Telephone and Telegraph Company Marie A. Hogan was re-elected Chamber secretary.

Elected treasurer was Paul E. Hazelrig, president, Kilpatrick's Bakeries, Inc. Robert M. Desky, deputy city attorney and president of the Junior Chamber of Commerce, was elected assistant treasurer.

While in Boston, Bird served a consultant to the Greater Boston Economic Study Committee and was member of the Executive Committee c the city's 100-man Committee for Civi Progress. He served as a member of th board of regents of the Institute fo Organization Management; was Edito of *The Journal,* national publication c the American Chamber of Commerc Executives, and is a former publisher c the Boston Chamber's *Greater Bosto Business* magazine.

BAY REGION BUSINESS

SAN FRANCISCO CHAMBER OF COMMERCE

VOLUME 20 • NUMBER 24 • DECEMBER 27, 1963

It's Dusk for 1963,-Dawn for 1964 .. Happy New Year!

. . . Financial district of San Francisco rises dramatically above the apartments of Telegraph Hill in this view from Coit Tower . . . .

S. F. Construction To Hit $180 Million for 1963

Total value of construction permits issued in San Francisco for the first 11 months of this year reached $176,666,414 according to Thomas W. Borek, manager of the Chamber research department.

The 1962 12-month total value for construction permits was $156,184,401. The 1963 11-month figure exceeds it by $20,482,013. "Clearly," Borek noted, "1963 will be another record year with total value of building permits to well exceed $180 million."

When compared with the 1962 11-month figure, Borek pointed out, "the upsurge in building permit valuation is dramatically emphasized" — an increase of $28,770,331 or 19.4 per cent.

Organization List Available at Chamber

An updated Professional Organization List — providing information on 246 groups active in San Francisco — is now available at the Chamber, according to Thomas W. Borek, manager of the research department.

The list, categorizes the organizations under 10 sub - headings; architectural, arts and letters, educational, educational alumni, engineering, legal, library, medical, dental and health, nursing and research-scientific.

Practical Politics Course is Scheduled

An action course in practical politics will be held for nine weekly sessions on Tuesdays beginning January 21, according to Randle P. Shields, Chamber public affairs department manager.

The courses will be held on Tuesday from 3:30 to 5 p.m. in room 200 of the chamber. Richard C. Smith, President, The Smith Company, will serve as discussion leader.

Chamber Job File Lists Varied Talents

The Chamber's research department has 20 resumes on file from professional and business people seeking employment. Resumes are held for three months.

Fields of experience covered by the 20 include general management, engineering, labor relations, public relations, advertising, personnel management, international trade, purchasing, sales, commercial banking, economic planning, evaluation and research.

...ble Center, January 22....

LEBATE is now engaged in "the life of a national news magazine." Issue of U. S. News and World Report to San Francisco via Slick each ...visiting one-day earlier circulation to ...customers in the Northern Cali....

RIVAL OF ONE ACTS will be presented by San Francisco State College Players' January 24 at 2:30 p.m. in the Little ...Theatre program: "The Measures Taken: ...Brecht; Three Sisters and Their ...Michel de Ghelderode, and "This ..." by Robert Corcoran....

...C Gas and Electric Company expects...in 1964 will reach a record high...at $150 million, it announced by ...Cordes, company president. This is ...a new gas and electric facilities will ...made of joins, he notes....

...J. A. JENSEN, chief executive officer ...lands Motor Vehicle Pollution Con-...will address the S. F. chapter of the ...ety Council Monday, January 6, at ...the Hall of Flowers, Golden Gate....

COMMERCIAL RECORDING of the ...College & Cappella Choir, ...for the Recording ...Music Library Records. The record ...including: "The Two Cities" ...Williams; two movements from Kreger ...ata "The Vine of Annihilation"; ...it's "Behold the Fowls of the Air"; ...Kodaly's ... from Mass Pictures....

...CLINE has been nominated, as are ...for 1964 presidency of the ...Bay Area Publicity Club. Others ...are Larry Lakey for first vice ...second by Dave Perry, ...treasurers and for the....

24....

been elected to the board of directors of Pacific Gas & Electric Co. filling the vacancy created by the death of Norman R. Sutherland....

EVENING SERVICE one night a week will be provided by the Department of Motor Vehicles, beginning April 1, according to Governor Edmund G. Brown. The decision to offer evening service was the result of a 90-day pilot program conducted in San Francisco and West San Fernando Valley....

CALLING CARDS printed in Japanese are now available to American businessmen before they depart for Japan, thanks to a new Name Card Service arranged by Japan Air Lines....

FOURTH ANNUAL Lucky International Open Golf Tournament will be televised live by KTVU from San Francisco's Harding Park course Sunday, January 26, from 2:30 to 4:30 p.m. The finest pros on the U. S. and international circuits will be competing for $35,000 in prize money....

JOHN L. MERRILL, president of the Merrill Co. Engineers, has been elected a director of United States Leasing Corp., Brooks Walker, Jr. president announced....

TWO SENIOR EXECUTIVES have been elected to the Bank of America's Managing Committee. They are D. Clair Sutherland, senior vice president in charge of business relationships, and Clarence H. Baumheister, vice president and cashier....

PAYROLL, LOCAL PURCHASES and other expenditures at United Air Lines' San Francisco Maintenance and Engineering headquarters reached a record $613 million in 1963 -- up $7.5 million from the previous year....

CALIFORNIA WINE SALES for 1963 will be in the same range as the all-time high of nearly 135 million gallons reached in 1961, according to Ivan W. McCulley, president and manager of the Wine Institute in San Francisco....

PHOTOGRAPHY CENTER is offering a package, January-February Beginner's Quickie Photography Course, including a three-weekend WORKARAMA in February. The Center is a service of the city's Recreation and Park Department....

up the population of the city's famous 'Chinatown.'"

CHARLES C. MILLER, Chrysler Transportation Department Manager, has been appointed Chairman of the National Industrial Traffic League Intercoastal and Coastwise committee. He also was named to the NITL's aeronautics committee and the import-export committee for 1964....

THE AEOLIAN ENSEMBLE — a new chamber group including Boris Blinder, cello; Isabelle Henselberg, piano; and Paul Renzi, flute — will open "the Intimate Concerts" January 12 at 2:30 p.m. in the Little Theatre of the San Francisco Jewish Community Center, 3200 California street.

TAX COST of the Bay Area Rapid Transit District system is going to be considerably less than the amount approved by the voters in the 1962 election, according to Thomas J. Mellon and A. Haldord Moffitt, Jr., co-chairmen of the Committee for Rapid Transit Now. This month's sale of $50 million in general obligation bonds, at an interest rate of 3.27 per cent was below the 5 per cent on which the campaign was based, they noted, and the ultimate savings on the total ($792 million) bond issue in interest costs alone could be nearly $119 million. ...

WELLS FARGO BANK'S board of directors elected two new members -- Peter T. Sinclair, president of Crown Zellerbach Corp., and H. Stephen Chase, executive vice president of the bank - according to bank president Ernest M. Cook....

FAIRCHILD SEMICONDUCTOR formerly opened its new headquarters building at Mountain View this month and also announced plans to build an addition of approximately 100,000 square feet to its research and development facility in Palo Alto....

A NEW NATIONAL BANK is due to open in San Francisco next year. Commonwealth National Bank of San Francisco has received approval of its charter from the U. S. Comptroller of Currency, according to attorney Joseph Martin, Jr....

Directors Endorse 47½ Ft. Height Limitation For SF

A 47-foot height limit generally for northern and northeastern bay frontage buildings has been endorsed by the board of directors of the Chamber, according to G. L. Fox, executive vice president.

The limitation supported by the Chamber exceeds that recommended by the San Francisco Department of City Planning in its plan. It would be applicable along the northern waterfront of the city and in the northeast area, with certain exceptions.

The Chamber board's vote was taken in response to recommendations of Edward C. Sequeira, chairman of the Chamber civic development committee, and Norman Impelman, chairman of the capital improvement and land use section.

The Chamber, which has traditionally opposed blanket limitations on building heights in San Francisco, noted that a 40-foot limit on the bay front would restrict new construction largely to wooden frame buildings. "This type of building has a place in our city, but should not be the only type."

Increasing height limit to 47½ feet would result in more lasting or concrete structures. Such structures would be better designed because one could build four-story residential units which would call for the use of concrete and more permanent materials, thus eliminating many of the wood-frame structures.

Calendar

January 7—Jr. Chamber Board of Directors. Room 200, 1:15 p.m.
January 8—Contact Club. Joint Finance. Board Floor. Signature Room, 351 California. 10 a.m.
January 8—World Trade Assn. Luncheon Meeting. World Trade Club. 12 noon.
January 8—Joint Meeting. Industrial Development Committee and Street, Highway & Bridge Section. Room 200, 10 a.m.
January 9—Transportation Committee. Room 200, 2 p.m.
January 10—Jr. World Trade Assn. Meeting. Room 200, 12 noon.
January 10—Intercity Section Luncheon Meeting. S. F. Commercial Club. 12 noon.

"Whither is Business Going in 1964?"

"Where Is Business Going in 1964?" A few educated guesses on that question will be invited on the KRON-TV panel show, Money in Motion, Sunday Dec. 29 at 2 p.m.

Participants will include William M. Burke, senior economist, Federal Reserve Bank of San Francisco; Frank Davis, director of research, Sutro & Co.; and Dr. Theodore J. Kreps, emeritus professor of business economics, Graduate School of Business, Stanford University.

SALUTE TO SF INDUSTRY

City's Largest Industrial Employer

The San Francisco Naval Shipyard at Hunters Point is both the city's largest industrial employer — 7,000 civilian workers — and one of the nation's top rated yards for efficiency of operation.

Reprint available at the Chamber Research Department, 333 Pine Street.

Aviation Section Urges Helicopter Relocation

Support for a plan to relocate the heliport of San Francisco-Oakland Helicopter Airlines away from the transbay terminal at First and Mission streets has been voted by the aviation section of the Chamber.

By Joe Haughey

MEMBERS of the San Francisco Bay Area roadcasting Association, plus many other stations, joined in observing a "Minute for Peace" at Sunday, according to G. L. Fox, executive ce president of the Chamber, which cooperated with the City and County of San Francisco in initiating the ceremony. Through the publicity department of the Chamber, releases ere sent out to newspapers and radio stations throughout the country inviting persons in communities throughout the United States to join the observance marking the ending of the period of official national mourning for the late resident John F. Kennedy. A telegram was ent to President Lyndon B. Johnson by Harry . Lee, president of the Chamber, seeking White ouse participation. . . .

"ALCATRAZ — PAST, PRESENT AND ?", comprehensive collection of materials submitted by architects and artists (professional nd amateur), will be exhibited at the Main ibrary, Civic Center, January 3-31. . . .

SLICK AIRWAYS is now engaged in "a major airlift of a national news magazine." Weekly editions of U. S. News and World Report are flown to San Francisco via Slick each unday, providing one-day earlier circulation to ubscription customers in the Northern California area. . . .

A FESTIVAL OF ONE-ACTS will be presented by San Francisco State College Players' Club January 3-4 at 8:30 p.m. in the Little Theater. The program: "The Measures Taken" by Bertolt Brecht; "Three Actors and Their Drama" by Michel de Ghelderode, and "This Way to Me" by Robert Corcoran. . . .

PACIFIC GAS and Electric Company expenditures in 1964 will reach a record high, stimated at $255 million, is announced by Robert H. Gerdes, company president. This investment in new gas and electric facilities will reate thousands of jobs, he notes. . . .

DONALD A. JENSEN, chief executive officer f the California Motor Vehicle Pollution Control Board, will address the S. F. chapter of the National Safety Council Monday, January 6, at p.m. in the Hall of Flowers, Golden Gate 'ark. . . .

FIRST COMMERCIAL RECORDING of the San Francisco State College A Cappella Choir, n association with the Society for the Recording f Contemporary Music, is being exclusively eleased on Music Library Records. The recording is an anthology including: "The Two Cities" by Darius Milhaud; two movements from Roger Nixon's cantata, "The Wine of Astonishment"; 'eter Sacco's "Behold the Fowls of the Air"; William Ward's "Listen, Lord," and Kodaly's Movements from Matra Pictures.". . . .

CARL BRUNE has been nominated, on an unopposed slate, for 1964 presidency of the San Francisco Bay Area Publicity Club. Others the slate are: Lorcy Lokey for first vice resident; Bob Harris, second VP; Dora Perry, secretary; Dudley Creed, treasurer; and for the oard — John McCombs, Katherine Pavia, Gil Dean, Dennis Richter, George Learned and Dorothy Gallyot. . . .

ONE JACKSON PLACE has completed leasing agreements with U. S. Leasing and Crocker-Citizens National Bank, according to Walter Landor, industrial designer and co-owner of the building with Joseph Weiner. . . .

FEDERAL BUSINESS TAX returns must include correct taxpayer identification number, it was reminded by Joseph M. Cullen, San Francisco District Director of Internal Revenue. Identification numbers are a necessary part of the IRS switch to electronic processing equipment, he explained. An employer who has not applied for an identification number should obtain a Form SS-4 from the district director, it was stressed. . . .

GREYHOUND'S annual 30-day Mardi Gras — Florida — Nassau Escorted Tour will leave San Francisco and San Jose on February 2. A visit to Carlsbad Caverns in New Mexico is one of the features of the first week of the tour, returning to S. F. on March 2. . . .

LEONARD P. DELMAS, president of Delmas & Delmas Jewelers, has been elected treasurer of the Yacht Racing Association of San Francisco Bay. . . .

THIRTY-THREE DOCUMENTARIES, all locally produced, are available to schools in the Greater San Francisco Bay Area and may be obtained from KRON-TV, according to Tom Mullahey, public affairs director for Channel 4. . . .

CHARLES DE BRETTEVILLE, president, chairman of the executive committee and chief executive officer of the Bank of California, has been elected to the board of directors of Pacific Gas & Electric Co., filling the vacancy created by the death of Norman R. Sutherland. . . .

EVENING SERVICE one night a week will be provided by the Department of Motor Vehicles, beginning April 1, according to Governor Edmund G. Brown. The decision to offer evening service was the result of a 90-day pilot program conducted in San Francisco and West San Fernando Valley. . . .

CALLING CARDS printed in Japanese are now available to American businessmen before they depart for Japan, thanks to a new Name Card Service arranged by Japan Air Lines. . . .

FOURTH ANNUAL Lucky International Open Golf Tournament will be televised live by KTVU from San Francisco's Harding Park course January 26, from 2:30 to 4:30 p.m. The finest pros on the U. S. and international circuits will be competing for $55,000 in prize money. . . .

JOHN L. MERRILL, president of the Merrill Co. (Engineers), has been elected a director of United States Leasing Corp., Brooks Walker, Jr., president announced. . . .

TWO SENIOR EXECUTIVES have been elected to the Bank of America's Managing Committee. They are D. Clair Sutherland, senior vice president in charge of business relationships, and Clarence H. Baumhefner, vice president and cashier. . . .

PAYROLL, LOCAL PURCHASES and other expenditures at United Air Lines' San Francisco Maintenance and Engineering headquarters reached a record $67.3 million in 1963 — up $7.7 million from the previous year. . . .

CALIFORNIA WINE SALES for 1963 will be in the same range as the all-time high of nearly 135 million gallons reached in 1961, according to Don W. McColley, president and manager of the Wine Institute in San Francisco. . . .

PHOTOGRAPHY CENTER is offering a package, January-February Beginner's Quickie Photography Course, including a three-weekend WORK-O-RAMA in February. The Center is a service of the city's Recreation and Park Department. . . .

ONE of the original water colors on the history of the Chinese in the United States, executed by noted Chinese-American artist Jake Lee for restaurateur Johnny Kan, is on exhibit in the Gum Shan Room of Kan's Chinese Restaurant at 708 Grant avenue. Chinese immigrants arrive by ship to begin a new life in early-day San Francisco and the rugged West. Some journeyed to the gold fields, some became railroad builders, others remained in San Francisco to make up the population of the city's famous 'Chinatown'."

CHARLES C. MILLER, Chamber Transportation Department Manager, has been appointed Chairman of the National Industrial Traffic League Intercoastal and Coastwise committee. He also was named to the NITL's aeronautics committee and the import-export committee for 1964. . . .

THE AEOLIAN ENSEMBLE — a new chamber group including Boris Blinder, cello; Isabelle Hesselberg, piano; and Paul Renzi, flute — will open "the Intimate Concerts" January 12 at 8:30 p.m., in the Little Theatre of the San Francisco Jewish Community Center, 3200 California street. . . .

TAX COST of the Bay Area Rapid Transit District system is going to be considerably less than the amount approved by the voters in the 1962 election, according to Thomas J. Mellon and A. Howard Moffitt, Jr., co-chairmen of the Committee for Rapid Transit Now. This month's sale of $50 million in general obligation bonds, at an interest rate of 3.37 per cent was below the 4 per cent on which the campaign was based, they noted, and the ultimate savings on the total ($792 million) bond issue in interest costs alone could be nearly $119 million. . . .

WELLS FARGO BANK'S board of directors elected two new members — Peter T. Sinclair, president of Crown Zellerbach Corp., and H. Stephen Chase, executive vice president of the bank — according to bank president Ransom M. Cook. . . .

FAIRCHILD SEMICONDUCTOR formerly opened its new headquarters building at Mountain View this month and also announced plans to build an addition of approximately 100,000 square feet to its research and development facility in Palo Alto. . . .

A NEW NATIONAL BANK is due to open in San Francisco next year. Commonwealth National Bank of San Francisco has received approval of its charter from the U. S. Comptroller of Currency, according to attorney Joseph Martin, Jr. . . .

Directors Endorse 47½ Ft. Height Limitation For SF

A 47½-foot height limit generally for northern and northeastern bay frontage buildings has been endorsed by the board of directors of the Chamber, according to G. L. Fox, executive vice president.

The limitation supported by the Chamber exceeds that recommended by the San Francisco Department of City Planning by 7½ feet. It would be applicable along the northern waterfront of the city and in the northeast area, with certain exceptions.

The Chamber board's vote was taken in response to recommendations of Edward C. Sequeira, chairman of the Chamber civic development committee, and Norman Impelman, chairman of the capital improvement and land use section.

The Chamber, which has traditionally opposed blanket limitations on building heights in San Francisco, noted that a 40-foot limit on the bay front would restrict new construction largely to wooden frame buildings. "This type of building has a place in our city, but should not be the only type."

"Increasing height limit to 47½ feet would result in more lasting or concrete structures. Such structures would be better designed because one could build four-story residential units, which would call for the use of concrete and more permanent materials, thus eliminating many of the wood-frame structures."

Calendar

January 7—Jr. Chamber Board of Directors, Room 200, 2:15 p.m.
January 8—Contact Club, John Hancock Bldg., 3rd Floor, Signature Room, 255 California, 10 a.m.
January 8 —World Trade Assn. Luncheon Meeting, World Trade Club, 12 noon.
January 8— Joint Meeting, Industrial Development Committee and Street, Highway & Bridge Section, Room 200, 10 a.m.
January 9—Transportation Committee, Room 200, 2 p.m.
January 10—Jr. World Trade Assn. Meeting, Room 200, 12 noon.
January 10—Intercity Section Luncheon Meeting, S. F. Commercial Club, 12 noon.

"Whither is Business Going in 1964?

"Where Is Business Going in 1964?"

A few educated guesses on that question will be invited on the KRON-TV panel show, Money in Motion, Sunday (Dec. 29) at 2 p.m.

Participants will include William M. Burke, senior economist, Federal Reserve Bank of San Francisco; Frank Davis, director of research, Sutro & Co., and Dr. Theodore J. Kreps, emeritus professor of business economics, Graduate School of Business, Stanford University.

SALUTE TO SF INDUSTRY

City's Largest Industrial Employer

The San Francisco Naval Shipyard at Hunters Point is both the city's largest industrial employer — 7,000 civilian workers — and one of the nation's top-rated yards for efficiency of operation.

The annual civilian payroll at the yard runs at $59 million. $66 million is spent locally on materials and supplies. Last year $27 million in military pay went to 500 officers and men based at the yard, 1042 aboard fleet ships home ported here, and about 4,400 attached to ships assigned here for repair.

During the 22 years since the Navy Department took over Bethlehem's Hunters Point Drydock 11 days after Pearl Harbor and built it into the San Francisco Naval Shipyard, the site has grown, through tideland reclamation, from a half-barren 48 acres to 979, six drydocks, four miles of deep water berthing space and 490 buildings. Hunters Point itself is a peninsula with a hard rock base, which gives the yard a natural advantage and a logical position.

Navy Boards and Congressional committees since 1910 have consistently and repeatedly stated the need for a Navy repair base at Hunters Point. A Navy harbor study in 1962 called the shipyard site "one of the finest in the world."

Growth has come about through necessity. Fully aware of the growing crisis in the Pacific, the Navy made the initial purchase in 1940 (for $3,900,000). Development funds, however, were not granted by Congress until war came. Soon thereafter a nucleus of Mare Island men began a frantic preparation for the expansion to come at San Francisco. Fortunately, there were two good drydocks, one of which could handle the largest battleships damaged at Oahu. It had been built in 1916 — on the site of the monster 465-foot dock constructed 47 years previously by the city's fabulous promoter, W. C. Ralston, builder of the Palace Hotel, for commercial use.

Before long a hill containing five million cubic yards of earth and rock was dumped into the bay to form more land. Piers, buildings and shops were quickly put up. Eventually, an 1,100-foot drydock was constructed.

Today, the yard is one of the two low-cost Naval yards in the country. It just set a new record of 69,000 man-days for a destroyer major rehabilitation project. The previous record was 72,000 man-days. Some shipyards take up to 100,000 for identical jobs.

The superior natural advantages of the yard include navigable waters on three sides, an unrestricted approach channel with minimum water of 60 feet leading up to piers and drydocks, the large deep-water anchorage of protected San Francisco harbor, its strategic location in the Pacific Basin and quick access to the open sea through the Golden Gate.

Reprints available at the Chamber Research Dept., 333 Pine Street

---

Aviation Section Urges Helicopter Relocation

Support for a plan to relocate the heliport of San Francisco-Oakland Helicopter Airlines atop the trans-bay terminal at First and Mission streets has been voted by the aviation section of the Chamber.

The action, in the form of a recommendation to the board of directors of the Chamber, was announced by Edwin M. Wilson, vice president of Thompkins & Company, chairman of the section.

M. F. Bagan, president of SFO Helicopter Airlines, was one of three speakers.

Also addressing the group were Dr. E. J. Barrett, president of Barrett Transportation, Inc., who discussed the parking situation at San Francisco International Airport, and E. W. Lassers, of

United Airlines, chairman of the Society for the Preservation of Commercial Aircraft.

The section's vote on the heliport matter was taken moments after Bagan completed his presentation in which he reiterated an earlier warning that, unless his company can find suitable heliport facilities after December 31, San Francisco may find itself without helicopter service to the airports.

The present heliport at the Ferry Building no longer is adequate and, in fact, presents some hazards and objectionable features, Bagan indicated. He called the site no longer "socially acceptable", in that taxicab service is difficult and the area is not the safest after dark.

San Francisco Rediscovered in Events Calendar

It takes newcomers, sometimes, really to scover San Francisco. Two housewives, rently arrived from the East, met here, made me mutual discoveries, put their heads tother and, presto!—something truly beautiful sulted.

The source of inspiration: Mrs. Norman lber and Mrs. Richard De Filippi. now dba e Filippi and Binni. Their work: A San rancisco Calendar of Events for 1964, illusated with magnificent photographs of the ty's persent and past, 11x14 inches between rong pasteboard covers, a splendid example the lithographer's art.

A calendar to keep when the year is done, it the forerunner of new issues to come each ar and functions as a normal, day-to-day ilendar, plus providing fixes on the dates of gnificant cutural and civic events in the city roughout the year.

As Mrs. Zilber—the "Binnie" of the new 1siness team—explains it: "We kept reading out events in the newspapers after they oc- irred—there was so much to do in San Fran- sco and we were missing it! We saw the need r a calendar of events."

They saw the need and went to work, despite e demands of home and children. At first, hotographers and printers came to their omes, bringing their wares and works to the isy homemakers.

When they had dummied a four-page mock- p of their proposed calendar, De Filippi and

Binnie approached the big downtown depart- ment and book stores. Response was more than simply enthusiastic — purchase orders were sufficient to guarantee printing costs.

The first printing is already sold out— throughout the Bay Area—and a second press run is scheduled for November to catch the Christmas trade.

Photographers represented in the calendar include Fred Lyon, Phil Palmer, George

Knight, Bruce Williams, Jerry Stoll, Bob Hol- lingsworth, Dick Erath—all by magnificent pictures of the city's many facets—and one of the incomparable pre-1906 Chinatown photos by Arnold Genthe.

Designing of cover and opening page is by Owen Welsh and the work is printed by George Lithograph Company. The calendar is obtainable from department and book stores throughout the Bay Area.

OHNNY KAN (l.), famed restaurateur dis- 'sses the new gourmet book, "Eight Immortal 'lavors" with co-author Molly Leong, and Paul :lder of the Retail Merchants Association.

Walk the City, See the World

The Heritage of Nations

With a population of 742,855 (1960 U. S. census), representing a great diversification in its racial and national origins and influence, a walk around San Francisco's neighborhoods is like a trip around the world.

San Francisco owes its cosmopolitan origin to the early Portuguese, English and Spanish freebooters of the 1700's. Don Gaspar de Portola was the first white man to see San Francisco's awe-inspiring 450-square mile bay (1769).

After the Spaniards, Russians, Mexicans, English and Americans came to rule or be ruled by San Francisco's enchantment, the city—then a sleepy village called El Paraje de Yerba Buena, or the Little Valley of the Good Herb, by its Spanish founders—saw the Stars and Stripes replace the Mexican national flag July 9, 1846. With the discovery of gold in a millrace on the American River near the foothills of the mighty Sierra Nevada mountains, a variety of races and nationalities poured into San Francisco. There are now more than 600,000 Caucasians, about 76,000 Negroes and more than 62,000 Orientals in San Francisco, including more than 36,000 Chinese.

Leading national groups—including native and foreign-born—(in round figures) are: Italians, 41,000; Chinese, 36,000; Germans, 29,000; Irish (Eire), 21,000; English, Scotch and Welsh, 22,000; Canadians, 16,000; Russians, 16,- 000; Mexicans, 16,000; Swedish, 7,000; French, 7,000; Polish, 6,000; Austrians, 5,000; and Portuguese, 2,000.

In the heart of downtown San Francisco is one of the world's most amazing communities—Chinatown.

A city-within-a-city, Chinatown is the largest Oriental settlement outside of Asia, containing about 30,000 Americans either Chinese-born or of Chinese descent.

Next to Chinatown—where Columbus Avenue slants into Grant Avenue— is the Italian section, "Little Italy," the world of Neopolitans and Tuscans, Romans, Sicilians and Venetians and assorted paisani "from the toe to the knee of the Italian boot." It was here that Amadeo Giannini founded the Bank of Italy, later to become the Bank of America N.T. & S.A.—largest bank in the world and fourth largest corporation in the country.

Reprints available at the Chamber Research Dept., 333 Pine Street

BAY REGION BUSINESS
PUBLISHED BY THE
SAN FRANCISCO CHAMBER OF COMMERCE

HARRY A. LEE, President
C. L. FOX, Executive Vice President
M. A. HOGAN, Secretary
JOSEPH I. HAUGHEY, Editor
CHARLES F. AYRES, Associate Editor

Published semi-monthly and owned by the San Francisco Chamber of Commerce, a non-profit organization, at 333 Pine St., San Francisco, Zone 4, County of San Francisco, California. Telephone EXbrook 2-4511. (Non-member sub- scription, $5.00 a Year.) Entered as Second Class matter April 26, 1944, at the Post Office at San Francisco, Cali- fornia, under the Act of March 3, 1879.

Circulation: 7,500